To Leif,
Enjoy... to
the seven... were
you doing?
Love + Peace, *Peggy*

THEN I WON'T SEEM SO FAR AWAY

Aérogrammes to My Mother

Peggy O'Toole

Peggy O'Toole

Lamb Publishing House (USA)

ISBN: 1499641680
ISBN-13: 9781499641684

THEN I WON'T SEEM SO FAR AWAY

To my father
"You can do whatever you want in life."

Contents

Part One: My Year Abroad

Contents

PREFACE

We had a few francs left, but not enough to stay in a hotel, so we waited until after dark and then walked down the stairs to the quay of the Seine to sleep. The clochards huddled over their trash can fires, eyeing us suspiciously as we set our backpacks against the wall and unfolded our sleeping bags, marking our spot. Ignoring their gruff voices, my boyfriend and I sat down on the damp embankment, dangling our feet over the water. We ate our baguettes and shared a bottle of cheap red wine, feeling smug that we were not like the other tourists who floated by on the bateaux mouches.

August 1971

Mom's burgundy satchel

Introduction

IN MY LETTERS HOME, I never told my mother about sleeping next to bums, nor did I mention hitchhiking, heartbreaks, or nearly dying. I sheltered her from the full truth and wrote home about school, the beautiful French countryside, and the kind people who helped me.

My letters arrived weekly at first and eventually tapered off to once a month. No one kept in constant touch like today—overseas telephone calls were cost prohibitive, and the reception was like talking underwater. The telegram, precursor to the text message, cost a dime per letter, and a dime was worth a half dollar. The least expensive way to communicate from abroad was to send an aérogramme, a lightweight sheet of pale-blue paper that folded into its own stamped envelope.

Five years after my mother died, I found the letters I had written to her in my early twenties. In the months after her death, I didn't have the heart or desire to sort through the personal items she had kept in an old burgundy satchel. Those were *her* memories, not mine. And anyway, I was busy with three teenage daughters, taking them to their track events, soccer games, and college tours. I stashed Mom's stuff on a cane chair next to my bed in my cottage at the shore and forgot about them. One evening, after all my kids had moved out, I was alone in the house, sipping a glass of wine as the sun set over the Pacific Ocean. I found the old satchel buried under a pile of clothes, books, and papers.

A fine white dust had coated the leather, and the salt air had corroded the zipper, making it difficult to open all the way. Reaching inside, I pulled out the contents: letters, children's drawings, Christmas cards, grocery lists written on the backs of photos, recipes torn from *Better Homes and Gardens*, holy cards, and church bulletins. Wedged at the bottom I found a large manila envelope labeled in my mother's wide, looping cursive: *Peggy Anne's letters from France.*

She had saved my letters for more than forty years, which surprised me. She had rarely written to me during the time I spent in Europe.

Not knowing what I would find in the letters, I hesitated, set them down on the long kitchen table, and poured myself another glass of wine. I watched the waves crash over the seawall, spraying foam high into the air like fireworks on the Fourth of July. I'd never been sure if Mom had even gotten all my letters, but now twenty of them covered the table, viscerally bringing up a guilty feeling. I had left her soon after Dad died, and I'd stayed away for such a long time to travel with my boyfriend.

I began to read them.

The feathery missives, written in my own hand and held by my mother, were like holy relics, an intimate connection to my past. My words, locked in time, read softly: *Please, Mom, sit down with a cup of coffee and write; send photos of the family with Dad in them. Please make me a cassette with your voices; I miss hearing them.*

The words saddened me. Why hadn't my mother written to me and shared news from home?

I didn't know what life was like for Mom after Dad died. I was in France and never asked her, and she never told me. She had been widowed at fifty-five years old, the same age I was as I sat reading the letters. I had written the letters when I was in my early twenties, the age my daughters are now. I had simply accepted the fact that Mom was just too busy to write while raising the last of her ten children. But now I can't imagine not phoning or e-mailing my daughters, who are away at college or traveling the world. My mother forwarded my bills and bank statements, often scribbling brief notes on the back of envelopes, saying, *I'm catching the bus in a few minutes, will write later. XOXO, Mom*

I will never know why she didn't write, but I never questioned her actions, and I never questioned her love.

As morbid as it might sound, I keep the last voicemail or e-mail my daughters send me in case it turns out to be the last one. I wonder whether Mom kept my letters in case I never returned, or whether she read them over and over, so I didn't seem so far away.

During my fifteen months abroad, I missed my family, but over time my loneliness waned. Untethered, I recreated myself, trying on new personas, pushing my limits, changing from a good Catholic schoolgirl to a liberated woman of the seventies—or so I thought. In my twenty-year-old mind, life back home had frozen, and only *I* was changing.

After graduating from an all-girls' Catholic high school in 1968, I attended the University of California–Santa Barbara against the advice of the nuns who said I would be corrupted. They were right. Like Alice falling down the rabbit hole, I entered a political world of anti–Vietnam War demonstrators, Black Panthers, and Students for a Democratic Society (SDS). I was free falling in a tunnel of psychedelic drugs, peace marches, and free love, to the deafening music of Led Zeppelin, the Stones, the Doors, and Jimi Hendrix. In spite of the radical noise swirling around me, I couldn't shake my parents' voices echoing in my head.

The aérogrammes transported me back to my days and nights on the road as a student with wanderlust in the hippie days of hitchhiking, revolution, and love.

It was after midnight when I finished reading the last letter. The moon had cast a path across the ocean, beckoning me outside. A wave lifted high, like the twirling skirt of a young girl, before closing in on itself. The letters lifted the veil of a time forgotten, a time that had folded onto itself.

I like this young girl—her pluck, her indomitable spirit, and her sense of adventure. She has stories to tell, and I am ready to tell them.

PART ONE

My Year Abroad

Summer 1970

CHAPTER ONE

Summer of Love

June 15, 1970
Dear Mom,
    Sorry I won't be home this summer. I've got a job and have to
finish a class. Hope you're okay
PS Please take care of my cat.

THE STREETS OF ISLA Vista were eerily quiet after the tumul-
tuous months of rioting and student demonstrations. The
police crackdown and the death of Kevin Moran, a student
shot during the infamous burning of the Bank of America,
had left more than just scars on our landscape. The police
had brutally beaten peaceful student protestors and fired
tear gas canisters point-blank into the crowd. Classes had
been cancelled before the end of the quarter, and most of
the students living in this college town next to UCSB had
cleared out, leaving an excessive amount of trash, old sofas,
beer cans, and junk.

In spite of the mass exodus, I stayed in Isla Vista after my sophomore year to enjoy my last summer with Bill before he graduated and I headed off to Europe. My parents didn't know I had plans to live with my boyfriend. They considered cohabitation with the opposite sex to be "living in sin," and I didn't want to disappoint them.

I stayed partly because I wanted to be with Bill, but also because I didn't want to return home for the summer. Life at home had become unbearable since my father had started drinking again.

Bill was my first love—a tall, blond surfer with Popeye arms, a droopy mustache, and a laughing smile. He owned a van, stereo equipment, a surfboard, and a pet hawk named Gandalf. I loved the whole package. We signed a lease for the bottom floor of a two-story yellow stucco duplex in the primo spot on Del Playa, across from the cliffs where the stairs went down to the ocean. We made plans to run on the beach and surf side by side every day. It was to be my summer of love. I was twenty years old, young, and naive, without the wisdom of experience to envision what was to come.

I enrolled in a summer class to complete a requirement I needed to get off the waiting list for the Education Abroad Program to France. There wasn't any scholarship money coming in over the summer, so I increased my hours teaching at Devereux, a school for emotionally disturbed children. I knew not to expect any money from home; Dad had a hard enough time putting food on the table for the kids still living there. Bill took a night job driving a taxi so he could surf in the daytime and finish a class project in the Tehachapi Mountains on the near extinction of the California condor. We were working opposite hours and going to school, miserable failures at following Timothy

Leary's advice to "turn on, tune in, drop out." Despite my hippie rhetoric, we'd become a conventional couple—not what I'd envisioned.

Move-in date arrived, and Bill and I filled his van with our belongings, drove a few blocks to our new place, and discovered it uninhabitable after the recent riots. The windows were broken, with jagged edges of glass left in the frames. The past occupants had left filthy clothes and personal belongings strewn about the house. The residue of tear gas permeated the orange paisley curtains, the olive green shag carpet, and the lumpy mattresses abandoned in the bedrooms.

The landlord promised to clean up the apartment building over Father's Day weekend, expecting that both of us would be going home to be with our families. I hadn't planned to go home, but now I needed a place to stay until the apartment was ready. I walked to the phone booth next to the market with a chunk of change and called home. No one answered, which alarmed me. Someone was always home. Mom didn't drive. She should've been home, or one of the kids should've answered if she were busy. There were no answering machines or services to leave a message in those days, so I gathered the dimes and nickels from the return dish, put them back in the coin slot, and tried to reach my older sister, Nola, who was already married. Again, there was no answer. I hit the phone a few times to get the coins back and then called my brother Terry. No answer.

Perplexed, I returned to our apartment.

"No one's home! Guess they all went on a family vacation without me," I tried to joke. "I can't go home, Bill. No one's there."

"You can come home with me. My mom wants to meet you. Just don't tell her we're living together."

"As if I would!" I didn't want his parents to know I was living with him.

That night, we slept uncomfortably on the floor of our apartment on the pad from the back of Bill's van. I had a dream in which my father spoke out loud to me: "I'm not your father anymore; your brother Terry is." I sat up, disoriented, trying to discern where the voice had come from—it was clearly my father's. Slipping out of bed, I went to the bathroom and got a drink of water from the faucet to quiet my fears. Returning to bed, I curled up under the blankets next to Bill to feel his warmth.

Morning came slowly as I lay awake, unable to go back to sleep. I was worried about my family, and I wondered if they were concerned about me. I tried to make sense out of my dream and eventually chalked it up to the restless sleep and my inability to contact anyone in my family. The malaise followed me throughout the weekend at Bill's home, even though I acted as though nothing was wrong and was too embarrassed to say anything about my family. They were polite and didn't ask why I wasn't with my father on Father's Day.

When we returned to Isla Vista Sunday night, I called home and found out that my father had been missing for three days. My brother Larry answered the phone and told me that Dad had been on a fishing trip in Montana with Jimmy, his fishing buddy.

"Both of them promised to dry out, and Dad told Mom he'd be back home in time for Father's Day to see his first grandchild."

I let that sink in. "Where's he now?"

Larry paused. "Dunno. He's been missing since Friday. Mom's holding up fine, but you know her; she won't let on how worried she is. Too bad Dad hasn't seen Nola's baby yet, but we think he's alive."

Putting the receiver back in its cradle, I saw an image of myself as a young teen, hearing my father moaning and painfully crying, quarantined in my parents' bedroom as he tried to stop drinking. The buried memories flashed back of my father going through the DTs, dealing with the night sweats that bled into the daytime, and seeing him fumbling, feeble, and weak in his underwear and skinny legs, barely making it to the bathroom to throw up.

On the Friday before Father's Day weekend, Jimmy had called from Montana to tell my mother the bad news. "Mary, Mike borrowed my car last night," he slurred. "He never came back."

He didn't know where my father had gone and had no more information. Apparently, Jimmy was on a drinking binge and didn't want to contact the authorities. My mother immediately called Terry, my oldest brother, and together they called the police and filed a missing-person report.

The police issued an all-alert search for him over the weekend, which ended with a few sad details given over the phone:

"Ma'am, your husband tried to admit himself to the hospital late Thursday night. He was delirious. No one knew him or where he was from. They sent him away. The last person to see him was the gas station attendant down the road. He said your husband was trying to find his way home. He was lost, asking for Colorado Boulevard in Pasadena. This is Montana, you know. We found the car he borrowed from his friend on the side of the road. There is no sign of your husband and no evidence of foul play."

Without further leads, the police stopped the search Sunday night. Early Monday morning, my two older brothers, Terry and Ted, left California to organize a new search party in Montana. After days with no results, they hired horses and went out to look for his body. It had been a week of searching, and finally, there in the wheat fields, where my father was born, my brothers spotted his body, facedown, his ochre-colored polo shirt and brown khaki pants blending with the wheat and earth.

Last family portrait on Shereen's wedding day

Chapter Two

My Father's Funeral

May 30, 1970
Happy Birthday Dad,
    You're 54 years old! Have a happy day (just kidding, I know
you hate that saying).
Love, Peggy Anne
PS Please stop drinking for me, your favorite daughter.
[The card was never sent.]

I RETURNED HOME, SOBERED by the death of my father, and found my family in the midst of preparations for his rosary vigil and funeral. My mother greeted me quietly at the door, dabbing her eyes with a tissue she kept in her sleeve.

"Can you help me find something to wear? Maybe do something with my hair?"

* * *

I hadn't spent much time at home since going away to college, except for the summer after my freshman year.

Every morning, Dad had driven me to my lifeguard job at the Gerrish Swim Club on his way to work at his parking lot in downtown Pasadena, where he had worked since I was a child. The commute had been a gift, a little time together when Dad was sober and pumped up on coffee. We talked a lot about his philosophy of life, his childhood, and the books he read.

"Just finished *Story of Civilization*. Ever heard of Will Durant?" He quizzed me about what I was learning in college, having never gone himself.

"I don't know Will Durant, but I took a history class on the Spanish conquests in the New World. Dad, why didn't you go to college?"

"Grandma and Grandpa needed me on the farm. They lost everything in the Great Depression. Couldn't risk losing the farm. Gave up a basketball scholarship to University of Iowa." He laughed as if he held no bitterness.

"I didn't know that, Dad. Were you good at basketball?"

"The best. Your old man is the best at whatever he does, even if it's drinking and gambling." He grinned his toothy grin with the gold cap in front, belying any trouble brewing inside. His baby blue eyes remained bloodshot, and his ruddy cheeks still had the rosy hue of a drunkard, but his mind was clear that summer.

"I'm not drinking anymore, Peggy Anne. I gave up the bottle for your mom."

"Yeah, Mom told me." I paused to carefully word the truth. "She also said you won't follow the doctor's advice and go to AA meetings."

The color rose in his face. "To hell with AA meetings. Only a bunch of knuckleheads go. I'm not going in front of those jackasses and say, 'Hi, I'm Mike O'Toole, and I'm an

alcoholic,' and have them repeat back, 'Hi Mike!' in unison.
It's a bunch of crap."

My silence wasn't meant to condone what he was saying. I just didn't want to upset him, having learned not to
question my father about his drinking. I'd seen him switch
from fun-loving Mike O'Toole to a real son of a bitch. But
I hoped this summer would be different. Maybe Dad had
mellowed out.

"Hey, Dad, have you ever thought of trying marijuana?
It's not addictive," I suggested the next morning on our
drive to work.

"Nah, I've enough demons. I don't need another vice."
There was no judgment in his voice, just a sense of weariness.

* * *

That was last summer, and I had thought there was a
chance for Dad, but now I'd come home to bury him. When
I walked in our front door, the house felt different. An unfamiliar hush replaced the usual ruckus of kids running and
playing, fighting and yelling. There was no crying—that
wasn't allowed. Our family covered up feelings and used
humor to deal with our grief.

At the dining room table, Nola announced, "We're going
to have an Irish wake in true O'Toole fashion. Dad would've
wanted that."

"No lamenting or sob stories," I added.

Mom chimed in, "We'll need to prepare the food." Her
eyes welled up with tears she held back.

Putting his arm around her, Larry said, "We'll get the Irish
records out, Mom, and do some Irish dancing and singing."

"And even a fight if we find the boxing gloves!" Ted
quipped.

On the day of the funeral, Mom came out of her bedroom wearing her black, polished-cotton dress, polished more by the years than intended. She held her head high as she donned the wide-brimmed black hat she wore on Sundays. Her thin, dry lips, arching eyebrows, and deep-set eyes, darkened by too little sleep, gave her a skeletal look. Seeing her made me sadder than missing my father. He died, but Mom suffered.

To lighten the situation, my brothers joked about what Dad had wanted us to do upon his death.

"Knock out his gold teeth!"

"It's a closed coffin. How do we know that the morticians didn't already take his gold teeth?" Pat said.

"Let's check the body. I'll bring the hammer and knock the gold out." Larry was ready for action.

"Or we could just blow them out with a firecracker!" Dennis, our youngest brother, was a prankster just like Dad.

We laughed, remembering Dad's practical jokes involving firecrackers. Looking up at our dining room ceiling, we could see the remains of the birthday cake Dad had blown up, knowing his children had inserted firecrackers in place of the candles.

"Stop it, boys," Mom said, biting her lip to squelch a smile that crept across her face. She knew Horace, his given name, would've laughed at his children's antics, but she always had to uphold her decorum, whereas Dad encouraged our silliness and bragged if any of the kids ever played a trick on him or got the best of him in poker. *A chip off the old block*, he'd say.

Three limousines arrived at our house, and we childishly scrambled for the front seat, making the younger ones climb to the very back. Once we were ensconced inside the plush interior, silence surrounded us.

The limos drove slowly down the tree-lined streets of my childhood, passing familiar houses and stores on the same route I had traveled every day on my bike to parochial school. We stopped in front of Holy Angels Catholic Church, where we had been baptized, made our first confessions, received our first communions, were confirmed, married, and had the funeral for our oldest sister, Shereen. Now, it was my father's burial.

I saw people waiting outside on the semicircular steps in front of the church. They watched us climb out of the limos as if we were celebrities. At first, I thought the church doors hadn't been opened, but then I realized the church was overflowing. Friends and relatives lined the steps. I walked the gauntlet, recognizing old friends, tears rolling down their faces, their arms reaching out to console me. *O'Toole babies don't cry,* my mother had told me since the first time I scraped my knee. I held my head high and passed, not shedding a tear.

All nine of us lined up according to age behind my mother: Nola, Terry, Ted, Larry, Peggy, Pat, Dennis, Kathleen, and the baby, Eileen, twelve years old. Terry grabbed our mother as she faltered on the step. We slowly began the procession behind the casket into the church.

Coming in from the blinding light of the sun, my eyes took a moment to focus. The cool of the morning lingered in the alcoves, with the heavy scent of flowers stifling the air. Upon hearing the organ dirges, my throat tightened as I remembered my sister's funeral eight years earlier. I cast my eyes down, the burgundy carpet so familiar from my childhood processions. Regaining composure, I looked up and saw the altar covered in huge bouquets of flowers draping down the sacristy stairs and overflowing to the side altars.

People filled every pew—not just family members and school friends, but also Dad's friends from the parking lot, who sat toward the back of the church. Scanning the crowd, I saw the newspaper guy with no legs who scooted around on a square piece of plywood. Every Saturday, after swim lessons at the Pasadena Athletic Club, Dad would send me to the corner Thrifty Drugstore to buy a paper from him.

"Tell him you're Mike's kid and say hi for me," Dad instructed, handing me a dime. "And then buy yourself an ice cream."

It scared me as a child to see a legless man, but I grew to look forward to his toothless smile.

Old Scoby sat next to the legless paper man in the church. He had put on a suit for the occasion. Mom always said he was up to no good when he hung around the parking lot selling tips on the races at Santa Anita and taking bets, but Dad considered him a friend.

The Japanese ladies who ran the beauty shop across from Dad's lot held hankies to their eyes. I recognized the one who had given me a fashionable short wig before I went to college. "You're Mike's daughter. He's so proud of you for going to college," she had told me as she handed me the gift.

Childhood friends came to remember their favorite parent, who had never judged them, only made them laugh and feel good about themselves...the outcasts, the troubled. Dad had time to talk to people, to listen to them, and he didn't discriminate according to wealth, color, or education. He always found something good in everyone, something he could learn from them or laugh about with them—unless of course, the guy was a *knucklehead*. Then Dad could *teach him a lesson or two behind the shed.*

Dad literally gave the shirt off his back if a guy needed it. We joked that the shoeshine man wore Dad's jacket to the funeral, and he probably did. If someone couldn't pay their monthly parking fee or needed to borrow some cash, my father always worked out a deal.

One Christmas, Dad sold Christmas trees to make a little extra money for the holidays. My sister Nola generously told the nuns, "My daddy's going to buy Christmas trees for all the classrooms." In fact, Dad had told her he would buy a tree for her class. So she could keep her word, he gave every class a tree and never mentioned the mistake.

All the nieces and nephews remembered him slipping them a silver dollar or fifty-cent piece when they came to our home or stopped by the parking lot. To this day, my cousin Agnes slips a dollar to the kids and grandchildren like my dad always did. "Uncle Horace always gave me money; it's my fondest childhood memory," Agnes told me as she tucked a bill into a child's pocket.

Dad, an honest man and a gambler, played fair, so people trusted him. There was always betting going on at the kiosk in his parking lot. Everyone knew about the pool for the big games, the Irish Sweepstake lottery tickets, and betting on the horse races. On any given day, you'd find my father with a deck of cards. "Hey, let's play a quick game of twenty-one." Or if there wasn't enough time, he'd say, "Just cut the deck, high card wins." If the cards weren't out, he'd fold paper dollars and play liar's poker with the serial numbers. He settled all kinds of debts and arguments this way and made a little extra money on the side. His handshake was his word, and that was better than any written contract.

We buried my father on June 25, 1970, next to my sister in the San Gabriel Valley Holy Resurrection Cemetery.

* * *

I choke up as I write these words about my father, but when I was twenty, I was thinking more about myself. Nothing was going to stop me from breaking loose from our large Catholic family, getting a college education, and traveling, not even my father's death. I had his blessing when I first left home for college. "You're smart. Work hard and make something of yourself," he told me as he handed me his copy of *The Prophet,* by Kahlil Gibran:

> Your children are not your children.
> They are the sons and daughters of Life's longing
>   for itself.
> They come through you but not from you,
> And though they are with you yet they belong not
>   to you.

Dad wanted a better life for me than he could give me, and he was willing to let me go find it. Without regret or tears, I returned to my life in Isla Vista a short time after the funeral, just as Dad would have wanted.

The next day, I stood in my gravel driveway gazing beyond the cliffs across the ocean, and my eyes settled on the tops of the Channel Islands, haloed in puffy white clouds. Snapping back to reality, I reached into my mailbox and shuffled through the junk mail, stopping at the envelope with the stamped seal of the University of California, Education Abroad Program. My fate was enclosed. Had I made it off the waiting list? I made the sign of the cross, kissed the envelope, and whispered a prayer to my father before reading the letter: "This is your official notification of acceptance to the EAP program Pau/Bordeaux for the academic year of 1970–71…" I paused as a shadow of doubt clouded my excitement. How could I afford this?

I read on. "California State Scholars and Work Study recipients will have money forwarded to them to cover any further fees and expenses for housing and food while in the host country."

A gift! I'd been working and saving since I was twelve years old: babysitting, teaching swimming, selling statues and bobbles. I'd be free to enjoy my year abroad without money worries.

My heart beat rapidly as I skimmed the rest of the page, my father's words echoing in my head: "Peggy Anne, you can do whatever you want in life. You work so hard." He had promised to send me to France with my high school French class, but of course I knew he couldn't afford to. "I know a guy who owes me a favor. I'll make a few extra bucks on the horses, win a few hands in poker...I'll get you to France somehow."

Looking at my acceptance letter, I felt a pang of sorrow that my father had died only a few weeks earlier, before I could tell him I was going to France. Rays of sunshine broke through the clouds where I imagined heaven to be. *Daddy, I'm going to France! Thank you for giving me permission.*

My mother at twenty-one years old

CHAPTER THREE

Good-Byes

August 12, 1970
Happy birthday, Mom!
Wish I could have cooked you breakfast in bed. Since you'll be at Nola's Friday for your birthday party, I'll go there instead of going home. Time is really running out. I wish I had another month or two before leaving.

Thanks for being so understanding and letting me go to Europe. PS You'll get to meet my boyfriend, Bill—he's coming too.

BEHIND MY WORDS OF gratitude, I felt guilty leaving Mom so soon after my father died. She had been the quintessential housewife of the fifties, dedicating her whole life to family, never holding a job outside the home, scrubbing floors, washing diapers in the toilet bowl, and toiling until the last child was in bed before she'd sit down next to Dad and read the newspaper. On summer nights, she'd water the plants on the patio, Dad yelling, "Mary, come in here and relax." I imagined she liked the coolness of the evening, the solitude of caring for flowers that didn't cry.

How was she going to provide for the last four children living at home?

I had no intentions of returning home, nor was I asked to. I couldn't wait to leave for Europe, to be far from home and away from the demands she had put on me as a child. I was the babysitter, dishwasher, laundress, and cook. My chores never seemed to end until I finally escaped to college on a full-ride scholarship and work-study program. Mom said she was proud of me being the first in the family to go away to college, but she chided, "You know, college isn't everything. You could stay home, get married, and have ten children like me." I never wanted to be in her position—a mother of ten and wife of an alcoholic, too many nights of arguing and yelling. But what really worried me was the thought that I might not return. I could die, like my sister, and cause my mother more sorrow.

* * *

I was thirteen years old the night my sister died. My younger brother, Pat, and I got to stay up past ten to watch the *Alfred Hitchcock Show* on that fateful Friday evening. My older siblings were out with friends, and the younger three children were in bed. The rain pelted the roof all evening and streaked the windows, obscuring the passing car lights on Rosemead Boulevard.

Inside, Pat and I, cozy in our pajamas, sat next to the fireplace while my parents reclined in their La-Z-Boy chairs.

A knock at the door startled me. Mom got jittery, rustling the paper on her lap. "Horace, answer the door."

"What the hell is someone thinking, coming over this late at night?" Dad grumbled as he walked across the room.

The man on our doorstep wore an overcoat, his hat low over his eyes, his voice somber, almost incoherent. It was Mr. Dietrich, my sister's father-in-law. I thought he was drunk.

My father invited him in. He refused.

"I can't come in," he said, standing under the awning. After a long silence, he took a deep breath, looked directly at my father, and said, "There's been an accident. Shereen was killed. My son is in critical condition."

My father clutched his heart and faltered back into the room, grabbing a dining room chair to steady himself. I don't remember him saying a word, just gasping for air. My mother crumpled in her chair, wailing, "Not my baby, not my baby, not my baby."

I froze in terror.

"She died instantly," Mr. Dietrich said, as if that would somehow be any consolation.

The torrential downpour had obstructed the flashing lights at the railroad crossing and muted the noise of the oncoming train as it slammed into their little red VW bug.

My mother and father left immediately to identify her body, leaving me in charge of my younger siblings. Mom instructed me not to wake them or tell them what had happened if they should get up.

Pat and I waited in the living room with the glare and blare of the TV on in the background, too numb to move or talk, until our pastor, Father McGovern, arrived to console us. He led us in the rosary, offering up the prayers melodically, "Hail Mary full of grace..."

In a trance we responded, "Pray for us sinners now and at the hour of our death..."

It was after midnight when Larry and Ted returned from their Friday night on the town, surprised to find the lights on and Father McGovern in the front room.

"Hello, Father. What happened?" Larry spoke, his hands clenched.

Ted's face went ashen. "Is it Mom?"

Father McGovern leaned near to their faces, spittle spraying gently, and in his thick Irish brogue told them, "Your sister Shereen has died." I don't know how much else they heard. "Take care of the little ones and your parents." He laid his hands on each of the boys' heads, incanting a blessing. They bowed in respect and opened the door for the priest to leave.

As soon as Father McGovern's car left the gravel driveway, my brothers gave in to their rage, throwing chairs, cussing, and yelling. I remained still and silent, a behavior trait I had observed in my mother when my father came home drunk and angry. That night in my attic bedroom, I denounced God and all the saints who had let this happen. If my beautiful, kind sister could die, then I was vulnerable—no longer could the angels save me from falling off a cliff, even if I said my daily prayers.

* * *

I put Mom's birthday card in the mail, thinking about Shereen's birthday the next day. If she were alive, she would have been twenty-nine, which seemed so old to me at twenty.

By the end of the week, I had everything ready to go. I sat on top of my suitcase on the bedroom floor, bumping up and down to squish my brown coat on top of a year's worth of clothing and forced the locks to snap into place.

Bill walked in and flopped on the bed. "One last hug?" He stretched out his big bear arms and I fell onto him. He wrapped his arms and legs around me and we held each other tight, rolling back and forth.

I looked into his clear blue eyes, hoping for a word of reassurance, a commitment, a promise.

"Watch out for those French guys. They're horny."

Squelched, I swallowed my true feelings. "I don't like French guys. They're too short."

"Yeah, too scrawny for my big, beautiful girl." He gripped me tighter and pulled me closer for a kiss.

"Are you going to miss me?" I sounded pathetic.

"Of course I am. Let's get going." He slid off the bed. "What do you want me to take?"

I pointed to the boxes that would be stored at my sister's house. He put them in his van along with my overstuffed suitcase. Closing the door, I said my last good-bye to our home on the cliffs of Isla Vista and headed south on the Coast Highway. Bill slipped in a John Mayall cassette:

Don't wanna leave California

The sun seems to never go down.

I sang the chorus, off-key but with heart: "California, I'll be back there before long."

I didn't want to leave Bill. I worried about being so far away from him for so long. Would I lose him? Would he be faithful? My stomach clenched. I knew I was blowing it.

The closer we got to Playa del Rey, the more nervous I was about introducing Bill to my family. My brothers had teased me unrelentingly in high school for never getting a date. *You're so tall and skinny, no boobs and big feet—you look like Olive Oyl.* I'd stuffed my bra with Kleenex and squished my feet into shoes a size too small, but I still didn't get asked out.

My mother consoled me on dateless nights, explaining, "Your friends get asked to the dances because they're from Latin countries. They mature faster." Dad yelled from the other room, "You're too good for those knucklehead guys."

You don't want 'em taking you out just because you got a big chest. Ahh, hell with it, you're the damn prettiest of them all."

We arrived at my sister's in the late afternoon, surprised to see a bon voyage banner alongside the happy birthday banner. All my brothers and sisters had come to say good-bye, and Mom prepared my favorite summertime meal, potato salad and fried chicken.

Bill walked in wearing his Spooner Hawaiian shirt and carrying a six-pack of Bud. He fit right in with my brothers, drinking beer, talking sports, and telling jokes. My little sisters whispered how cute he was, and Mom and Nola kept offering him more food.

Bill's grin spread across his face. "Sure, the potato salad is great stuff. Thanks so much."

At the end of the evening, Larry threw an arm over Bill's shoulder, ceremoniously slipping him a five-dollar bill. "Thanks for taking out my little sister."

Bill tucked the five in his shirt pocket and laughed. "Best money I've ever earned."

Mom smiled, but her eyes betrayed her. "Why do you have to go so far away? Maybe I'll come visit."

I had only seen my mother cleaning floors, washing clothes, and doing dishes. She wore the same thing every day: her old turquoise-blue pedal pushers, a button-down beige shirt, and a peachy-orange cardigan sweater with a Kleenex tissue rolled up in her sleeve to dab at the constant drip from her aquiline nose. She looked so different from how she looked in her portrait on our mantelpiece—a flawless Irish beauty with a porcelain complexion, wavy black hair, a distinctive widow's peak, deep-blue eyes, and a smile of confidence. I knew so little about my mother and her desires. She kept everything bottled up. I knew she wouldn't visit me, which made me sad, but deep inside I didn't want her to come anyway. Mom gave me her usual sermon as she hugged me good-bye. "Mind your p's and q's, say your prayers, and brush your teeth before going to bed." She had given me that advice since my first sleepover. "I trust you'll be good," which meant I wouldn't have sex. But this time she added, "Be safe." She couldn't say, "Don't die," but that's what I understood.

The burden to be safe overwhelmed me.

I pulled my rosary out of my fringed leather purse, dangling it like a rabbit's foot. "My lucky charm, Mom." And it may have been the charm that kept me out of harm's way that year.

I said my good-byes to each brother and sister and left for the airport with Bill to catch the all-night flight to France.

At the boarding gate, Bill kissed me and said he would see me soon, maybe Christmas, for sure by Easter. But he didn't say "I love you," and neither did I.

Our first French meal

Chapter Four

Arrival

August 25, 1970
Dear Mom,
    We arrived safely, but I am ready to crash now—I haven't slept since I saw you. The flight was really high class, two full meals: steak, duck, vegetables, champagne, wine, and any drink I wanted served all night long. I was full the whole eleven and half-hours it took to get here. When we landed in Paris it was rainy and overcast. The only sunny spot was over Ireland.
    Don't worry mom, everything is under control. Thanks for the wonderful send off. Take care, sorry for such a short note, but know I'm safe and all is well. I can't believe I'm here!
Love, Peggy

WHAT REALLY HAPPENED WAS that I stepped off the plane feeling sick from too much wine, rich food, and no sleep. I found the nearest bathroom and rushed inside before I met anyone from my program. My reflection in the mirror showed a tall, thin, pale young girl with sunken blue eyes and a strand of wet, dirty blond hair stuck to her cheek. Splashing water on my face, I swished my mouth with tap water and pinched my cheeks to bring the color back. Then I mustered a smile to hide my fear and walked out, dragging my huge suitcase. I shifted my carry-on to my other shoulder, tugged at my pants to make them longer, and walked stiffly across the concourse.

The airport smelled peculiar, a mixture of strong coffee, baked bread, and body odor. The familiar sounds of bustling crowds masked the fact that I didn't understand a word over the PA. Everything was in French: the signs, directions, and advertisements. It was so new and strange for a girl who'd never traveled farther than a few hundred miles from Pasadena.

Scanning the airport, I spotted a large group across the lobby gathering around placards labeled EAP. Trying to maintain my cool, I sauntered over to the group, gave my name to the official with the clipboard, and busied myself with my bags on the ground, occasionally looking up. From my vantage point down on the floor, it looked like everyone above me was in good spirits, chatting like they knew each other or clinging to a friend. For the first time since first grade, I didn't have my best friend, Carmen, at my side. We had made all of our decisions together: play punch ball or swing at recess, invite Bob or Pete to the dance, stay in Pasadena or go to UCSB. She always deferred to me, counting on me to test the waters. "Peggy, you jump first!" she yelled as I dove headfirst into the ocean. She had always been right behind me...until now.

A good-looking Frenchman in his twenties blew a whistle to get our attention and directed us to three waiting buses. Outside, the warm air and diesel fumes wafted into my nostrils, adding to my nausea. Once I was settled in my seat, I studied the young tour guide. He had wavy black hair, chiseled features, and tight pants that accentuated a very cute derriere. Standing at the front of the bus with his clipboard in one hand and leaning against the driver's seat, he introduced himself in a very sexy French accent. "I am Jean-Paul." *The French love those hyphenated names,* I thought. "I'll be your guide." Looking at his clipboard, he read aloud the itinerary for the next few days of touring. Then he put down the clipboard and looked directly at me. "I know you're all tired. We will go to bed soon, and in the morning I will knock you up."

Tittering erupted, and the guys hooted and snickered. I blushed, catching the twinkle in the young guide's eyes. Monsieur Carter, our elderly chaperone, stood up and clapped his hands.

"Now, now, please, quiet down. What he meant to say is that he will knock on your door to wake you up in the morning."

I got the feeling Jean-Paul knew exactly what he was saying, and I fancied the thought of his knocking in the morning.

From the airport at Orly, our group traveled south to Orleans, staying in empty dorms and eating in large cafeterias until we arrived at Chartres, where I experienced my first authentic French meal in a bistro across from the cathedral. The large banquet room had rows of long tables covered in white cloths, with baskets of bread and carafes of wine for every four place settings. After a noisy seating of a hundred American college students, Monsieur Carter made an announcement: "You must order in French and only speak French to each other." He gleefully added, "Nous sommes Américaines en France," in the worst American accent I'd ever heard.

Of course he's kidding, I thought, but to my dismay, everyone around me ordered in French and asked each other really stupid questions like *Comment allez-vous? Comment vous-appelez vous?* Language is meant for communication, and I wanted to get to know these kids and talk about more meaningful things than the mundane.

I looked at the menu, feeling like a two-year-old child who can't get the right words out. A tempest built inside me, readying for a tantrum to explode. I wanted to lie down on that restaurant floor, kicking and screaming. "Give me the fuckin' menu in English!"

The waiter stood over me and shrugged his shoulders. Tongue-tied, I pointed to the *Plat du Jour,* which listed several unknown items.

"Ah oui, coquilles Saint Jacques," he announced loudly so everyone knew I hadn't ordered in French.

Sheepishly, I nodded, thinking, *I should have listened to Mr. Allen last fall.*

✳ ✳ ✳

Mr. Allen, the affable, red-haired recruiter for EAP, had counseled me to go to an English-speaking Education Abroad program because I didn't have enough credits in French, nor any recommendations from my French professors.

"Peggy, you would do very well in Sweden. You even look Swedish; they're tall and blond and speak English."

I softened to the idea until he said, "During the winter months, it will be dark most of the day..."

He didn't need to go any further. I had lived my entire life in Southern California, basking in the February sun.

"Thank you, Mr. Allen, but I'm going to go to France. I'll take the required French class."

"Fine. I'll put you on the waiting list." He closed my file, smiled, and shook my hand. "Really, I'll do my best for you." It helped that he knew my family in Pasadena; he had even gone to high school with Shereen and dated Nola. I trusted he'd get me in, provided I did my part.

The next quarter, I took the required French class and got a D, an unacceptable grade for two reasons. First, I needed to maintain a 3.0 GPA or I'd lose my scholarship and loan money. Second, if I didn't pass the class with at least a C, I'd lose my place on the waiting list for Bordeaux.

Outside my French professor's office I rehearsed what I was going to say. I knocked.

Opening the door, the peevish man hurriedly asked, "Mademoiselle, what can I do for you?"

He was a small, dark, bespectacled man from either Senegal or Ghana who spoke English with a heavy accent.

So as not to tower over him, I slouched and explained my circumstances.

His response was less than flattering: 'I vill geeve you a C eef you prrromise never to take another French class in this universitee. I have a reputation to keep."

Shocked by the insult yet ecstatic about his proposition to change my grade, I quickly replied, "Oui, monsieur, I will never take another French class here. Merci—au revoir!" I skittered out the door before he could change his mind.

* * *

After lunch, we walked over to the cathedral in bunches of friends, chatting about—well, I didn't know what everyone was saying, since I couldn't understand French.

Inside the cavernous cathedral, our guide's voice echoed as he pointed to the vaulted ceilings and the rose windows, but what stayed with me was the moldy smell of the ancient walls mixed with my fear and loneliness. Before leaving, I lit a candle for Shereen and Dad and said a prayer to them. "Help me get through this year."

When Shereen died, my father decreed we would pray to her because she was closer to God than any goddamn saint or angel. Our family keeps our dead alive, beseeching them to guide us and intercede with the power one calls God. It's a constant dialogue in my head: the deceased's voice whispers, telling me what I should do and gently admonishing me for my sins…always there.

Feeling like an outsider among my own compatriots, I attached myself to the only foreigner in our program, Lisbeth, a pale, blond Swedish exchange student of average beauty with a sophistication that I hoped to acquire. She spoke five languages and didn't mind speaking English. Sex was Lisbeth's favorite topic. She told me about her lovemaking with older men, how many times she had done it before she was sixteen, and her interest in meeting an American boy, even though she had a boyfriend back home.

"I've never made love to an American. What's it like?"

"Oh, it's great, but I've only done it with my boyfriend. His name's Bill. We just started, you know, sleeping together, and we haven't done it that many times."

"Too bad. You can change. Frenchmen would like to make love to you."

"Oh no, I love Bill. We might even get married. I'm faithful."

"Pouf! Faithful? Why? He won't know."

"It doesn't matter. I'm Catholic, or at least I was. I don't want to cheapen myself." I was channeling my mother.

"Ahh, you're Catholic. That's good. I'm Catholic too. Just go to confession, and everything is forgiven."

Having had sex outside of marriage was a sin in the priest's eyes, but being disloyal to my boyfriend went against my *own* principles.

"I love Bill, and he's coming to see me at Christmas. I can't cheat on him." I was naive and wanted to believe what I was saying, but Lisbeth had sown the seeds of doubt.

Spanish cows in Basque country

CHAPTER FIVE

La Vache Espagnole

September 1, 1970
Dear family,
    It's so embarrassing, I can't speak French and everyone else
can. We had a week of sightseeing before we started school, vis-
ited the Cathedral of Chartres and toured Paris. I didn't get to
see everything this visit but I'll return, and hopefully with more
knowledge of the French language. I just began my intensive
language class at the University of Pau, and it's intense. Take
care and write soon.

EARLY SUNDAY MORNING, OUR group boarded the train at
Montparnasse bound for Pau, where we would spend the
next six weeks in an intensive language program. The engines fired, the whistle blew, and the train slowly moved
out of the station into full sunlight, picking up speed on
the outskirts of Paris, passing rundown *banlieues* into the
golden farmlands. I looked out the window as we passed
villages with church steeples soaring above cottages, and

rivers cutting huge ribbons across expansive wheat fields that rippled in the wind, triggering an image of my father lying facedown in the Montana wheat fields. No one knew exactly how long his body had lain there in the sun before he died. It was an unbearable thought, wondering if he suffered.

I didn't get to say good-bye to Dad. I hated him at that moment for dying, but my hate turned to sorrow. He had let me down, disappointed me, deserted me. I hated him again for not being alive so I could tell him I was in France. A lump formed in my throat. He wouldn't be at my graduation or walk me down the aisle or know any of his grandchildren.

Why couldn't he have stopped drinking? Why did he have to go fishing in Montana with his half-assed friend? Why didn't the damn hospital take him? My shoulders heaved as I held in a groan developing deep in my belly.

Sucking in my breath, I stared into my past and saw myself at twelve years old, holding my father's head as the fireman resuscitated him in his bedroom. It was his first heart attack. In their big, clumsy boots, the men carried my father away on a stretcher, his white hands dangling off the sides. He didn't die. Days later, when he returned from the hospital, he teased me. "Peggy Anne, I felt your tears on my face. You thought I was going to die!" He laughed, making fun of my emotions but unable to profess his own feelings. After that, I couldn't cry for him again—or for anyone else for that matter. I held everything in; it was easier than risking rejection.

Still, I sensed Dad had loved me, like an animal knows his master loves him, but I was rarely hugged or kissed. Dad avoided displays of affection and hid his emotions behind jokes, but I knew I was his favorite. He was my defender and supporter. To him I was special, different from the others, because I worked so hard caring for Mom when she was sick, doing the household chores, and still getting good grades. I wanted to please him, remain his special child, and never disappoint him. I wish I had told him I loved him. The tape recorder in my mind whirled out of control with regrets for what could no longer be. My father was dead. I released the air held in my gut in a puff, closed my eyes, and fell into a light sleep.

The rhythmic sound of the wheels on the track anesthetized me, but in that darkness each blow of the lonesome whistle brought back another death—my sister's. She had been killed by a train when her car got stuck on the railroad track in a rainstorm. So young, so innocent, she had been married only seven months. I had often thought that if she had been pregnant that would make her death *two* deaths. I mourned for my sister more than my father. She had no say in her death, whereas my father chose to drink. *Wheat fields and trains, heart attacks and crashes. How will I die?*

I stopped myself from crying, like I always did…unless I was alone in my attic bedroom, where I was safe from anyone hearing me. I had done enough grieving over my dead family members. I had to get on with my new life in France. It was my turn to live.

I couldn't pinpoint the ominous yet exhilarating feeling during the seven hours on the train. My family and friends faded into the background, muddled together as one entity, both living and dead.

When we pulled into the station at Pau, I stepped over a threshold into another world, distant and different from the one I had known. Beyond the platform, the snow-capped peaks of the Pyrenees stood watch over the fortified city, with its musk-scented moat and castle majestically placed on a hill at the edge of town. In clusters, our group followed the guides along the cobblestone road, lugging our suitcases and bags and stopping at a public bathroom before getting on the waiting buses. Outside the Turkish-style toilets, a black woman collected a fee to use the facilities. She wiped down the sinks, mopped the floor, and threw a bucket of water down the hole. It had always bothered me as a child when Thelma at the Athletic Club had to do the dirty work while I got to swim. She was black too. Dad had made sure I treated Thelma with respect. I never left my dirty towel on the floor, and I gave her the bottle of Jungle Gardenia perfume I had won on the TV show *Truth or Consequences* when I was in sixth grade.

The dark woman put out her dry, ashy hand. I smiled as I let the coins drop and her fingers grasped the centimes; her eyes flashed a kind recognition. *Dad, I'll make you proud.*

Late Sunday afternoon, we moved into the dorms at the University of Pau. Each student had his or her own room with one bed, a desk, and a small window. A paper with my class assignment was on the bed: Salle de classe No. 10; Monsieur Jean-Pierre Dupuy; Commencement Lundi, 8:00.

After dinner I went to bed early, worried about starting the six-week intensified language course.

The first day of class confirmed my worst fear. I was the dumbest in my class.

Monsieur Dupuy, a small but well-built man in his twenties, introduced himself by writing his name on the board with a flourish, turning and saying, "Je suis Monsieur Dupuy. Monsieur Dupuy! Répétez."

We obediently repeated, "Monsieur Dupuy."

He went down each row and asked the students to introduce themselves. The panic that had taken residence in my stomach the night before climbed to my throat. When it was my turn, I tried to be cute, which is hard for a five-foot-ten, skinny girl. I puffed out my lips, like the French girls do, and in very poor French said my name and where I was from. Monsieur Dupuy raised his thick eyebrows and adjusted his scarf, rakishly tied around his neck. "See me after class."

The class emptied. He walked over to my desk, looked down, and said, "Mademoiselle O'Toole, you will need more practice in speaking."

I nodded my head in agreement, thinking, *Yeah, asshole, that's why I'm here.*

"You come with me to a *boum* at my friend's house," he said with full authority, as if assigning me a lesson.

Boum? In my first-year French book, I remembered seeing a picture of kids dancing with musical notes circling above their heads with *boum* written under it. A party. I could handle that, even if he was a twerp. I might meet someone, as Mrs. Kenmore, my biology teacher, had advised us to do at the sophomore dance. "Go with a creep and look over the crop."

"Okay, where do I meet you?" There was no reason to try to speak French; his English was perfect.

"We can walk from the dorms. I'll come get you at five o'clock, *dix-sept heures.*"

At orientation, the director had warned the girls not to go alone with a Frenchman, but he had been talking about the guys from the local factories who hung around our dorm rooms, not the teachers. So I went.

Monsieur Dupuy instructed me to call him Jean-Pierre before escorting me into the house where the party was in full swing. Loud '60s music blared from the phonograph. Girls in form-fitting sweaters and suggestive, narrow skirts sipped pink Kir Royale cocktails. The guys, in tight red pants that accentuated their bulging crotches, drank a strange mix of beer and grenadine. Everyone smoked. Chatting, hugging, kissing, hands wandering over derrieres...I had walked into a classic French B-movie.

Jean-Pierre joined in the love fest, kissing girls who appeared totally enchanted with him. Attempting to mingle, I approached a small group of girls, but after a bonjour or two, I had nothing else to say. They turned and walked away giggling, pointing to my not-so-cool beige cowgirl jeans, baggy green shirt, and white tennis shoes.

Unable to understand a word and embarrassed by their snobby looks and sneers, I decided to leave.

Jean-Pierre was standing near the doorway. He put his arm out to stop me. "You can't leave now. Your French lesson isn't over. Meet my friends." He was already drunk.

I pushed his arm out of the way and opened the door. He grabbed me. I shrugged to dislodge his arm and told him to piss off.

The next day in class, Monsieur Dupuy (we were no longer on a first-name basis) wouldn't look at me or call on me. By the end of the week, so much animosity had built up that when I asked him a question, he yelled back, "Tais-toi, tu parles français comme une vache espagnole." ("Shut up, you speak French like a Spanish cow.") Stung by the remark, I retreated into my workbook, head cast down to avoid the stares of my classmates, hating the ones who laughed.

I walked back to my dorm room and decided to skip the welcome party downtown given by the mayor. Alarmed that I wasn't on the bus, our dorm supervisor, Mademoiselle Clara, came to my room.

"Qu'est qui ce passe?" She wanted to know what was wrong.

Lying on my bed under the covers, I broke down crying, sniffling, and coughing, unable to explain that I felt like shit, I missed my boyfriend, and my French sucked.

"Voulez-vous un médecin?" she queried with compassion.

"Medicine? Oui, s'il vous plaît," I replied, grateful for any kind of relief. Over-the-counter drugs in Europe were strong, and I needed a good fix for whatever ailed me.

A half hour later, Clara knocked at my door, this time with a man in a white coat. *Shit*, I forgot, the word *médecin* had a picture of a doctor, not a bottle. Why hadn't I studied harder?

The obese doctor put his bag down and motioned for me to unbutton my blouse as he waved his stethoscope. Clara explained it wouldn't hurt and would only cost fifty francs. *Ten dollars!* I had no extra money, and even if I did, I didn't want the fat, pug-breathing old man to examine me. Exhausted from trying to speak French, trying to understand French, and trying to be heard in any language, I whimpered, "I don't want a doctor. Go away!"

Ignoring my plea, the doctor started to unbutton my shirt. I screamed, "Don't touch me! I want medicine, like in pills, not a doctor!"

Shocked, Clara ran across the hall to find another sick student to help interpret. Redheaded Sheila came over in her pajamas.

"Please tell them I don't want a doctor, just medicine."

"Elle veut le médicament, pas un docteur," she said with clarity.

Why couldn't I have done that? The doctor made funny puffing sounds from his mouth and left abruptly without giving me any pills. Luckily, he didn't charge for the visit. Clara and Sheila stayed a moment to make sure I'd be all right. I told them how hard it was for me in class and how my teacher had called me a Spanish cow.

"Ah, non!" Clara was stunned. "I will tell the director."

After they left, I allowed myself to cry. I cried for my father, I cried for my sister, I cried for Bill, I cried for my mother, I cried for myself. I was so far from home and so lonely.

**Monsieur Albert, Marsha Le Brun,
Renée, Chris, and Peggy**

Chapter Six

Tea for Two

Le 15 septembre
Dear Mom,

I realize I haven't written for a while but the past two weeks slipped by so fast. I can't tell if I'm progressing much. My first teacher was awful, now I have a really nice teacher Renée who is teaching me a lot.

Let me know how you are, Mom. Send a letter about what everyone's doing.

ON MONDAY, THE LANGUAGE director called me to her office. "Mademoiselle O'Toole, we have changed your classroom." She briskly escorted me to my new class.

Mademoiselle Arnaud greeted us at the door. She was in her late twenties, friendly, and warm, not like the typical skinny, tight-skirted French chick. Rounded and voluptuous, she wore her henna-red hair in a top bun with ringlets that fell softly around her rosy cheeks. Her full lips were painted with glossy red lipstick, her big brown eyes darkened with kohl, her thick eyebrows penciled in perfect arches. Mademoiselle accentuated her Rubenesque figure with lace and frills. I had never seen anything like it outside of a musical.

After class, Mademoiselle invited me to go with her to her blind music teacher's house. In exchange for piano lessons, she would read to him in the afternoons. "It will be good for you to listen to me read in French," she suggested. I agreed.

As we left campus, she linked her arm with mine, leaned close to my face, and said, "Call me Renée. We'll be good friends."

The piano teacher lived in a drab, mustard-colored row house with a front door that opened onto the street. Standing on the single step, Renée knocked loudly, and an elderly woman dressed in the customary long, black widow's dress answered the door and led us to a darkened room where her blind son, Monsieur Albert, slouched on a faded red velvet couch. Hearing Renée's voice, he sat up straight, his mouth turned up in a mechanical Howdy Doody smile. "Ahh, bonjour, ma petite Renée."

She greeted him with a kiss on each cheek and sat down close to him, letting him feel her face. Having never been around blind people, I assumed this was a greeting, a way for him to *see* how she looked. After a few prolonged and uncomfortable moments, he stopped touching her, and she began to read without introducing me. I sat down in a straight-backed Victorian chair across the room and observed.

Monsieur Albert was in his forties, with a receding hairline and greasy wisps of mousy brown hair hanging behind his ears. He had a large, Romanesque nose with coarse, dark hairs poking out and a bad set of dentures. His head bobbed as if marking time to his mother's footsteps as she left the room and closed the door. When the door clicked shut, he turned his attention back to Renée, following the words in his Braille book while his free hand rested against her left breast. His milky eyes rolled back in his head as he let his hand fall until it lay between her legs, and then he slowly and rhythmically caressed her. I couldn't pay attention to the story as I watched his hand move up her skirt. She gently guided his hand back to his lap. I sat quietly, wondering if he even knew I was in the room. Their duet appeared well practiced. Renée didn't miss a beat as she read and repeatedly pushed his hand away. A half hour later, Renée put down the book, leaned over, and kissed him good-bye on each cheek, allowing him to skim her breasts with both hands.

'Au revoir, Monsieur Albert." She brushed away his hands. "À demain."

The old woman reentered and led us out the door into the bright sunshine.

Upset at having witnessed such strange behavior, I walked ahead of Renée. I didn't understand whether this overt sexual attention from her blind piano teacher was acceptable in French culture or Renée just didn't stop him out of respect for her elders. Or maybe she enjoyed it.

"Ça va, Peggy?" She innocently asked if I was okay.

I stopped and turned. "He's a pervert, Renée. Why do you put up with him?"

"He's blind. He doesn't mean any harm, Peggy. I like to help people."

The next day, Renée invited me downtown to have tea and practice speaking French, after she took her piano lesson. I agreed to meet her for tea but not the piano lesson.

Arriving early, I waited outside the tearoom, shifting from foot to foot and looking up and down the street, painfully aware of being a tall American girl in blue jeans and white tennis shoes. A group of adolescents smoking

Gauloises approached me. I gave them an *if I'm nice, you won't hurt me* smile.

"Keeess me, pleeease! American keess," the runt of the pack shouted as he skidded on his knees in front of me, his head upturned, hands on his heart, and lips pursed. I turned away and another guy kissed me on the lips to the delight of the puerile group.

In my best and most forceful French, I yelled, "Ne me baise pas!" which I thought meant "Don't kiss me!"

The boys' taunts increased, "Baise-moi, baise-moi."

By the time Renée arrived, the hoodlums had circled me, encouraging each other. I yelled louder, "Ne me baise pas!"

Renée scowled and gave them a quick tongue-lashing. The youths ran away, leaving me forlorn but relieved.

"What did you say?" I asked.

"*Bas les pattes*; it means 'down with your paws.' They're like a pack of dogs. Pouf, little boys, so bad," she said, releasing air through her pouty lips.

"Oh, I'll remember that. I was being too nice."

"Ah no, Peggee. You were not being nice; you were telling them, 'Don't fuck me.'" She laughed. "And they were yelling, 'Fuck me, fuck me!'"

My lesson for the day: *baiser* means "to kiss" when a mother kisses her baby, but when said to a boyfriend, it means a whole lot more. *Damn French!*

Red-faced, I entered the tea salon and sat stiffly on the tuck-and-roll red velvet banquette seats, watching the sophisticated crowd through the gilded mirrors surrounding the brightly lit room, with garish chandeliers above each table. The waiter, severe in demeanor and dressed in a tuxedo, rolled the pastry table over and described each item in detail, *chocolat* this and *chocolat* that, all covered or filled with Chantilly crème. As a child, I had dreamed of eating cream puffs and chocolate éclairs that didn't come wrapped two to a pack by Hostess.

* * *

I had only been to one other tearoom: Bullock's on Lake Street in Pasadena. I was nine years old. After Thanksgiving dinner at my aunt Peggy's house, she took me aside and whispered, "Ask your mother if you can stay the night. I'll take you shopping tomorrow and to the Bullock's tearoom to watch your sister Shereen in the fashion show."

I got a tingly feeling. I wanted to go so badly, but I worried that I'd hurt my mother's feelings. My stay-at-home mother never learned to drive and could only take me on the bus downtown to shop for clothes for school and sometimes Christmas and Easter. I'd overheard her say to my father, "My poor sister, Peggy. She can dress up and have a fancy Cadillac, but no children." I had sensed a bit of jealousy in my mother's voice.

Finding Mom in the kitchen doing the dishes, I pulled at her apron to get her attention. "Can I stay the night with Aunt Peggy?"

"Of course, Peggy Anne. I packed your blue organdy dress with the pink sash and your Mary Janes."

When it came time for my family to leave, Mom handed me my homemade clothes in a brown grocery bag. "Mind your p's and q's."

My stomach dropped. This was my first night away from my family.

The next morning, Aunt Peggy's house was quiet. There was no one yelling for socks, no baby crying with a wet diaper, no brothers fighting over the toy in the bottom of the cereal box. I sat by myself at the breakfast table eating Cheerios and drinking Tang while Aunt Peggy straightened the kitchen. She wore an indigo tweed pencil skirt and matching jacket with deep purple velvet cuffs, collar, and covered buttons over a frilly white blouse. Her trademark three-inch heels in slate patent leather clicked on the Formica floor. Mom never dressed like that, and in my child's mind, this was my fault. With ten children, Mom was too busy to take care of herself.

We arrived at Bullock's and took the elevator to the third floor. It opened onto the tearoom. A man in a dark blue suit showed us to our table, which was set with linen, silverware, and china teacups. The emcee called out each designer as the models entered the stage. Shereen waited in the wings. My heart thumped when she walked down the runway wearing a beautiful cocktail dress with layers of ruffles in the purest white and thin spaghetti straps, displaying her long neck and flawless skin. I beamed and squirmed in my seat. At the end of the runway, she tilted her head toward me and winked. I wanted to say hi, blow her a kiss, stand up, and let everyone in the room know she was my big sister.

"Shhh, Peggy Anne," Aunt Peggy whispered, squeezing my hand and leaning close to my face. "Put your napkin on your lap and take only one item from the pastry tray."

* * *

Recalling that afternoon of both delight and terror of embarrassing my aunt, I chose one item from the pastry tray. Renée studied the pastries, pronouncing each one for me: *millefeuille, tarte au fraises, petit four, profiterole, baba au rhum.* "Hmmm, which do you want, Peggy?"

I chose the largest, a profiterole—a decadent, oversized pastry shell filled with a thick yellow crème and smothered in chocolate sauce with a side of vanilla ice cream to soften the richness.

Over the following weeks, Renée and I became closer. We often went out after class and drank Pernod, the sweet licorice liqueur that made water a foggy yellow and set my head spinning. She taught me how to pull snails from their soft shells and part the tiny frog legs to eat the succulent meat.

I questioned why she spent so much time with me. Didn't she have other friends? Perhaps I was another one of her projects, like the blind music teacher. She told me she understood my social awkwardness and empathized with my inability to speak the language.

"I was lonely in San Francisco when I was an au pair. I made many mistakes in English, like you do in French." She laughed. "I told them I was gay, which I thought meant happy. Like now, I'm gay with you." There was a twinkle in her eye. I wasn't sure how to take her remark.

Stairs leading to the disco in the Casino Barrière

CHAPTER SEVEN

Chocolate

Le 2 octobre 1:30 a.m.
Dear Mom,
    It seems as if I have only been in school a week, and here it is—already a month has gone by and only 13 more days left of this intensified language program. Last Friday, our class went on a tour of a chocolate factory. I sampled all the bonbons on the conveyer belts and stuffed my purse full of the rejects, just like in I Love Lucy. Needless to say, I was thoroughly disgusted with myself afterward. I'm up late cramming cuz I was gone all weekend. Write soon.

ON THE BUS RIDE back to the dorms from the chocolate factory, I sat next to the Swedish girl, Lisbeth, all dolled up and looking like she had walked out of *Seventeen* magazine. Leaning close to my face, she whispered, "I met a boy last week from the aeronautic factory, and he invited me to Biarritz this weekend. He's bringing a friend! Do you want to come?"

These boys weren't boys; they were men—engineers working on the fastest jet in the world, the Concorde. Most of them were married, with one intention: to get the California girls in bed.

"I'll think about it," I said. Only two weeks were left to learn French well enough to take classes alongside native speakers, and I knew I should stay in the dorms to study. My cohorts had progressed enough to pass leisurely afternoons speaking French in cafés and drinking with friends in the evenings. They spent their weekends shopping or on side trips to Spain, the Pyrenees, Biarritz, and the vineyards. I often joined them but made the mistake of conversing only in English, embarrassed at how little of the language I knew.

But if I go with Lisbeth and the French guys, I'll be forced to practice my French, I rationalized to myself.

Lisbeth pleaded, "You'll have a good time, and I already told them I'd bring a friend. We'll stay with his family. Pulleeese!"

I need to immerse myself in the language, not stick around Americans. "Okay, I'll go."

As the bus turned onto campus, Lisbeth pointed to a fancy red sports car parked under a tree with two men leaning against the hood. They were smoking filterless Gauloises and wearing *la mode*—tight purple pants, red shirts unbuttoned to show flashy gold jewelry, and pointed shoes. It was like a flashback to a scene of the Puerto Ricans in *West Side Story*.

"There they are. Aren't they adorable? The dark-haired one is mine, Didier," she squealed, waving from the window. I took another look. Didier was a Neanderthal; at least *mine* didn't have facial hair. My guy was tall and lean, his blond hair hanging over one eye. He was a James Dean look-alike.

"Meet me in fifteen," Lisbeth said. She ran off the bus to get her already packed oval suitcase. In my room, I tossed a few things in a bag: pajamas, bathing suit, change of underwear, my rosary, and a toothbrush. Throwing my fringed purse over my shoulder, I left without telling anyone where I was going. I felt naughty sneaking off but exhilarated to be whisked away to the famed surf spot, Biarritz. It did cross my mind that they might want sex, but I was confident I could ward off any advances. Being raised in the middle of five brothers, I could hold my own.

As I approached the car, Lisbeth yelled, "Vîte, vîte!" and flung herself onto Didier's lap, wrapping her arms around his neck. Instinctively, I recoiled. *Was this a mistake?* She was dressed for nightlife, not a weekend at the shore.

Without being introduced, I got in the backseat and moved as close to my window as possible, pretending to watch the scenery. My date pulled out a pack of cigarettes from his shirt pocket and offered me one.

"No, thanks." I rolled down the window.

He leaned forward and offered Lisbeth a cigarette and rattled off something in French, which I assumed translated to something like, "Why did you bring the skinny bitch?"

Lisbeth scooted closer to Didier, patted the seat, and Monsieur James Dean climbed to the front, sandwiching Lisbeth between them. The entire two-hour drive, they chain-smoked and spoke an incomprehensible slang, giggling and tickling, guffawing and snorting. Occasionally, Lisbeth would turn around to ask, "Ça va?"

The sun had set by the time we got to Biarritz. A purple haze settled in the sky, the horizon a deep orange hue against the slate blue ocean, and the lights twinkled in the windows of the scarlet and cream Hotel du Palais.

Instead of dinner, we went directly to the disco in the Casino Barrière on the promenade of the Grand Plage.

Lisbeth flashed a smile and grabbed my arm in full French mode. "We'll have a good time. Just be nicer to Laurent." Funny, I hadn't even realized that was my date's name.

Walking through the lobby, we passed the roulette tables and descended the spiral staircase. A large disco ball spun in the middle of the dance floor, splattering silver white light over the gyrating bodies moving to the worn-out song, "Louie, Louie." At the bar, men in tight black suits and gold chains fawned over women who looked like porn stars in sequined pantsuits, their cleavage on display. *So...these are the beautiful people,* I thought.

I was instantly self-conscious. I was wearing the same old green button-up blouse tucked into tan jeans, a gray cardigan, and sneakers. I stayed in the shadows, hugging the periphery of the room and wondering, *Do I matter to anyone here?* No one gave me a second glance. If I hadn't walked in with Lisbeth and her friends, the bouncer probably wouldn't have even let me in—I looked like a peon.

I needed a glass of wine, a beer, anything to relax me. Timorously, I walked up to the bar and ordered. "Un verre du vin blanc."

"Trente francs," the barman said, wiping the bar with a white towel.

"Trente francs?" A glass of wine cost more than a week's meal ticket! "Un verre d'eau, s'il vous plaît." I was still overcharged: ten francs for a lousy glass of fizzy water in a fancy green bottle.

I watched Lisbeth and her new beau on the dance floor, Didier dipping her under his legs, throwing her over his shoulder, and spinning her like a rag doll. *So high school.* Laurent kept his distance from me—he was on the prowl, chatting up the scantily clad French women. He'd definitely get lucky tonight, even if he had to pay for one of the fancy call girls.

Escaping to the balcony, I peered into the dark, looking at the Atlantic Ocean for the first time. I drifted back to the Pacific coast, thinking of Bill and the cliff across from our apartment in Isla Vista. The huge October waves crashed against the silvery sand. Moisture gathered beneath my eyes, and I couldn't tell the difference between my tears and the delicious taste of salt spray.

A man who had been standing in the shadows approached me and said softly, "It's beautiful, isn't it?"

"Yes. You speak English."

"Yep, I'm American—a pilot for Pan Am." He put his hand out to shake. "I'm Ted. What's your name?"

"Peggy. It's nice to meet you." He had a sincere grip. We talked about ordinary things: the ocean, the weather, where I was from, and what I was doing in France. He told me about himself. "I live part time in Miami, graduated from Dartmouth, and have a terrier named T-Rex." He didn't whistle between his teeth or grope me or make innuendos about going back to his place. There was no spark, just a friendly, warm feeling.

"I've got a flat here. If you come back to Biarritz, stop by." He jotted his address and phone number on the back of a napkin and handed it to me. As he turned to leave he said, "Hang in there. The French aren't so bad, once you get to know them."

Inside the tepid disco, clouds of smoke swirled, and the music thumped relentlessly. I found a corner booth and curled up in a fetal position to wait. It must have been after two in the morning when Lisbeth finally stumbled over to the table and informed me she'd had enough.

"Time to go; Didier's waiting in the car." She looked like shit. Her hair had fallen into a stringy mess that accentuated a not-so-flattering head shape, and her makeup was smeared across her cheek. A missing fake eyelash gave her an off-kilter look.

On the way to the parking lot, she held on to me, swerving and dipping like a cartoon drunk. At the car, no one mentioned waiting for Laurent. We drove to Didier's family's home, a cramped apartment on the outskirts of town. In the entryway, the grandfather clock chimed four times. Didier gave me a blanket and pointed to a mattress pushed against a wall amid decaying magazines and musty artifacts left behind by his invalid father. Lisbeth disappeared into another room and Didier followed. The paper-thin walls did nothing to keep out their animal grunts and cries. I turned away from the sounds, promised Jesus and Mary I'd never get myself in another mess like this, and fell asleep.

**Marsha La Blonde, Francoise the
language teacher, and Valerie**

CHAPTER EIGHT

Moving On

Le 15 octobre
Dear Mom,

We left for Bordeaux this morning—I'll get settled, hopefully with a French family or some French girls, that way I'll be forced to speak French plus learn a little more about their culture, especially their cooking. After I get moved in, there will be nearly ten days to travel. I'll see a little of France, meet Claire (my high school friend) in Paris and really learn something. What's new at home?

IT WAS OUR LAST evening in Pau, and the mayor had invited the American students to a formal dinner with local dignitaries in the ballroom of the Hotel de Ville.

The California girls wore short skirts and minidresses in paisleys, bold oranges, and lime green, and the boys sported flared trousers, plaid bell-bottoms, and flashy ties. We sat intermingled among the French professors at tables covered in white linen and set with silverware, Limoges china, and crystal wineglasses. A handwritten menu was placed at each setting. The first dish was something called *Ortolan*.

Waiters bustled in and out of the kitchen carrying silver-domed plates, carefully placing one in front of each of us and with a flourish lifted the lids, exposing the smallest little songbird, baked to a crisp, sitting in a halved potato that resembled a nest. Screams and shrieks erupted throughout the dining room like popcorn popping. The Ortolan looked like the pet parakeet Bette Davis served her wheelchair-bound sister in the movie *Whatever Happened to Baby Jane?*

The French patrons stared aghast as we Americans refused to eat the delicacy of the region and groaned in disgust at the sound of the crunching of tiny bones as our professors ate the minuscule birds whole, licking their fingers and wiping the drippings off their faces, staining the linen napkins.

My attitude toward the French had changed since I'd first arrived. I no longer idealized them as the sophisticated, poodle-walking, café-au-lait-sipping, romantic stars as depicted in the movies. They were all that, yes, but they were also snail-eating, frog-leg connoisseurs and bone-crunching baby-bird eaters.

I saw myself differently too. I wasn't all that cool and groovy; in fact, I was awkward and in dire need of learning how to adapt to a new culture, beginning with learning the language and how to dress. I had hoped my shopping spree in Spain would have solved some of my problems, but it ended up being a painful memory.

* * *

It was our last weekend in Pau and the school had hired buses for an excursion to Zaragosa. We arrived around eleven and had the day to sightsee and shop. I followed Reuben, a self-proclaimed maven, and his pals into a camera shop. From behind the counter, the clerk brought out the sought-after camera, the Nikon F2. The price tag before the lenses was one hundred *US dollars,* not *pesetas!* I was out of my league. The savvy American students wheeled and dealed with the salesman, and three of them walked out with new cameras, lenses, batteries, and film for the price of a month's rent.

In private, I asked the clerk. "Do you have anything a little less expensive?"

"What's your price range?"

"About twenty-five dollars."

He looked at his inventory behind the glass doors. "Do you need an F stop?"

"I don't think so. I just need a camera."

He brought down a Kodak Brownie instamatic camera. "This one is easy to use and takes good pictures. You'll like it."

It was within my budget, so I bought it, happy with my purchase until the bus ride back. The rich kids checked out what each other had bought, showing off their purchases and bragging about the good deals they'd found.

"Hey, Peggy. What did you buy?" Reuben, the class prick, condescendingly asked.

I had on my new sweater and proudly pulled out the light tan suede jacket. "I got a good deal on it."

"Wow, that's really cool. What else?" He knew what else and was baiting me, knowing well and good I had bought a camera and it wasn't the Nikon F2.

He reached inside my bag and took out my new Kodak Instamatic Brownie and let out a whoop. "You bought an *American* camera in Spain? You paid too much for it, and you can't even get the film developed here!"

My cheeks flushed. I grabbed it back and mumbled, "It's the one I wanted, shithead."

* * *

After dinner the last night in Pau, I went back to the dorms and packed my bags. I layered my new purchases on top of my old clothes, the new me over the old me. I neatly folded my gray cashmere sweater on top and left the suede coat out to wear on the train. I checked my accounting of what I had spent and felt guilty about splurging on a new jacket when my corduroy coat would've been fine for the winter. On the other hand, I rationalized, if I wanted to hang out with the cool kids and make a good impression with the French students, I needed better clothes.

Ah shit, who gives a damn what others think? I thought. *I was so stupid!* I closed my suitcase, hoping the new clothes would somehow change me, but they only reminded me of the day on the bus returning from the shopping trip to Spain. I stuffed the shitty little camera deep inside my suitcase, burying my embarrassment. Why had I even come to France? I couldn't speak the language, I didn't have any friends, and I couldn't afford to be here.

Early the next morning, we left the little town of Pau in the beautiful Pyrenees. I was scared to death. I didn't want to be here, but I couldn't go home either—that would be failing.

The train pulled into Gare de St. Jean, a bustling station with soot-laden buildings and the smell of urine emanating from the walls. I found myself thinking, *How can I live here for nine more months?*

On doorstep at 77 Rue de l'Abbé de l'Épée

Chapter Nine

Rue de l'Abbé de l'Épée

Dear Mom,

I'm living in a mansion in the attic room next to Ernaldine, the Portuguese maid. My landlady is very Catholic and has crosses above every bed and statues in the corners. I feel at home. Please sit down with a cup of coffee and let me know what you and the family are up to. I miss you.

LEAVING THE BUSTLING TRAIN station, we loaded onto three large buses and drove through the grimy city streets of Bordeaux, past the cookie-cutter apartments of the suburbs, and into the countryside, with rows and rows of vineyards on both sides of the road. Fifteen minutes later, we arrived at the Talence campus of the University of Bordeaux.

The large, uniformly ugly cement block buildings, with rows of narrow rectangular windows, were a testament to the era of Russian architecture. In contrast, white puffy clouds dotted the azure sky, and a clean breeze offered the proverbial breath of fresh air to a rather dismal first impression.

As we got off the bus, the director of foreign students, Monsieur Garcia, greeted us by name, a small kindness that made me feel welcome. Rumors had circulated among the students that he had been a leader in the French Resistance, helping downed American airmen and French Jews escape across the Pyrenees. During our orientation, Monsieur Garcia spoke of his gratitude to the Americans for risking their lives, praised our country, and hoped for the continuation of good Franco-American relations.

Later, on the campus tour, it became apparent that his pro-American sentiment hadn't transferred to the next generation. Written across walls in dripping red paint were slogans I had yet to fully understand: "Contre la guerre de Vietnam. Bas les Amèricains! Vive la lutte!" There were no rainbow "peace and love" signs to be found on campus.

After the general assembly, Monsieur Garcia handed out our housing assignments. "Piggy," he addressed me in a heavy accent, "you and Marsha will live together in town with Madame Assemat, a very respectable woman." He leaned in a little closer. "I studied all the student photos, and you two look like sisters." This statement proved prophetic—Marsha married into my family thirty years later—but at the time we didn't know each other.

Marsha had a great many friends in the program, and I wasn't among them. I watched her hugging them good-bye, asking who they were rooming with, and seeing her face fall when Leslie, her best friend, said she was living with their other best friend, Valerie.

"I asked to be both of your roommates," Marsha whispered, nearly in tears. "But it's okay, I got Peggy." She turned to me and lightheartedly said, "Okeydoke, let's go, ain't getting nowhere standing here."

I felt sorry for Marsha for being left out, but I was secretly thrilled to be her roommate. She attracted male attention with her long, blond hair, blue eyes, and sexy body. She was cool and hip, the epitome of a "California Girl." Maybe it would rub off on me.

During the taxi ride to our new home, we chatted about what it would be like to live in a big city far from the ocean or mountains. I had grown up in Pasadena, with views of the San Gabriel Mountains and horses next door. Marsha had grown up in Encinitas, a small beach community in Southern California. We both had lived on the beach in Isla Vista.

The cab turned onto Rue L'Abbé de l'Épée, a narrow cobblestone street lined with attached gray stone houses and protected by lion's-head door knockers on fortresslike wooden doors.

Standing in front of the imposing entry with our luggage at our feet, Marsha nudged me. "You knock."

"No, you knock. You speak better French."

"I don't speak French; I just read and write it."

"Okay, fine." I knocked several times but got no response. We peered up at the windows on the top floor and saw a young girl dressed in a white uniform who was shaking out billowing sheets and pillows.

"Allo!" we shouted with our best French accents.

Leaning out the window, the maid smiled broadly and called back, "Un moment, je descend."

The large door opened, and the dark-haired maid welcomed us into an exquisite foyer, with black-and-white floor tiles, faux marble pillars, a red tufted entry seat, and a crystal chandelier.

A short, plump, middle-aged woman bustled past the maid.

"Bonjour, Peggy? Marsha?" she greeted us in a high melodic voice. "Je suis Madame Assemat."

"Enchanté," we replied politely.

"Entrez, entrez," she declared, waving her hand.

After exchanging a few niceties, she introduced Ernaldine, the Portuguese maid, and asked her to take us to our rooms. The docile young girl grabbed a bag from each of us and trotted up the three flights of stairs to the attic rooms with us following. Madame Assemat slowly mounted the stairs, breathing heavily, muttering about clean linens and keeping windows closed so as not to let the heat out.

Ernaldine whispered, "N'inquietez pas. Elle vient pas souvent dans les chambres," assuring us that Madame Assemat rarely came up the stairs to our rooms.

The home had the affectations of old money: Persian rugs; heavy, ornate furniture; and gilded sconces on the walls. Madame's spinster sister, Mademoiselle Margaux, lived on the third floor across from us. Their invalid mother, Madame Margaux, remained on the second floor in a separate apartment.

Margaux. I had heard that name connected to the great wines of Bordeaux and wondered if there was a connection.

Mademoiselle Margaux, a small and birdlike spinster, kept to herself. Rarely, if ever, did I see her, and when we did cross paths, we exchanged few words. *Bonjour, Mademoiselle... Bonjour, Mademoiselle.* Her eyes cast down, she'd lock her door, squinch her face into a smile, and leave early in the morning for an office job. She returned for lunch in her upstairs studio across the hall from me, went back to work, and returned in the evening. I could smell food cooking and hear the low hum of a television set from behind her door.

"Mademoiselle Margaux est très gentile, mais triste," Ernaldine confided. Her sadness stemmed from a lost love. She'd been engaged to a soldier before the war, but something had happened over the years of occupation and fighting, and the marriage was called off. She never had any interest in another man, or at least, that's what I understood.

Madame Assemat had stopped on the second floor to check in on her mother, who was wailing. Marsha and I looked at each other quizzically. Ernaldine gave the universal sign for "crazy," circling her finger around her temple. Marsha whispered, "*la folle*," which became our pet name for the senile old woman whom we never met in the year we lived there.

Her door stood ajar. The old woman in black lace sat in an ebony rocker facing the French doors that opened onto a balcony overlooking the street. A lace skullcap covered her wispy gray hair, making her resemble a living version of *Whistler's Mother*.

Madame spoke harshly in an attempt to settle her mother down, and then she rang a bell for La Folle's private maid. In seconds, a matronly woman in black with a white apron and nurse's cap scurried out of another door with a tray of tea and into the mother's room. The door closed behind them, and the wailing stopped.

I couldn't imagine what caused her to be in such a dismal state, rocking and moaning. Was she crazy, or did she suffer a great loss of fortune and loved ones? At times, I would catch a glimpse of La Folle in her rocking chair, like Mrs. Bates in the movie *Pyscho*.

In any case, it saddened me that the old woman was so isolated, never invited to dine with her daughters and just cared for by a maid, which was so foreign to me. We always took care of our own. Grandma came for Sunday dinners. I visited her in her little apartment on Saturdays after swim lessons, and eventually, she came to live with us, sharing our lives. We certainly didn't leave her alone in her bedroom.

Huffing, Madame Assemat arrived on the third floor to show us into our rooms. "You'll have to decide which one of you will get the larger room." She spoke slowly and clearly in French, having been familiar with Americans staying in the two attic rooms next to the maid. Marsha and I flipped a coin, and Marsha got the large room with a fireplace, two big windows overlooking the street, and a large walnut bed with a feathery duvet and puffy pillows. I got the tiny room.

"Peggy, you can come over anytime," Marsha offered with a tinge of guilt in her voice.

"Thanks, Marsha, but don't feel bad. I like my room. It's cozy like my room at home."

✳ ✳ ✳

I flashed back to my little room in the attic of our house on Rosemead Boulevard. There were ten of us living in a two-bedroom home that my mother and father had bought when they had three small babies. Children kept coming, and my mother made do with what she had.

I slept in the playroom with my baby brother, Pat, who was in a crib; I was in a daybed pushed up against our library wall. At naptime, I pulled down encyclopedias and looked at pictures of naked Africans, tall Watusi, little Pygmies, and strange people with painted faces and Ubangi lips, but my favorite photo was of the Siamese twins. My two older sisters slept in the sunroom, my three older brothers in the unfinished attic, and my mother and father on a hideaway sofa bed in the living room with a bassinet next to them. At five years old, with so many people under one roof, I felt secure, the breathing at night a comfort that no one was too far away if I should wake up in the middle of the night and need to go to the bathroom or get a drink of water. When my mother became pregnant with their tenth child, my father decided it was time to build the extra room he had promised her when they first moved to Rosemead Boulevard. During the construction of the "boys' room," my father decreed, "Peggy Anne is a young lady and deserves a bedroom of her own, not with the boys."

Dad fixed up one side of the attic and painted it in my favorite colors of pink and blue. I loved that little room with the window overlooking Mr. Latham's garden next door and the San Gabriel Mountains in the distance. It was a place of solace and solitude when things heated up over money or when tempers flared and angry words preceded the slap of a belt or the back of a hand.

✳ ✳ ✳

Snug in my new room in Bordeaux, I flung open the window, looked down, and watched an old man lock his door, and amble down the street, like a grandpa. Melancholy overwhelmed me. *Grandpa died, but he was old. But my dad won't grow old.*

Potted geraniums hung from the window ledge across the way, clusters of red flowers falling gently to the ground, slowly dying as winter approached. I sensed a part of me dying. So much had changed. I had left home. Dad had died. My little attic room was no longer mine. My childhood was over. The old man turned the corner out of sight. I looked out over the ancient city—its red roof tiles and black chimneys—remembering my brother's sage words. "Take advantage of being in Europe; it's going to go by fast." I resolved to make the most of my time here. What would my life be like in France? Surely different from anything I had known.

Now I had my own room: *a place to hang my hat,* as my mother would say.

I closed the window lest I get caught for letting the heat out into the brisk autumn air. The tiny room had everything I needed and more: a bed, an armoire, a sink, and a bidet, something I'd never seen before but discovered that every French woman thought it was a necessity. Unpacking my bags, I folded my sweater and extra pair of jeans in the bottom of the armoire, hung my two blouses next to my new jacket, filled two small top drawers with my underwear and the second drawer with a couple of soft cotton shirts, and placed my clogs and tennis shoes under the bed. Perfect. It all fit.

I lay down and my feet dangled off the end of the short European bed. I propped the pillows behind my back, grabbed a pen from the side table, and wrote a postcard to Claire.

Peggy, Howard, Claire, and Clifford in Paris

Chapter Ten

Paris in Autumn

Le 15 octobre
Chère Claire,
I'll meet you Friday the 23rd, late afternoon, on the steps in
front of the Jeu de Paume, Place de la Concorde.
Love, Peggy

"Have you ever done this before?" Marsha asked.

"No, but everyone says it's easy."

Being virgin hitchhikers, Marsha and I discussed various techniques of holding out our thumbs.

"I think if we stand one in front of the other and hold our thumbs really high, we'll have a better chance of being seen," I suggested.

"Okay. Let's try." Marsha had that worried little girl look on her face, her long blond hair pulled back tight with a headband, creases showing along her forehead.

Men in sharp-looking business suits and fashionably dressed women in tight skirts and high heels bustled past us on their way to work, turning their heads in disdain. At first I thought it was my clothes that warranted French condescension, but Marsha looked good, almost French, with a scarf tied neatly around her neck, a crisp white blouse underneath her navy blue sweater, and tight jeans. That's when I realized the French turned their noses up to all foreigners. They collectively felt superior in most areas, possibly because of their good wines, gourmet food, beautiful countryside, haute couture, and thin, lithe bodies. In my mind, they were haughty and unapproachable.

Marsha stepped away from the curb. "I can't do this! Let's take the train with Leslie and Valerie."

Defiantly, I raised my hand higher. "You said you'd go with me. Everyone else does it." This wasn't true, but I couldn't afford a train ticket after spending all that money in Spain.

Just then a sleek Citroen braked, causing the traffic to stop. Horns blared and angry drivers shouted out their windows. "Merde alors!" A red-faced fat guy swerved to miss the stopped Citroen in front of us.

"Get in! You can't *autostop* from here!" A young man in a gray-striped suit and red paisley tie got out of his car, opened the passenger door, and motioned for us to get in. Grabbing our bags, he ran around to the back of the car, unlocked his trunk, and threw them in, giving the annoyed drivers the Italian salute, one arm in the crook of a bent elbow, equivalent to "the finger."

Safely back in his car, he laughed, "You must be American hippies. Blond hair, tall, beautiful like in the movies." He paused. "Too bad you act stupid like Americans too."

Dumbfounded, we didn't know how to react to the compliment and rude comment rolled into one.

"Where do you go?" he asked.

"We're going to Paris."

"Okay, I'll take you across the bridge to the A10. You'll get a ride very quickly there."

He dropped us off at a rest stop on the outskirts of town, gave us our packs, lit a cigarette, and shook his head. "Be careful with French men. I was nice."

After he had driven off, Marsha scowled and took out her map. "The jerk was right. The A10 will get us to Paris." The distance was about the same as from Los Angeles to San Francisco. We could make it before nightfall.

Again, we stuck out our thumbs and within minutes a truck lumbered to the side of the road, kicking up dust and releasing a hissing sound as it came to a complete stop ahead of us.

"Do you think it's safe to go with a trucker?" I wondered aloud, remembering the ax murderer on Isla Vista beach who hadn't been found. Hesitating, I thought of the truck-driver who molested and killed a young girl he picked up hitchhiking along the northern coast of California.

Marsha shook her head and waved him on.

He looked down on us and swore, "Putains, alors." The truck swerved back onto the highway.

"Let's not put our thumbs out until we see a nice car, one with a family," Marsha pleaded. "I don't like being called a whore."

Agreeing to be more discreet, we waited, leaning against our packs on a small knoll off the road. We tore off pieces of baguette and smeared the morsels with *La vache qui rit* (The Laughing Cow), the soft comfort cheese. An hour later, a Spanish family pulled into the stop and set up a morning picnic on a large red-checkered tablecloth, inviting us to join them.

In broken English, the mother told us not to hitchhike. "Come with us to Poitiers. You'll be safe." We accepted.

By early afternoon, we had only gotten as far as Poitiers, halfway to Paris. Another Citroen stopped, this time with an older businessman, a fatherly type. We asked where he was going first, a safety measure so he couldn't just say he was going where we were going.

"Orleans," he replied, which was at least two hundred kilometers closer to Paris!

We climbed into the backseat, holding onto our bags in case we needed to exit quickly. The hydraulics slowly raised the car, making the ride so smooth it felt like we were floating on air. After a few kilometers, the gentleman smiled in his rearview mirror.

"You're American, no? My daughter is your age, studying in New York City. My name is Monsieur Clement."

Being in the company of American girls seemed to make him feel a connection to his daughter. I thought of my own father and imagined he was looking down from heaven, happy to see me in a safe car with a nice man instead of a trucker.

Monsieur Clement delighted in telling us about each region, the wines and cheeses, the chanterelles and foie gras.

"Ah, it's better for you to taste than just talk." He pulled into a *Routier,* a truck stop with the ubiquitous red and blue circular sign out front. The parking lot was full of trucks. After a filling family-style meal, we had a thick, black espresso in a demitasse, and a crème de menthe *pousse-café* to digest the food before facing the final leg of our trip. We still had two hours left to go.

"Bon route!" Monsieur Clement flashed us a peace sign and drove off.

By three o'clock, we had caught our last ride with an older gentleman, a World War II veteran. He loved Americans. In fact, he said he owed his life to the American soldiers who liberated France.

We reached the *périphérique* in Paris by late afternoon, the sun hidden behind the rows of tall apartment buildings, the air brisk with excitement, and lights beginning to twinkle in street lamps.

The old man wanted us to see Paris as he had seen it as a young man after the war. He crossed the Seine with a view of the Tour Eiffel, maneuvered the busy roundabout of the Arc de Triomphe, triumphantly sailed down the Champs-Élysées, circled the Place de la Concorde, skirted the Tuilleries, and dropped us off in front of the Louvre.

"Amusez-vous bien, mes filles Américaines." He waved good-bye with a warm smile.

He had gone an hour out of his way to get us to our destination, talking about the days of occupation and the camaraderie with the Americans who had liberated Paris, conjuring up the iconic black-and-white photo of the American soldier kissing the French woman. World War II had ended only twenty-five years earlier, five years before I was born. I didn't have any memories of the war, and having not been fought on US soil, there weren't any constant reminders, yet everywhere in France was a living history of the war. The monuments, the streets, the people, the cemeteries—all held stories. I was being sucked into the past and home, my point of reference, was slowly fading.

I liked the old man. He made me feel good to be an American, but that feeling didn't last.

Walking down the treelined gravel path of the Tuilleries toward our meeting spot, we ran into Marsha's friends, Leslie and Valerie. They swooped her up into their conversation, hugging and dancing around like playmates in a schoolyard.

I hurried ahead, hoping to find Claire, my high school friend who was studying in Aix-en-Provence. "I'll meet you at the end of the park, on the balcony overlooking the Place de la Concorde."

Nothing short of a miracle, Claire, in her fashionable knee-high boots and black peacoat, was leaning against the wall, talking to a group of students from our program.

"Salut, copains!" I cried. Giddy with laughter, we had a group hug. Marsha, Leslie, and Valerie ran to join in, all amazed and relieved we had found each other on the steps of the Jeu de Paume. We linked arms around each other, scarves and coats blending, one body overlapping the next.

We took the Metro to the Rive Gauche, the Left Bank, and found a rundown hotel on Rue Saint Jacques near the Sorbonne in the Quartier Latin (Latin Quarter), where the students lived. Entering the dark foyer, we rang the bell on the desk and an old woman in a black dress with a white apron waddled out from a back room, the aroma of croissants trailing her.

Clifford and Lise, a Bohemian couple from Berkeley, negotiated the room rates, while Claire and I stood nearby. The rest waited outside.

"Avez-vous deux chambres, pas cher?" Clifford's curved pipe dangled from the corner of his mouth.

The woman eyed his wild Einstein hair and mustache and then looked at Lise in her long, voile skirt and army boots.

"Vous êtes marié?" she demanded.

Lise's eyes twinkled. "Oui, c'est la lune de miel," she replied, lying that they were married and on their honeymoon.

"Oui, Monsieur, Madame. C'est cinq francs chaque chambre."

"Avec une douche?" Clifford asked if the shower was included.

"Sans douche, Monsieur. C'est pas cher."

We paid five francs, the equivalent of a dollar, for each room—no shower—and went to join the others outside.

Tall Howard was toking a joint. "Your friends left. Couldn't dig the scene."

I understood why Marsha had left. She hated drugs and any kind of smoke, but I felt ditched again, and that left Claire and me with Tall Howard, an affable stoned giant.

The woman handed us two heavy metal keys attached to chains and pointed to the stairwell.

Unlocking the small door, Claire and I entered the attic room with slanted ceilings and a little nook where we stashed our packs. Two twin beds fit snugly against a single flat wall with a reproduction of an Impressionist painting overhead and a dormer window that opened onto a view of tiled rooftops. Howard tucked himself under the eaves and pulled out a sleeping bag.

"This okay with you?"

I could see the disappointment in Claire's face. She had stayed at the Intercontinental when she'd arrived in Paris a month ago, so the Hotel Saint Jacques was a bit below her standards.

"For now, but maybe we'll find our own place tomorrow."

Leaving the hotel, we walked down Rue des Écoles to Boul Mich, the shortened form of Boulevard Saint Michel, where the students had torn up the cobblestones and hurled them at the police during the 1968 student uprisings. The street cafés bustled with activity, and crowds of people strolled while soldiers with machine guns stood at the ready on the street corners. I put my hand inside my purse, feeling around for my student ID card. It was the law to carry personal identification at all times or risk incarceration.

Monsieur Diament, the liaison of the Faculté d'Étrangères, had warned us that anyone could be stopped without reason and searched. "Do not participate in any type of covert activity, be it a political meeting or demonstration, and by all means stay clear of Communist organizations or risk deportation."

From the corner of my eye, I stared at these urban soldiers, studied their faces beneath plastic face shields, and checked out their weapons with curiosity, as if looking at a rattlesnake. I didn't show them my fear. Ill feelings resurfaced—I had experienced the Isla Vista riots, the killing of Kevin Moran, the searches, the tear gas, and the mishandling of peaceful student protestors. *Pigs,* I thought.

In a bookstore window, a series of black-and-white posters chronicled the protests: a long line of French students, arms joined, resisting the gendarmes who held metal shields, their grenades and rifles at the ready and tanks in the background; riot cops lobbing tear gas canisters into the crowds; mayhem, young students fallen in pools of black blood, others running; police holding fire hoses unleashing torrents of water at the students, who were hurling rocks. I was standing in the same place where these photographs had been taken only a couple years before.

Avoiding further contact with the gendarmes, we dipped into an alley, winding deeper into the Quartier Latin, following the smell of sticky sweet pastries and smoky barbecue, past a myriad of vendors selling pizza, slicing rare pieces of meat off large haunches roasting on spits, and wrapping up

Tunisian burgers in waxy paper. The brightly lit pedestrian streets had a carnival-like atmosphere, with brightly dressed Africans, swarthy Arabs in traditional robes, and a mélange of student types, from well-appointed youths carrying book bags to rag-clothed dilettantes.

We moved in a wave, following Clifford's Einstein hair and Tall Howard's dark, wavy hair, both of which we couldn't miss bobbing above the crowd ahead of us. Bumping shoulder to shoulder with the crowds, the guys led us through the streets until we found the student café Clifford had been looking for.

"Be cool. This is a hangout for the Marxist students."

"How do you know?"

"I met this French guy, Giles, at Berkeley and he told me to come by here when I got to Paris." Tall Howard nodded his head in approval, pulled out a hash pipe, lit it, took a hit, and passed it to Lise and Clifford. Claire and I held up our hands in protest, not wanting anything to do with dope, especially out in the open with the police only blocks away.

Howard slipped the pipe back into his pocket. A young man sitting on a stool in the doorway checked our student cards, charged us five francs each, and gave us meal tickets before descending the narrow staircase into the cavernous student dining room.

Waiters streamed in and out of swinging kitchen doors, carrying huge pots of soup and placing them on the long tables in front of Baudelairean students wearing heavy jackets and vests over dark, baggy clothes. The guys sported beards and long, scraggly hair. The girls pulled back their long, flowing hair with bandeaus and headscarves, revealing bangle earrings and Indian beads. Claire and I looked like all-American sorority girls in comparison to this edgy, political fringe of anti-American students.

On the other hand, Clifford, Lise, and Howard fit right in and swaggered over to a table, interrupting a group in deep conversation. After muttering a few words, Clifford flicked his head toward us, indicating to sit down at the table. Lise passed the breadbasket, and we started speaking in English—American English. It was like waving a red flag in a bull's face. A bearded guy in a black beret and red scarf turned to Clifford and said something curtly about the Vietnam War and baby killers.

Clifford responded with a nearly perfect French accent, "Je suis révolutionnaire, contre l'état."

With a thud, the waiter set down the soup terrine. Lise lifted the ladle to serve the steaming brew and in midstream turned to the heckler and said in her perfect French, "Nous sommes communistes."

Claire's eyes widened; she motioned to me that we should leave.

Before I could get up, a radical guy with goofy, stoned eyes looked directly at me and asked, "Et toi? D'oú viens-tu?"

Caught off guard by his accusatory tone, I was afraid to say anything to incite these rough intellectuals. But he had asked an easy question: Where was I from?

"Je viens de Santa Barbara, Isla Vista," I replied tentatively.

"Isla Vista? Santa Barbara? Le Banque d'Amérique était brulé la bas." He knew about the burning of the Bank of America! I had my chance to show I was one of them.

"Oui! I was there. I burned the Bank of America!" Redemption.

I became the center of attention for having accomplished such a feat. The French activists thought the "Bank of America" was the central bank of the United States, like the Fed. I kept talking, bullshitting about the Chicago Seven,

the riots, the SDS meetings, the fuck rallies, and the sit-ins;
I even impressed Clifford.

* * *

I had stood at the edge of Perfect Park and watched students ram the door of the small bank with an old couch.

Earlier that day, the police had shut down a riot emanating from the football stadium after William Kunstler, the lawyer for the Chicago Seven, had spoken and incited the students to "take back the streets." Later that evening, a bonfire burned in the vacant lot adjoining the bank. People gathered, warming their hands over the campfire, as if waiting for marshmallows to soften for s'mores. I walked back to my apartment to tell my roommates the bank was going down. We had all protested Bank of America's involvement in the war by withdrawing our funds—which in my case amounted to a total withdrawal of $3.75.

By the time I returned to the scene, the bank door had been busted open, the windows were broken, and people were inside throwing furniture, papers, and ledgers out the gaping holes to fuel the bonfire. A Molotov cocktail finished the bank, and I watched the flames dancing high into the black sky. Mobs of kids, dogs, and transients worked themselves into a frenzy, chanting, "Burn, baby, burn!" for an unseen team, as if attending a football rally. Some others freaked out like they were on a bad acid trip. No police or firemen showed up to bring order to the anarchy. By early morning, an unsettling quiet had descended. All that was left of the bank was a smoldering pile of trash and the acrid smell of burning rubber.

* * *

The next day in Paris, Claire and I left our dope-smoking, radical friends and found a little hotel near St. Germaine. We visited museums, ate in outdoor cafés, and strolled the Jardin du Luxembourg.

By the end of the week, our vacation time had run out along with our money. I convinced Claire that hitchhiking was safe in pairs, so we decided to go south toward Lyon until our paths parted, at which point we would take the train, Claire continuing east to Aix and I west to Bordeaux.

Standing on a busy corner on the Champs–Élysées, our bags and suitcases at our feet, we studied the map with a forlorn look that announced to every passerby, "These American girls are lost."

Out of nowhere we heard a voice say, "Don't I know you?" A strapping, embarrassingly American-looking guy yelled from his seat under a café awning. He shouted even louder, "Don't you live in Isla Vista?" and took a swig of his *pression*, draft light beer. He motioned for us to come over.

"Yeah, I live in IV. Do I know you?" I said, giving away the fact I had no idea who he was.

"I own the apartments across the street from where you lived last year." He stood up, all six-two inches, and pulled out two chairs for us. "I'm Craig. You're Peggy, right?"

"Oh, I remember you," I lied. "This is my friend, Claire."

We sat down to have a beer with him and told him we had to find our way out of Paris to hitchhike back to school.

"Well, I'm leaving today, heading south. I could give you a ride as far as you like on my way to Spain."

Out of all the thousands of corner cafés in Paris, luck would have it we stopped there and met Craig. Once again, living in the dumpy, seaside student enclave of Isla Vista had proved to be a lifesaver in Paris. When serendipitous things happened, I imagined that God was pulling my puppet strings, sometimes laughing at me, but still I felt safe in his hands...or maybe it was Dad's hands.

That afternoon, Claire and I left Paris in Craig's VW bus. We traveled through the countryside of central France, drinking wine, eating at the roadside Routiers, playing the Who "All aboard the magic bus..." on his funky cassette player, and enjoying being Americans.

Arriving at school

Chapter Eleven

Fall Semester

Le 9 novembre
Dear Mom,

The French are so unorganized. It usually takes three times as long to get anything official done over here. My courses won't be definite until the end of November and then they've been known to change them as late as January. I plan to take twelve units in Sociology, eight in French Literature and eight in Art history. My intensified language course counted for twelve units. Ha, I learned more French traveling with Claire. Please write a long letter, I miss you and everyone.

CLASSES STARTED IN LATE fall. The days were warm and the early evenings cold, with a hint of winter in the air. I attended class regularly, but I couldn't understand the professors, read the material, or do the assignments. I was hopeless. French coursework is structured so that each year of study builds on the previous year and is universally taught throughout France. By university level, every French student has already read the *Lagarde et Michard* textbooks, which cover a sampling of French literature. They have memorized important events and dates in French history and can identify artwork and artists from prehistoric times to the present. My professors frequently made references to this bank of knowledge. I sat through class after class wondering if anything would ever sink in. The other American students didn't appear to be stressed by all the schoolwork—they gabbed away in French, spoke to the professors after class, and hung out in cliques making plans to go shopping, stop by a café, or view an art exhibit. Occasionally I tagged along, but I never felt I belonged.

At break one day, I spotted Marsha and her stylishly dressed friends sitting on the wall, looking like the cast from *Love Story*. They'd picked up the French flare for throwing on an expensive sweater, squeezing into tight pants or a pencil skirt, and wrapping a scarf casually around the neck. The guys hung about them like flies to raw meat, goofing around, jumping off the wall, doing just about anything to get their attention.

I've got to make some friends. I've got to fit in somewhere. I'm so stupid. My mantra turned over and over in my head. I approached them, wearing my dorky, huge white tennis shoes, my bright blue cowboy jeans (still rolled up from the morning bike ride), and a god-awful, striped button-down shirt. What in God's name made me think that would make a fashion statement I will never know, but there I was, taller than the guys, my skinny legs accentuated by the slim-fitting jeans and my long brown hair tightly knotted into two braids down my back.

Reuben, the class prick with the curly black hair and trimmed mustache, called out, "Hey, Piggy, I didn't know there was going to be a flood!"

Forever gullible, I looked up at the robin-egg blue sky with Magritte-like clouds, puffy and white, perky in the glowing sun and replied, "I don't think it's going to rain."

An embarrassing silence ensued, followed by chuckling from the group. Marsha shot them a dagger look and made room for me on the wall. That evening at our house, she offered to take down the hem on my pants and add a band of braid.

"Your pants are too short; they're floodwater pants. That's why they were laughing."

"Jeez, I didn't know that. I appreciate you telling me," I said, even though it seared my heart to hear it.

"Take them off," she said, laughing, "and don't wear black socks with your white tennies either. You look like a marine."

* * *

Being made fun of in my short part legs brought back childhood memories. I had grown at an enormously fast pace in eighth grade, which meant many of my skirts and dresses rode above my knees and my sleeves were never long enough to touch my wrists, no matter how much I nervously tugged at them.

Mom couldn't afford to get me new clothes when I outgrew the old ones, but one year she surprised me and let me open two gifts on Christmas Eve, an unheard of privilege in our family.

"You need something nice to wear tomorrow for Christmas mass."

I opened the Broadway gift box and pulled out a red wool jumper and a white lacy blouse.

"It's perfect, Mom!"

I put the outfit on, and the dress hem hit above my knee.

"Mom, I can't wear my new dress to sing in choir. It's too short."

She reassured me, "You look beautiful, Peggy Anne. It's not too short; you just grew too fast."

On Christmas morning, my parents dropped me off at the back of the church to climb the choir stairs while the rest of the family crowded into the long pews in the side section of the nave.

Sister Eileen stopped me at the door to the choir loft. "Kneel down, Miss O'Toole." Obediently, I went down to the floor, my hands tugging at the hem of my dress. "Too short. Go find your parents. You can't sing in choir today."

* * *

The next day, I sat with Marsha and her friends discussing the literature class and planning where to eat cheaply. No one invited me to go to lunch. They hopped off the wall and left, leaving me alone at the *Centre d'Étrangères*, which literally means "Center for Strangers" but translates to "Foreign Center." I was both a stranger *and* a foreigner.

Determined to meet French students, I walked over to the student dining hall on campus and filed into the cafeteria. Students in the back of the line started pushing and shouting, bullying to get to the front. The ones in front held strong, causing a backlash. Being caught in the whip-like motion frightened me. When people fell, the students trampled over them. I maneuvered out of line to avoid being crushed and walked outside. There had to be another way to meet French students.

Even though I attended classes, I was unable to keep up with the work and considered dropping the large sociology class, but my TA, an American in his late twenties, encouraged me not to give up. "You must go to the lectures. Professor Ellul is the most renowned French Marxist of our time."

"But I don't understand what he's saying."

"You will in time."

Professor Ellul lectured like a politician, raising his voice, clenching his fists, inciting the students and proletariats to throw off the chains of capitalism. The lecture hall rocked with the energy of change. After class, a student, wearing torn jeans and a dirty T-shirt with Che Guevera's face on it, approached me and asked if I would join the Communist party and attend the workers' meetings in the town hall Wednesday nights.

Communist party? Communism was feared back home in the United States, but here the leftist students embraced and propagated it.

"Sign here." He pushed the ledger into my hand, shaking the pen. "Act now."

I wanted to be part of the youth movement and flirted with the idea of joining the student political group. Was I willing to become a Communist and go wholeheartedly against the establishment, my government?

Not that day.

The "Marché des Pousses" is where I got all the junk stuff I am sending home — I figure it has to be authentic French if it's at their flea market. All the open markets are fun to walk around.

Booklet I sent home for Christmas

Chapter Twelve

Long Letter from Bordeaux

Le 1 decembre
Dear Mom,

Maybe if you can see the places I pass everyday then I won't seem so far away.

(On a cold, dreary November morning, armed with my Brownie camera, I set out on my Solex to photograph my days in Bordeaux.)

The Marché des Pousses is where I got all the junk stuff I'm sending home. I figure it must be authentic French if it's at their flea market.

THE OLD CARAVANS, DELIVERY trucks, and tents formed a circle in the Place de Quais along the river. On Saturday mornings, Marsha and I would cruise the lot, picking out hand-laced nighties, linen undergarments, wooden tissue boxes, small cast-iron irons, and antique coffee grinders, *Moulins au Café*, smelling of coffee grounds. The vendors' ages matched their wares.

As we passed, a wrinkled woman cackled, "Viens ici, ma petites crottes." She wanted us to buy something from her little card table—a hanky, an embroidered cloth, a crocheted arm cover, all stained and yellowed.

"She just called us 'little turds'!" Marsha chuckled. "It must be an endearment."

The old lady smiled, holding out a delicate handkerchief in her bony hand. Marsha gave her a few centimes and walked away with a story.

I pasted the photos I took on blank white stationery, folding the pages in half to make a book. I trimmed the edges with yellow, green, and purple markers and carefully labeled each picture with a story.

Not far out of Bordeaux you can find countryside, farms, little villages and Romanesque churches, chateaux and Maison du vins. Marsha and I take our Solexes out when the days are warmer than it has been for weeks. After getting cultured we have good food (wine, bread, cheese and fruit), French style by the side of the road.

I motored from one place to the next, stopping to take photos, imagining my mom next to me, even though I knew she would never get on a bike. In fact, she didn't even know how to ride one. She couldn't swim or play baseball or tennis either, but she could dance Irish sets all night. I wondered what she was doing now.

Mom, you'd love the "jardin publique." It was beautiful this fall, fantastic colors, but now the trees are bare, it's cold and there's a different charm about it.

De Gaulle just died and it's Armistice Day so France has put her flags out along the streets. Our director, Monsieur Carter, lives on the other side of the wall and Marsha and I live a few blocks away to the right. The cathedral can be seen in the mist at the end of Rue Vital-Carl at Place Pey-Berland where I catch the bus to the university in Talence.

I was sad and alone when I took the last photo.

Across the bridge is a beautiful view of Bordeaux's façade, especially at sunset or through the fog. Merry Christmas, Mom!

I found the little book forty years later, tucked inside a white envelope labeled "Peggy Anne's Long Letter from Bordeaux." It pleased me that Mom had saved my handiwork, but at the time what I had really wanted was news from home. I had added a note on the flap of the envelope so as not to ruin the content of the book.

Please write and let me know what the family's up to. Make it a long letter.

* * *

When my mother wrote me a letter, it felt like a to-do list.

Dear Peggy Anne, I'm making the beds, laundry is in the washer, and I have a hair appointment. The mailman's here, I better say good-bye. Love, Mom

The short missives, written on the back of an envelope, a torn sheet from her telephone directory, or a half sheet of lined school paper, always felt like an afterthought, an intrusion on her busy life taking care of household chores and kids. Her refrain was "I don't have time to sit down like other mothers who go to coffee klatches and have maids to help." Her better-than-thou attitude was a cover-up for her lack of confidence in the world of educated and wealthy women. Mom didn't drive a car, hadn't gone to college, couldn't shuffle a deck of cards, and had no interests outside the home. She would boast, "I'm not like those other mothers who go gallivanting around in their Cadillacs and serve frozen dinners in front of the TV."

As most children do, I thought my mother was the "best mom ever," even though I longed for her to be like Rosie's mother, Mrs. Liberto, who dressed up, went to PTA meetings, played bridge, and drove a pink Cadillac. I loved going to the Liberto house and being served TV dinners on TV trays while watching TV.

Mom made sure we had clean clothes and ate healthy, fresh food that she cooked herself, never frozen, except Friday nights when we got Mrs. Paul's frozen fish sticks. But I don't remember her making time for meaningful conversation. She never spoke of anything deep or personal. Our dialogue was perfunctory.

"Peggy Anne, after you do the dishes, sweep the floor."

"It's not my turn."

"Please do it for me; your sister has a cold."

When she asked about my friends, often the answer was in her question. "Now, Claire comes from a nice family, doesn't she?"

We never had the conversation about my changing body or sex. I was an awkward thirteen-year-old, too self-conscious to undress for gym class. I didn't understand why my chest remained flat while the other girls had full breasts. But I did have underarm hair and the hormones to go with it. I questioned Mom about what she called the birds and the bees.

During Mom's sick time of the month, I lay on her bed and lifted my arms above my head, stretching to make sure she saw I had grown hair.

"Can I shave my armpits and legs?"

She answered abruptly. "Use the word *underarm;* armpit makes you sound like a truck driver."

"Well, can I?"

"You don't need to shave. You're not Italian."

Mom had it in for Italians, who developed too young and could lead me astray with their wild ideas and over-sexed desires. She never said those words, but I knew that's what she meant. As my body matured, so did my thoughts about sex. I leaned on my elbows at the foot of her bed and probed for information about periods, boys, and making babies.

"You're too young to know those things. I didn't know about that until I got married."

Mom's written communication wasn't much better than her spoken. She sent my loans and scholarship papers with her signature and an occasional note attached to a package reminding me she loved me and to "watch my p's and q's." My birthday card had a little cat on the front, and inside she had underlined meaningful words like *to my beautiful daughter* and *loving mother* before signing it at the bottom.

Rarely, if ever, did I receive a newsy letter from home. Not once did she mention my father. No one spoke or wrote about Dad or even said if they missed him. Did they miss me or talk about me? It was as if I had wandered off into the field with my father and vanished.

I never told my mother I was lonely, sad, and overwhelmed living and going to school in France. I wanted her and the family to believe I was adapting well, becoming fluent, and having the time of my life. I might have had a better attitude if Bill had written, but he was busy too.

✳ ✳ ✳

By December, I was fully immersed in classes—or more like drowning, because I was nowhere near being competent in the language. For my midterm papers, I lifted sentences from the texts with a few wispy conjunctions to disguise my plagiarism. The teachers returned them with red lines crossing out full paragraphs and question marks where I attempted to express original ideas in incomprehensible French.

Grades for the year were based solely on the final exams in June. With a devil-may-care attitude, I balled up my graded midterm papers, threw them in the trash can, closed my books, and left for vacation.

Claire was waiting for me on the other side of France.

Strasbourg, Christmas Eve

Chapter Thirteen

Christmas at the Base

Le 18 décembre
Dear Mom,

Merry Christmas and Happy Hanukah! I'll be traveling with Claire over Christmas vacation. Tonight I'm taking the night train to meet her then maybe go skiing in the Alps. I mailed a few gifts home for the kids but want to get you a special doll from Provence, a Santon.

I miss you all. I'm doing fine, school's out so I won't think about studying till I get back.

I ARRIVED EARLY SATURDAY morning at the dorm in Aix-en-Provence only to find out that Claire's friend Jamie had convinced her to change plans without consulting me. "You can come with us too and stay with my cousin, Jack. He's in the army in Germany." Jamie was a twit.

I looked at Claire for an explanation. "Jamie has a place for us to stay," she said, as if a free place trumped our time together.

"Jack told me to bring a girlfriend, but there're a lot of guys, and he won't mind if you come too," Jamie prattled.

I immediately disliked Jamie, a nondescript girl with brownish bobbed hair, plaid skirt, and loafers. She seemed uptight and prissy, the type of Catholic schoolgirl I didn't want to associate with. Besides that, I didn't want to share Claire and I didn't want to go to an army base.

The next morning, all three of us caught the train to Germany.

As promised, Jack met us at the station and we drove to the American base, bypassing the old town of Baumholder with its quaint homes, wreaths on the doors, and Christmas trees in the windows. At the security gate, handsome Private Jack flashed his smile and ID card. The guard waved us on under an arching sign that read Welcome to Little America, referring to a subdivision of tract houses with postage-stamp-sized front yards. The sterile neighborhood appeared void of life and warmth, a stark contrast with the villages.

In front of the canteen, a lanky soldier with a southern drawl greeted us. "Welcome, girls, to the good ole USA! Y'all hungry?" He held the door open to a large mess hall set up with folding tables and metal chairs, and decorated with shiny green and red streamers attached to the light fixtures. In the corner was a tall plastic crèche and fake Christmas tree.

My stomach clenched at the smell of canned green beans, fried hamburger meat, and baked cookies, reminding me of the awful dorm food I had eaten freshman year, which resulted in irritable bowels and indigestion. I had wanted to try bratwurst, sausages, thick brown breads, and German beer, not shitty American food.

Lining up cafeteria-style, we loaded our plates and joined the other soldiers and their families at the folding tables.

One of the wives, a petite, washed-out blonde, spoke softly. "Welcome." She looked at me, doe-eyed. "Hope y'all have a good time here. Safer than out there." Her eyes glanced toward the door and tall windows. "I just don't trust those Germans," she said. She took a spoonful of peas, put them in her child's mouth, and wiped the green spittle off his chin. "How're the French? They don't bathe, do they?"

I could barely swallow before answering. "They have different habits."

The southern accents and provincial attitudes of the soldiers and their wives annoyed me; it was a prejudice I carried from childhood. Slow-talking, soft-spoken drawls belonged to ignorant people, and television reinforced that belief, as untrue as it was.

"Don't y'all miss a good burger and fries?" lamented a soldier with no facial hair.

"Not really. I like the baguettes and ham." By now, my polite veneer was wearing thin.

"What we need here is a McDonald's "Jack laughed. "I'm going to bring the Big Mac to Germany when I get out of here." He offered to get us some peanut butter, jelly, white bread, pancake mix, and chocolate chips at the commissary. "Whatever you babes like."

"Wow, thanks! PB&J and chocolate chip pancakes!" Jamie squirmed with excitement as if she was about to pee in her pants. I cocked my head and looked dumbfounded at her. How could she be so simple? I hated her syrupy sweet, all-American enthusiasm.

I was a protestor against the war. I had marched downtown State Street carrying banners against the Vietnam War and blocked the Santa Barbara airport runway when Governor Reagan arrived. My brother-in-law had ridiculed me for being "Red," but I stood strong in my conviction against the war and its corporate sponsors. Now I kicked myself for being at the army base, fraternizing with these GIs. But then I thought of my brother, Ted, who had spent two years serving in Germany. *Maybe I should try to be kind,* I thought. I bit my tongue and excused myself to go to the bathroom.

* * *

Outside, dark clouds concealed the sun, threatening a rainy Christmas week. I wondered what was happening at home; it would be the first Christmas without my father. He had always made the holidays magical for all ten of us kids, somehow saving enough money to buy what we had asked Santa to bring: a shiny two-wheeled black bike for me; a red wagon for my younger brothers; two soft dolls for my baby sisters; boxing gloves, pogo sticks, and stilts for the older boys. How did my father buy all those toys when we had so little money? I knew I would miss Christmas Eve—my brothers and sisters opening one gift, going to midnight mass, and hanging stockings before going to bed. But Santa wouldn't be there.

* * *

When I returned to the table, the conversation had changed to where we would spend the night. Jack announced that he had a *big surprise*. "Let's go, girls!" We piled into Jack's car with his friend Joe and drove through a snow-covered forest to an old castle near the border of Luxembourg.

Passing through the wrought iron gates, we drove slowly over the crunchy gravel driveway that wound up to a Gothic castle, now an all-girls' prep school.

"Surprise! You get to stay in your very own castle for Christmas vacation."

I wasn't so sure if this was a good idea; we had no other transportation to and from the castle besides Jack and therefore would be dependent upon him for the rest of vacation.

"Thanks, Jack, this is fantastic," Jamie said. She looked at us. "Isn't this fabulous?"

Jack got the keys from the caretaker and led us up the path, the ice-laced leaves scrunching under our feet. With the turn of the old brass key, the lock clicked and the metal-studded door creaked open. Inside was dark and dank, smelling of mildew and strong cleaning solution. The electricity, gas, and water had been turned off for the holiday break. By flashlight, we climbed the winding staircase to the second floor. At the end of the hall, we entered a small room vacated by Sophie, Jack's girlfriend, who had gone home for vacation.

"We could stay to keep you warm," Joe half-joked.

"No, thank you," we all claimed.

"Gotta go," Jack said. "We'll pick you up in the morning. Sleep tight."

We heard the main door slam and watched through the leaded glass window as their car rolled out of the driveway. The small, prisonlike room had posters of James Dean and Marlon Brando hanging on the cement walls. The three of us stared at the two twin beds covered by woolen blankets and no sheets.

"I'll take Sophie's bed," Jamie announced.

Claire and I glanced at each other, resigned to the fact she had the upper hand. "Sure, Jamie, you deserve your own bed since you got us here." I don't think Jamie caught Claire's sarcasm.

We took turns using the flashlight to go to the bathroom down the hall. I stayed up late pondering how to dump Jamie and the GIs.

Looking out the leaded window to the snow-laden yard below, I watched the dark shadows of the trees shimmer under the moonlight on the newly fallen snow. Taking the flashlight, I crept out of the room into the hall, where I had seen an old-fashioned telephone on the wall. I wanted to call home. I turned the crank, but the line was dead. Later I wrote: *Dear Mom, I tried to call but I was in a chateau and couldn't reach you…*I started to cry.

Shivering, I returned to the room and wrapped myself in all of my clothes. I climbed into bed next to Claire, head to toe, and said my rosary until I fell asleep. The mindless repetition of the familiar prayer soothed me, taking my mind off the day and my lousy predicament. I asked the Blessed Mother to help me be more understanding of the poor guys in the service, and then I added, "And give me the strength to leave tomorrow."

Praying was part meditation and part making deals. I pleaded and bargained with Jesus and Mary: "I'll do this if you give me that." I just hoped they would pull through on getting me out of here tomorrow.

Late the next morning, we heard Jack's car rolling over the crispy snow and bolted for the door with our bags packed, not willing to spend another cold night in the castle. Jamie sulked, knowing both Claire and I didn't appreciate all her cousin was doing for us, but she didn't want to stay there alone.

"Hey, girls, how was your night in the castle? Did you sleep like little princesses?" Jack had that *cool guy* demeanor I found so nauseating. Did he really think it was a treat to stay in a cold, deserted dorm?

"Oh, thanks, Jack, it was so exciting staying in a real castle," Jamie cooed.

"Jeez Louise, I'm so sick—" I didn't finish my thought aloud, *of your goddam high girly voice.* "Really, I'm sorry, Jack, but I have to get back to Bordeaux. We'll stay in town tonight and catch the train tomorrow." Claire nodded over Jamie's protests.

"But you'll miss Christmas Day and New Year's!" Jamie turned to her cousin. "I'm staying, Jack. I'm sure they'll change their minds."

Jack shrugged. "We got lots of plans, girls. Give it a thought."

Back at the barracks, we picked up a few more guys before continuing on to Strasbourg to celebrate Christmas Eve in the bars and discos. But first Jack wanted to have an early Christmas dinner in the mess hall.

"The food is free and much better on the base than in town. Holiday turkey dinner." It was the saddest turkey dinner I've ever had—not like our Christmas dinners growing up.

*   *   *

On Christmas morning, Mom would get up early to prepare the turkey, as large as the current baby, the kitchen full of kids and new toys. Each of us got a turn to pat the turkey before Mom stuffed the bird. I can't remember why, but it was a ritual slapping of the large bird that each year morphed into some new and more elaborate twist. One year, Pat twisted the head off my old Kewpie doll and stuck it in the neck cavity. Dennis grabbed a wing and I took the other as we flew the bird through the house before Mom demanded we let her place it in the oven. Christmas day rolled by as slowly as the turkey cooked; we waited for cousins to come over and the feast to begin. Daddy carved the turkey. I was his helper, learning how to carve against the grain so that each tender piece was uniformly angled and then placed on Mom's special gold-rimmed Haviland platter. The dining room table was covered with an Irish lace tablecloth and set for twenty with fine china plates, crystal glasses, and Mom's wedding silverware. Dad lit a fire in the hearth. We all sat down, said grace, and passed the stuffing, gravy, potatoes, homemade breads and pies, and Mom's special fruitcake stored from the previous year, dripping in rum.

* * *

I willed myself back to my family home, the ghost of Christmases past. I said a silent grace and ate the Ocean Spray canned cranberries, instant mashed potatoes, real turkey, and prepackaged gravy.

My mother's homunculus jumped on my shoulder: *Be grateful and think of the poor starving children of Armenia.*

Okay, Mom.

That evening, we left in two cars and crossed the border into France. As we approached Strasbourg, the streets narrowed and the old buildings rose up and closed in on us like a tunnel. Getting out of the car, Jack and his friends grabbed our arms in a protective but possessive way, marching us along the dark streets and then descending into a disco in the basement of a warehouse. A group of US soldiers lined the bar. They gave us girls the once-over and greeted the men with slaps on the back, bantering back and forth like fraternity brothers. Jack made a quick introduction and ordered us drinks.

Christmas Eve in a cellar nightclub with GIs, foreigners, and unknown faces, all sloppy drunk on German beer, depressed and angered me. The GIs expected to dance with me, even when I said no. *Why do I have to put up with this male chauvinism crap?* After an hour, my head ached from the pounding music, and my eyes stung from the cigarette smoke. I found Claire. She looked distressed too. Nodding toward the exit, we broke away, coming up for air in the crisp winter night.

Church bells were ringing in the distance, coming from an illuminated spire piercing the inky sky.

"Midnight mass!" Entwining our arms, we ran down the narrow cobblestone street until it opened to the Place de la Cathédrale. Altar boys holding large sacristy candles circled the plaza, leading a procession of black-robed priests and bishops in their tall miters and white flowing robes, blessing the people with holy water, incense wafting from silver thuribles. We threaded our way through the crowds and entered the church under the carved stone portal.

Inside the nave, lit by candles and chandeliers, the ancient organ filled the church with chords of power and joy. The angelic voices of the choir lifted our spirits as we sang along, "Gloria en excelsis Deo,' harkening back to our roots. The high mass in Latin was as familiar to us as our mothers' voices, the intonations soothing, "Sanctus, sanctus, sanctus."

After receiving Holy Communion we left mass to get back to the disco before Jamie and the others noticed us missing. Joe met us on the stairs. "Got to go. Curfew is one a.m. for us."

Feeling guilty, we said our thanks and good-byes. Jack dropped us off at a hotel, and Jamie stayed with her cousin and the guys from the barracks.

That night, in a cheap hotel by the cathedral, Claire and I stayed up late talking about home. We missed our large families and our friends, but we were excited to be together and eager to see what tomorrow would bring.

The morning after the storm

Chapter Fourteen

Snow on the Tracks

Dear Mom,

After Claire and I left Strasbourg, a cold but beautiful town, we tried to head south. The night we left, a storm hit France, the worst since the 40s and the hardest hit was where we were traveling from Lyon to Valence. We spent 19 hours on that damnable train in snow that blocked the tracks. I went crazy when I woke up and realized we hadn't gone even halfway. I hate trains!

* * *

On Christmas morning, we woke to the cathedral bells chiming the hours. From under the covers I counted the strokes: one, two, three, all the way to eleven o'clock.

"Claire, wake up. It's late! Merry Christmas!"

"Merry Christmas," Claire responded, still half asleep. "Shall we get up and look under the tree?"

"I think we got coal for Christmas," I chided. "We must have been bad to get stuck with those GIs last night."

Over a café au lait in the hotel lobby, we hatched a plan to catch a train to the south of France to salvage our vacation. "It'll be warm in Marseille," we promised each other.

Unfortunately, we didn't have enough money for a train ticket to Marseille plus hotel and food. We set aside a few francs for necessities and each bought a thirty-franc ticket so we could board the train with a plan to stay on the train for as far as we could go until discovered. We found an empty cabin, collapsed on the bench seats, and let out a sigh of relief, giddy to be on the road again, this time by ourselves.

We sang Christmas carols as the train rolled through the snow-covered forests and passed icy lakes, with the towering Alps in the distance dressed in their winter cloak. It was late afternoon when the train slowed to a stop in a village outside Lyon. The attendant ushered in a group and then opened the door to our cabin and checked our tickets. He waved his hand and told us to get off, muttering his disapproval of student tricks: *un sale tour d'étudiante!*

"Not bad, four hundred kilometers for six bucks!" I whispered to Claire. Pleased with ourselves, we got off, took the stairs to the urine-soaked underground passageway, and exited onto the street. Our good humor soured as we walked along deserted streets lined with barren trees, the branches shaking like skeleton bones. Our footsteps echoed on the cobblestones, the air cold and heavy with a still, quiet emptiness. We were hungry, and all the stores were closed, even the bars.

"It's a Catholic country; it's probably against the law to be open on Christmas."

To get out of the cold and wind, we went into a Romanesque chapel in the village square, lit a candle, and said a prayer for our families, friends, and our safe journey.

"Let's eat in here; it's too cold outside," Claire suggested. "Churches are sanctuaries for lost souls. I think we qualify."

Resigned to a Christmas dinner of leftovers, we found a half baguette, two wedges of la vache quit rit, and four squares of chocolate at the bottom of our purses and bags.

"Church mice. We're eating cheese in church." I nibbled the soft cheese with my two front teeth.

"I'll bless the bread." Claire held the stale, half-eaten loaf above her head. "The body of Christ."

"Protein." The jokes lightened the moment.

In her soprano voice, Claire sang, "Come, they told me, pa rum pa pum pum, A newborn king to see, pa rum pa pum pum."

I joined in, my off-tune alto making the duet humorous. "I am a poor *girl* too, pa rum pa pum pum."

It was not yet four in the afternoon and already dark when we left the church. Not wanting to spend money on a hotel, we walked back to the train station in the silent night.

"We can take the night train," Claire suggested.

"Yeah, maybe get something to eat on the train too."

No one was at the window selling tickets, and no one stopped us from getting on the train that pulled into the closed station after six in the evening. We found a vacant cabin and closed the curtains, hoping to stay out of view of the conductor. Stretching our legs out on the cushioned seats, we settled in, pleased with our second heist and prickly with trepidation of getting caught. At the next stop, I peeked out the window and saw dark Arabs or perhaps Spanish people, mounting the stairs, and then we heard them knocking against the corridors with their luggage opening and slamming doors to the cabins. Heavy-set, kohl-eyed women in robes carried bundles of stuff wrapped in blankets and babies in slings tied to them. The men carried baskets of food and opened thermoses of steaming liquid. Cloaked children trailed them. They crowded into their own cabins, leaving a sticky smell of grease, mint, and honey drifting under our sliding door. The curtain fell closed, leaving me with the eerie feeling of having witnessed a scene from *The Seventh Seal*, a Fellini movie I had studied the year before in film class: *the march of death, the search for meaning in life when all is lost.*

"Jambon, fromage, baguette, café, boissons..." A sleepy-eyed attendant passed our door, pushing the food and beverage cart down the corridor. Cracking open the door, we checked up and down the hall to make sure the train conductor wasn't around, and then we snuck out and bought a ham and butter baguette sandwich to share. The food attendant continued down the hall, his voice fading and blending with the clinking of the bottles and the blowing of the train whistle. The train rumbled on into the black night. Claire and I fell into a deep sleep, hopeful that by the time we woke up we would be in Marseille, as far south as we could go in France, away from the cold, northern countryside.

A screeching sound of brakes, a jolt, and cars bumping together woke us up. Over the loudspeaker, a crackly voice bellowed, "Attention, Mesdames and Messieurs, il faut descendre." We peeked under the shades. It was still dark outside, but the voice was telling us we needed to get off the train.

"Oh my God! Claire, did you see the snow?" I gasped.

Outside, the snowdrifts came up to the train windows, a blanket of undulating white covering the countryside.

"Where are we?" Claire asked, still drowsy from her deep sleep.

"I don't know, but it's not Marseille."

The porter knocked on our door and ordered us to get off the train. "Il y avait le pire orage du temps. Tous les trains sont arêtés depuis minuit." The train hadn't budged since midnight due to the worst storm of the century. What we had heard was the disconnecting of the cars.

We gathered our stuff and filed behind the overburdened families onto the cold stone platform to wait under the awning until the tracks could be cleared. We stood shoulder to shoulder with the dark-skinned people who had a peculiar smell of animal, spice, and sweat. Their shielded eyes made me wary, and I moved as far away from them as I could and sat wrapped in a train blanket next to Claire.

I didn't trust the swarthy foreigners and was afraid to sleep for fear they would steal my things or try to harm me. Even the children scared me. I didn't understand their cries or the harsh voices the parents used to soothe them. Yet at the same time, it bothered me that my instinct was to avoid contact with them I was ashamed when I came to the realization that I was no better than the army wives and soldiers who isolated themselves and judged the Germans without getting to know them. Still, I couldn't change the way I felt. I didn't want to be near them.

* * *

During the fifties and sixties, I had been sheltered from different cultures, especially the dark, ethnic groups. In Arcadia, where I attended Catholic grammar school, a curfew existed for Negroes, which at the time was the polite racial designation for African Americans. The black maids, butlers, jockeys, and stable workers at Santa Anita Racetrack, and even our visiting priest with dark skin from India, had to leave town before dark or risk going to jail. Not understanding the impact of words as a child, I used racist slang, calling Mexicans "wetbacks," Japanese "gooks," Italians "wops," and Jews "kikes."

My mother would admonish prejudiced behavior, yet she held her belief that the Irish were a superior people. "We should love everyone, even the Mexicans and the less fortunate." She also told us her parents wouldn't allow her to date a Mexican or a Jew. She could only marry someone Irish or at least a white Catholic, like my aunt Peggy, who married a Croatian Catholic. There was no tolerance for the darker races or other religions, only condescension and pity. How could I not have recognized that my upbringing reinforced discrimination? Racism coursed through my blood, and I had thought I was tolerant.

* * *

By morning, we were back on the train, moving slowly forward behind a snowplow that had been sent to rescue us. Claire and I were both irritable and groggy when we reached Marseille at nightfall the next evening.

Claire in Marseille

CHAPTER FIFTEEN

Return to Bordeaux

Dear Mom,

We arrived in Marseille, a port on the Mediterranean Sea, and for the first time in years, it snowed there! The locals said it was "une occasion rare," like we were lucky to get snow, not sun!

When I got back to Bordeaux I received your Christmas card and presents. Thanks for the pictures of the family, the fruitcake, my boots and money. That was too extravagant considering the shipping cost.

Send some old pictures with Dad in them. I would love any and all home pictures. Sorry you couldn't hear me when I called from Aix, but I heard you and everyone. Made me nostalgic.

Please write, make a tape of your voices. Don't forget your suffering daughter in Europe, maybe someone can come visit me.

AFTER OUR NINETEEN-HOUR JOURNEY, we dragged ourselves to the nearest low-rent hotel in Marseille across the street from the train station. Station hotels are often bordellos, and this one was no exception. We snickered at the footsteps on the stairwell outside our door but were disgusted when we started to hear noises coming from the other side of the thin walls. Pulling back the blankets, we noticed stained spots on the sheets, so we slept on top of the covers in our clothes, rolling up our jackets for pillows.

The next morning, ice covered the windows. The storm had followed us to the Côte d'Azur, bursting our dream of sunny blue skies and swimming in the fabled Mediterranean Sea. Claire and I walked to the beach, snapped a few photos, put our feet in the frigid water, and returned by train to Aix to stay in her dorm. The next few days, Le Mistral, the icy cold wind from the Alps, whipped our faces, stung our legs, and pierced our clothing as if we were naked. Bundled up and pushing against the wind, I did my Christmas shopping in the little stalls that lined Cours Mirabeau, buying presents for my mother: Santons (dolls dressed in the traditional costumes of Provence), foie gras, and fine Camembert cheese.

A deep sense of loss and melancholy overwhelmed me when I returned to the cold, loveless mansion on Rue de L'Abbé de l'Épée.

Claire was a touchstone to my past, providing a respite from my pining for home. But once I was back in Bordeaux, loneliness and the weight of class projects wore me down. Final midterm papers were due in less than six weeks, and my French had barely improved. In a desperate attempt to finish my semester, I spent my free time in libraries, even on weekends, hoping to get something accomplished.

One late Friday afternoon in mid-January, I looked around the empty library and hit rock bottom. My schoolmates had already left town for the long weekend. I started thinking, *Maybe I should just throw in the towel.* Defeated, I left my books on the table, walked out of the Central Library, and sat in the stairwell with my head in my hands, drained of hope.

A group of French students stood on the landing, the guys smoking Gauloise unfiltered cigarettes, looking cool in ragged jeans and oversized jackets. The only girl, a sultry blonde with a scarf around her neck, asked me if I was American.

"Yes," I replied, doubtful that this could go anywhere good.

"Where are you from?" she asked.

"California." To calm my frayed nerves, I boldly asked, "Can I have a cigarette?"

"Sure, California." The blonde shook a cigarette out of her pack of Marlboros. "What's your name?"

I put the cigarette in my mouth, cupped my hand around her lighter, inhaled deeply, and then exhaled slowly, eyeing the group. A tall, skinny, goofy-looking fellow with long, sandy-brown hair kept shifting from one foot to another. Next to him was a dark-skinned guy with black hair and chiseled features. He held my gaze with his piercing brown eyes, and I stared back, my heart skipping a beat. The third one was gorgeous—tight-bodied with asymmetrical masculine features—but aloof.

"Peggy," I answered an octave higher than normal. Fearful they would ridicule me in my pitiful state—alone in the stairwell, unable to communicate in their language—I spoke politely. "What's your name?"

"Marie-Paule. Nice to meet you." She put her hand out and then turned to the boys and introduced them. "This is my brother Marco and our friends Jacques and Pierrot." They nodded, continuing to joke around, talking so fast I didn't even recognize the language to be French.

"Nice to meet you," I said, my head cast down, my hair covering the sides of my face.

"Why are you so sad?" Marie-Paule took a hit off her cigarette and then blew smoke out of the corner of her mouth.

Why did she care?

"I have a lot of work to do for my political science class. I don't write well in French, and I'm having a hard time understanding."

"No problem. It's Friday. No school tomorrow. I invite you to dinner with my family. Everything will be okay, California. Come skiing with us for the weekend."

Is this for real? I couldn't imagine anyone, let alone French people, would want to be with me in my miserable state. My inner voice fought back the urge to refuse and crawl back into my shell.

"Okay. Where should I meet you?"

"Le New York Bar on Rue Pasteur in town next to the Faculté de Droit. See you tonight at dix-huit heures? Six o'clock, you say."

I nodded.

"Good. Afterward, I take you to my family's home." Marie-Paule snuffed her cigarette into the cement with the toe of her fashionable cowboy boot. "Would you like another ciggie?"

I took the cigarette, put it in my shirt pocket, and watched them leave: Jacques sliding down the bannister, Pierrot jumping two steps at a time, and Marie-Paule and Marco walking close behind. The heavy door slowly closed shut. I returned to the library table, gathered my books into my pack, and left, wondering if I was cool enough for them.

Outside Le New York Bar with Clifford and Howard

CHAPTER SIXTEEN

Le New York Bar

Le 10 janvier
Dear Mom,

I met this French family and they're so nice—there's eight kids in the family, a couple are married, and the one I met first is my age, Marie-Paule. She introduced me to all of her friends. Really nice people—they remind me of my California friends—they surf and ski, play hockey, and aren't snobby.

ARRIVING BACK AT MY house, I ran upstairs to my room, threw off my clothes, and took a "French bath," straddling the bidet as it filled with warm water. I wrapped a towel around my body and leaned over the sink to look closely into the mirror as I applied eyeliner and mascara. Color had come back to my cheeks. Was it the cold wind, or was I alive again?

My father's voice reminded me: *First impressions are lasting impressions.* This was my one chance to make a good impression. Brushing my long, brown hair, I counted to a hundred as Shereen had instructed when she brushed my hair as a child, pulling at the tangles, telling me, "Hold still if you want to be beautiful." I thought of Mom getting ready for her Saturday date night with Dad. She would wiggle into her girdle, smoothing her belly flat, and then pull her slip over her fancy bra before applying her coveted Estée Lauder perfume, not the cheaper eau de cologne. *Put a drop on each wrist and a dab behind each ear—not too much, Peggy Anne. You don't want to appear cheap.* Finishing my toilette, I splashed the lemon scented Jean Naté on my wrists and behind my ears...not too much.

Opening the armoire, I rummaged through my stacks of folded clothes and fingered through the few shirts and jackets on hangers. I had two choices of pants: tan jeans or blue jeans. I hadn't brought the Levi 501s that shouted, *You are a cool American.*

Muted colors felt right. I grabbed the tan pair, coupled it with my beige button-down shirt and my high-top construction boots Mom had sent at Christmas. I grabbed my new suede coat, gave a final approval to my image in the mirror, and ran down the three flights of stairs, out the door, and onto Rue de l'Abbé de l'Epée.

I arrived at six o'clock *précise* and waited for Marie-Paule under the yellow sign with the words *Le New York* tucked beneath a silhouetted Manhattan skyline and a martini glass in the corner. The beautiful people—intellectuals in buttoned-up Nehru jackets, preppy students, and hippies—mixed together at tables, all deep in conversation.

A white-aproned waiter bustled by me with his arm above his head holding a serving tray full of beers, whiskey tumblers, and tall glasses with fresh lemon juice and little pitchers of water. I squeezed past him to find my way to the bar.

"Je voudrais une bière," I said, enunciating every syllable.

The bartender ignored me, snickered, and then took the order of the guy next to me. When he returned with the drinks for the other guy, I repeated myself, "Je veux une bière."

"Whadda ya want?" the bartender barked loud enough for others to hear him speak English.

"I'd like a beer," I acquiesced to English.

"Hmmph, what kind—*Pression? Blonde? Noir?*" He listed the numerous selections, all in French.

"Blonde," I said, not knowing what I was going to get. Within a few minutes, he placed a bottle of light beer and a mug in front of me.

"Deux francs." He set the tab down with a slap of his hand.

"Voila." I took two francs out of my fringed purse and put them on top of the receipt.

"Merci, Mademoiselle." He swept the coins into one hand, tore the receipt to show I had paid, and left to deal with the other patrons.

"Jerk," I said under my breath. I poured my beer, placed the empty bottle back on the bar, and walked outside.

A seat had opened up at a table.

"Excusez-moi," I said, and before I had finished asking to sit, the man in the Nehru jacket nodded his approval and turned back to his conversation and friends.

I sat down and nervously looked around for Marie-Paule. It was now six fifteen. I had already learned that when the French say, "Meet around six," it could literally mean around the full hour, so any time before seven would be socially acceptable.

Out of the corner of my eye, I saw the waiter barreling toward me.

"Qu'est-ce que vous faites ici!" he yelled. "Il faut quitter le table, immédiatement. Il y a pleine de monde."

What am I doing here? Leave the table immediately? I didn't know what his problem was. "Excusez-moi? J'ai payé," I explained, indicating that I had paid for my drink.

He spit his words back at me: "Vous n'avez pas le droit de s'assesoir."

I have no right to sit? What did I do to lose my right to be here?

"Je ne comprends pas." I pleaded the fallback excuse of not understanding.

"Oh la la, les bêtes Américaines." Stupid Americans. I was used to the slur.

Heat rose in my cheeks, first out of embarrassment then anger. Defiantly, I didn't budge and sipped my beer, praying that Marie-Paule would appear. The waiter plopped the drinks on the table for the other customers, left, and came bustling back with a heavyset man dressed in a suit. "You deed not payee pour zee place to seet." He spoke worse English than my French.

"Oh, I didn't know. Sorry." I got up, took my beer, and went back into the bar. I stood in the far corner with one eye glued to the front door.

"Voila, Peggy!" I turned to see Marie-Paule coming from the back room. "We are in here, Peggy. Ça va?"

"Oh, I was waiting outside but got kicked out of my seat. Do I have to pay to sit?"

"Oh, it's so stupid, but we have to pay to sit in France, even in the parks." She shrugged. "We even pay to go to the WC."

The room at the back of the bar housed the games: darts, baby-foot (foosball), and a couple of beautiful Pachinko pinball machines from Japan. Pierrot, the tall, dark, and mysterious one; Jacques, the goofy guy; and Marco, Marie-Paule's handsome brother, were playing an intense match of baby-foot. Marco flailed his arms, spinning the wooden soccer players attached to movable sticks, smashing the ball down the miniature field. Pierrot intercepted the ball and passed it to Jacques, who flung his wrists and scored, yelling, "Goooooooooal!"

"This is not very interesting to watch," Marie-Paule said as she rolled her eyes. "Do you want to sit down?"

We sat down at a large round table with straight-backed chairs. I didn't know what to say, and if I did, whether I should practice my French or just keep speaking English.

Marie-Paule smiled, shifted in her chair, and broke the ice.

"My sister lives in California. Venice Beach. Do you know where that is?"

"Sure, I know Venice Beach," I said, even though I had never been there. "I live nearby in Pasadena, but I usually go to Huntington or Newport Beach."

"Oh, Huntington Beach! I know surfers from there. Do you know Nat Young? Billy Hamilton? Mike Diffenderfer?"

"They're famous. How do you know them?"

"I met them in Biarritz. I surf." She flipped her long golden bangs out of her deep-set blue eyes, her face angular with a broad bone structure. Her English didn't have the usual French accent, or even an English accent. It was an American accent, with a twang and inflection unique to her.

"Why do you speak English like an American?"

"It's a long story. Genetics." She leaned in closer. "My family does not like to talk about it. During the war, my grandmother had a child, my father, with an American soldier. He promised to come back." She looked up to make sure no one was listening. "My grandfather never came back to get her. If he had, I'd be American. I'm going to find my grandfather. I love Americans."

"Wow, that's sad." I didn't tell her about my father, not yet.

"How many brothers and sisters do you have?" I asked, wanting to tell her about my family.

"Oh, many! Marie-Helene, Marie-Christine, Marie-Jean, Marco—you've met him—I'm next, then my younger brothers, Francois, Xavier, and the baby, Marie-Pascale."

"You must be Catholic!" I hated when people said that to me, but I blurted it out like a *gesundheit* to a sneeze.

"Everyone is Catholic in France."

"I'm Catholic too. Ten kids in our family."

"Ha-ha, you win!"

Our conversation stopped when the guys joined us, each greeting me with a kiss on both cheeks. This intimacy had initially shocked me, but *le bise* was the standard French greeting, and eventually I got used to it.

I sipped my *pression*, the preferred beer of students, with a touch of grenadine or mint, and listened to the rapid banter of French *l'argot*, an incomprehensible language mixed with slang and innuendos. I didn't understand a word. Marie-Paule occasionally explained what was being said and why they were laughing, but the humor didn't translate. At least they weren't laughing at me.

We finished our drinks and headed over to Marie-Paule's home, the guys on their motorcycles and Marie-Paule and me in her *Deux Chevaux*, the ubiquitous two-horsepower car with the turning radius of a motorcycle that was driven by students and farmers throughout France.

The Delannes lived in a chic neighborhood on Boulevard Wilson, in a beautiful, stately old home with an unusually large backyard for the city. Across the yard above the garage was Marie-Paule's bedroom, in a separate guesthouse. We found the boys there, lying on low couches with overstuffed pillows, passing a hash pipe. A lava lamp pulsed to Jimi Hendrix, "Purple haze, al in my brain…" The blinds were pulled down, the windows were shut, and the room vibrated peace, love, and cool.

"Do you want a hit?" Marco said melodiously as he passed the pipe. His short hair and clean-cut look didn't jibe with his dope smoking.

"Really?" He seemed pleased that I was shocked. I took the pipe and inhaled the sweet, rich hashish. "Where did you get this shit?"

"Morocco. It's good, no?" Marco smiled. He was already clearly stoned.

"Yeah, and strong." Dizzy, I sat down, choking back a cough.

From the kitchen steps below, a voice rang out across the garden, "Marie-Paule? Marco? A table!" Chantaille, their half-daft French maid from the countryside, sang her words, calling us to dinner.

"On arrive!" Marie-Paule cried back.

Marco extinguished the pipe and hid it under the pillows. That's when I noticed his army boots. He was in the French service, home on leave during the weekends. He explained, "I'm against zee war, but inscription is *obligatoire*."

The family gathered at a formally set table in the main dining room, so different from my home where the ten children sat at a bar that lined two walls of our kitchen. Monsieur Delanne sat at the head of the table, Madame Delanne at the other end, and the younger blond and blue-eyed children on either side of them. The children reminded me of my younger brothers and sisters. The three oldest siblings no longer lived at home. Pierrot took Marie-Jean's seat, Jacques sat next to him in Marie-Helene's chair, and I sat where Marie-Christine's napkin ring marked her spot.

Monsieur Delanne picked up a bottle of red wine to serve but stopped in midair, looking at me. "C'est qui?"

Marie-Paule introduced me, "C'est Peggy O'Toole de Californie!"

"Ahh, de Californie! I have a daughter there. She looks like you!" I liked him right away. He had the rosy cheeks of an Irishman, the good looks of a movie star, and my father's grin. "Le vin?"

"Oui, merci," I replied as he filled my glass.

In understandable French, Madame Delanne asked if I was a student.

"Oui, je suis une étudiante."

"Avez-vous des frères et souers?"

"Oui, il y a cinq filles et cinq garcons."

"Oh la la. You have ten!"

This was going well. They knew how to talk to foreigners, *dumb foreigners*, using a mix of English and French, and they spoke slowly. But after the initial introductions and niceties, I couldn't follow the conversation and quietly observed the family's interactions.

Madame Delanne rang the servant's bell, and Chantaille appeared with the first dish, sliced tomatoes and onions sprinkled with olive oil and wine vinegar, followed by *coq au vin et les haricots verts*, and finishing with *un plat du fromage*, salad tossed lightly at the table, and chocolate mousse. I felt like I was in a Shirley Temple movie, an orphan dropped into a rich family, and my part was not to make a mistake and to be very polite. In my home, we ate everything off one plate and I was the server. Nothing had prepared me for the etiquette of eating a seven-course meal served by maids.

Madame poured espresso in the delicate Limoges demitasses while Monsieur Delanne opened various bottles of liqueurs. "Do you like whiskey?" asked Monsieur Delanne. "You're Irish with a name like O'Toole, non?"

"I'm Irish, but I don't like whiskey, thank you," I replied politely.

"Good, you'll like this." He poured me a cordial of strong Basque liqueur, Manzano, which had the perfume of a green apple and the taste of pure grain alcohol.

"Drink it like this," he instructed. He poured the liqueur down his throat. Of course, I had no choice but to take the shot and belt it down, burning the lining of my throat.

After the table was cleared, Madame sent the children upstairs with Chantaille to get ready for bed, while the older siblings stayed to plan the weekend ski trip. I tried to follow the gist of the conversation. *A caravan to the snow?* I imagined a Spanish caravan, gypsy carts being pulled by cars up the winding steep hills of the Pyrenees. But it turned out the caravan was a small motor home. I could imagine what it would have been like to go with them, huddling together at night for warmth, sleeping next to each other. I wish I had gone, but at the time I was bound to my studies.

Marie-Paule, Marco, Bibiche, Madame Delanne, Xavier

CHAPTER SEVENTEEN

After Dinner

Le 20 janvier
Dear Mom,

I have a checking account at home that does me no good, so I'm enclosing a check for you to buy a new girdle or at least a haircut to pay you back for that long collect call I made. As long as we're on the subject of money, I'm turning twenty-one soon, so send me the address of Social Security cuz I think they should be sending me money after Daddy died. I'm becoming a Socialist and feel the state owes me something. (Just kidding but I don't think they should be screwing us around and everyone here hates capitalism.)

I'd love to hear from everyone, or at least someone. Take care.

THE TABLE CONVERSATION CONTINUED in rapid-fire French, mostly about politics. Madame Delanne was very animated about *Le Parti Socialiste,* deriding the Gaullists, heralding a new age for France. Marco, in his melodious voice, casually condemned his older sister for being a Communist, while Marie-Paule fought back with verbiage from the Trotskyites.

I battled with myself. Was I a Communist? A Trotskyite? A Socialist? Definitely, not a Capitalist.

Unable to follow the discussion, my eyes glazed over and I spaced out, until I noticed Pierrot's eyes fixed on me. I recognized that language. A jolt of electricity ran down my spine and settled between my legs. I glanced away, and when I looked again, our eyes met. He smiled, as if he could read my thoughts.

Excusing myself, I found the WC tucked under the staircase in the hall. The room was tiny; I had to squeeze between the sink and the toilet in order to shut the door. Feeling faint, I fanned myself and opened a small window to let in the cool air. The noise from the busy Boulevard Wilson obscured the conversation outside the door. I pulled down my jeans, sat on the porcelain commode, and took a deep breath, tipsy from the wine…or Pierrot's gaze. *What a great turn of events—new friends, good food, finding a family and a crush,* I mused, when suddenly the door opened, causing me to jump up and come face-to-face with Pierrot, my pants around my ankles.

"Oh! Excusez-moi," he stuttered, but his eyes held mine for what seemed like time without end.

"It's okay," I mumbled, fumbling for my pants and pulling them back up. I had never seen such deep, brown, clear eyes and a smile so gentle and sincere.

He closed the door. I felt mortified to be caught in such an awkward position. Composing myself, I fixed my hair in the mirror, and checked my makeup. A smile crept across my face. Did he like me?

I left the bathroom, my cheeks flushed and heart pounding, when I heard voices in the hallway. I had hoped to sneak by unseen, instead I ran into everyone saying good night.

Marie-Pascale, in her long white nightgown, bobbed blond hair, and big doe eyes, came up to me, her hands behind her back. "Devines, qu'est-ce que c'est?"

I looked at her blankly. She repeated herself several times and then stamped her foot. I understood her to say in French, "That lady is older than me and doesn't speak as well as I do." Her eyes fixed on her mother, she added, "Elle est bête!"

Oh my God, she's only five, and she just called me stupid!

"She wants you to guess what's behind her back," Marie-Paule explained.

"C'est un chien." I guessed a dog.

She laughed, either at my joke or my stupidity.

"Non, c'est une fleur pour toi." She handed me a flower.

Leaning down I took the flower and said good night using her nickname, "Fais dodo, Bibiche." She wrapped her little arms around my neck and gave me a kiss, prolonging the time before she had to go upstairs.

Jacques and Pierrot had put on their jackets, kissed everyone on each cheek twice instead of once, affection reserved for family and close friends, and headed for the back door. Pierrot stopped, turned to me, and asked how I was getting home—at least that's what I thought he said.

"À pied." I told him I had to walk.

"Viens avec moi." He suggested I go with him. I agreed with a slight nod.

I too said my good-byes, kissing everyone twice on each cheek, and followed Pierrot across the backyard to the alley. He pushed his motorcycle upright, got on, kick-started the engine, and motioned for me to climb on the back. "Tiens moi." I wrapped my arms around his waist, and we sped down the darkened streets, flashing headlights at the intersections, a brisk wind in my hair, and warmth inside that I had never felt before.

My twenty-first birthday

Chapter Eighteen

Breaking Loose

Le 25 janvier
Dear Mom,

Thanks for my birthday check (too much) but mucho appreciated since I spent it in advance when I was in Spain, so I'll thank you for the suede jacket. It's the natural color of the hide, soft and light beige, not too practical for the cold nights here, but perfect for California and summer here. And thanks for sending my construction boots! They're great for riding my Solex on the icy roads, in case I slip, (which I did once but didn't get hurt), and also for on the back of a guy's motorcycle. Just kidding.

Love you and please send more photos, I need some of brother Pat, and the cats, Freddy, hope he lost some of his grotesque fat and if Corina approves. (Are the cats getting along? Any illicit relationships?)

IN THE SILENCE OF the late night, the noise from the motorcycle reverberated off the buildings, trailing behind us and echoing down the narrow streets of the posh neighborhood where I lived. In front of my house, Pierrot revved the motor before killing the engine, put his bike on its kickstand, and got off, cautioning me not to touch the hot exhaust pipe as he helped me down. The curtains were drawn, the shutters rolled down, and the lights out. *What will Madame Assemat say if she catches me out past my curfew?* I imagined her *tsking,* saying under her breath, *Proper young girls need a chaperone and belong home by ten, definitely not on the back of a motorcycle of a boy they hardly know.*

Looking up at the ominous facade with fancy corbels and gargoyles, Pierrot whistled between his teeth and shook his left hand, "Ooh la la, Piggy, c'est une belle adresse. You must be rich." With a theatrical scoff he flicked his nose, deriding the old money and capitalists. "Le con bourgeoisie!"

My street address didn't carry any significance for me, but to the Bordelais, it was where the "old money" upper class lived. I didn't tell him my own family had a simple background and I was far from wealthy. I let him think I was rich.

The awkward on-the-doorstep moment ensued. We looked longingly into each other's eyes, but neither of us made a move to embrace.

"On entre?" He raised his eyebrows, questioning why we didn't go in.

My landlady had made it clear not to entertain boys in her home. I could invite them in, but not beyond the black-and-white tiles in the foyer.

I opened the door and stepped inside. The lights from the street illuminated the entry with its high arches and marbled columns. A passing car's headlights danced over the sculptures.

"I can't invite you in, because—" I rambled in incomprehensible French.

"Pourquoi?"

"La Madame ne veut pas."

I turned to say good-bye and waited expectantly for a kiss. He nodded, jumped off the top step, got on his bike, and rode off down the dimly lit street.

That's it! I can't live like this. Look what I just passed up. How utterly foolish and childish to live under such strict rules! My weekend's ruined, and I'll never see him again.

And it was a miserable weekend. My friends had left town, and I spent hours at the library working on my term paper. No one stayed home, not even Ernaldine the maid, who had gone to visit her family on the outskirts of Bordeaux. She had left a map and an invitation to come meet her parents. After feeling sorry for myself, I decided to go see her.

On Saturday afternoon, I followed the map. The streets narrowed, garbage cans overflowed, and laundry hung out of tenement windows. I found her address. Her father, in a white T-shirt and suspenders, looked out from the street level window and called, "Ernaldine! Ton amie," referring to me as her friend, which made me feel good. Within minutes, the door opened and her family welcomed me into the small room that housed the kitchen and beds. Ernaldine introduced me to her sisters, her brothers, her mother, her father, and her grandparents, all living under one roof. She wasn't self-conscious about the poverty and didn't hide behind false airs. She hugged her father, extolling his good fortune of finding work as an immigrant worker in the vineyards. She, her mother, and her sisters had found jobs as maids. "Nous avons la chance, merci a Dieux." They were lucky.

When I returned to school on Monday, all the students had turned in their papers and were hanging around the Centre d'Étrangères, talking about their weekend adventures

in Spain, the Netherlands, the beach resorts, the mountains—anywhere but Bordeaux. Even though I had stayed
home, except for my visit with Ernaldine's family, I still
hadn't finished my paper and needed help.

I approached the smartest kid in class, Marsha *Le Brun*
("the brown-haired"), a super-intellectual, cool Berkeley
coed who partied and hung out with the French druggies
yet still aced every assignment. The poetic difference was
that my roommate, Marsha *La Blonde,* had light hair and
was angelic, kind, and dependable, whereas the dark-haired
Marsha was daring, provocative, and self-centered.

"Hey, Marsha, can you help me finish my term paper?"

"Of course I'll help you. It only took me an hour to do
mine."

Cringing at her savoir-faire, French-speaking, know-it-
all manner, I feigned a casual attitude. "Great. Where can
we meet?"

"I just got my own apartment on Rue Judaique." She
turned to the others to make sure they were listening. "I
couldn't stand living in the dorms." Having got their attention, she laughed as if about to tell a joke. "Peggy, how can
you stand living with that old lady?"

"Now that you mention it, I can't stand it."

Later that afternoon, I walked to her apartment a few
blocks from my "nunnery." I heard her calling, "Peggy, je
suis ici!" Marsha Le Brun, naked from the waist up, leaned
out of the second-story window overlooking a very busy
street and waved.

Shocked, I yelled back, "What are you doing?"

"They love it! Look at those guys with their tongues
out!" Sure enough, I turned and a group of street cleaners
leaning on their brooms and passersby gawked.

"I'll be right down." She ducked back into her room, closing the window.

Standing on her doorstep, I heard her running down the stairs. She flung open the door wearing a flowing robe that was opened to expose her breasts.

"Entrez!" she cried flamboyantly and whisked me into her chambers.

"What the hell are you thinking?" I asked, annoyed by her impudence.

"I'm celebrating my freedom. I can do what I want in my own apartment. Fuck the rules."

I envied her at that moment. She was smart and funny, and though she was not beautiful, she knew how to capture a guy's attention. I felt like a child around her.

"Well, show me what you've got," she said, referring to my term paper. I handed her my exposé on "Tristan and Iseult."

She read the first page and glanced at the rest. "This doesn't make any sense, Peggy. Can't you write in French?"

"I can't write in French, and I can't speak French. Please, just help me."

"Okay. Tell me what you want to say, and I will write it for you *en français*." She rolled her *r*'s with a deep guttural flare.

"I didn't really get the story. I don't read French."

"You're *pénible*," she said, a synonym for stupid, annoying, burdensome, and tiresome.

How could I have been in France for six months and still be unable to write a simple paper?

I had to dig down deep inside myself to hold on to my belief that I wasn't stupid or a lost cause or a total loser. I had to prove it to Marsha.

"Just help me a little bit, and I'll buy you a drink at Le New York Bar, where my friends go."

"You have friends at Le New York? That's where the drug dealers and the Maoists hang out." Clearly, she was surprised I had friends there.

"Yeah, I know," which wasn't altogether true. The drug dealing was news to me, but I put on my cool act. "My friend, Marie-Paule, has a really cute brother and these cool friends, one really gorgeous guy I like." Marsha took the bait.

"I'll do your paper if you introduce me. I met some drug dealers in Holland last week. They hang out at Le New York. Maybe they'll be there."

"Sure, but can you do my paper tonight?"

"No problem." She changed the subject to more personal interests. "Did you know you can get any drug you want on the streets in Amsterdam? No one gets busted. The hard part is getting it into France without getting caught."

"Wow, cool." I had a premonition that I shouldn't be hanging out with her, but I needed her to write my paper. "Marie-Paule told me to meet around six, after classes. Can you make it?" Naive and trusting, I opened my world to her.

That evening, we went to Le New York, as promised, and Marsha met my friends. She immediately charmed them with her fluent French and radical political ideas. She flirted with Marco. He didn't invite her home for dinner, just to the apartment above the garage. I got a paper out of the deal; Marsha got a lover.

TV Scene of Sylmar Earthquake

CHAPTER NINETEEN

Earthquake in California

February 12, 1971
Dear Mom and family,

Glad *the old house is still standing. I saw the news on TV
and was a little worried whether or not LA fell into the ocean. I
was at Marie-Paule's house for her little sister's birthday dinner.
They have a daughter living in LA, so they tried to call her for
three hours while I was there, but they couldn't get through by the
time I had to go home. Next day we received news at the California
student center that all was well on the home front.*

*Write soon and send a cassette with your voices, I miss hear-
ing them.*

WHEN I ARRIVED AT Bibiche's birthday party, I found
the Delanre family gathered around the television set. On
the TV screen, I recognized the bright blue California sky
with the backdrop of the San Gabriel Mountains etched in
purple. The camera panned the area, showing collapsed
bridges, cars spewed helter-skelter across the freeway,
and buildings demolished in heaps of rubble. The news

commentator repeated over and over again, "Just before sunrise, a six-point-six earthquake struck the San Fernando Valley; bridges are down, telephone wires severed, hospitals have collapsed."

"Que'est-ce qu'il dit, Peggy? Ma fille, Marie-Jean, est là! Venice Beach!" Madame Delanne begged for news. Her daughter was living in Southern California. I watched the reporter intently as he gave the details of the destruction while the ticker tape below translated it into French. Breaking news interrupted, "Evacuate the area…"

A map flashed on the screen with red outlining the area for evacuation with the center circle pulsating at the epicenter.

"Ce n'est pas Venice Beach. C'est San Fernando." I reassured her that Marie-Jean was not at the center of the quake. But I didn't know if she was safe, and I didn't know how my mom, siblings, and friends had fared.

The rest of the evening, we watched the news from the dining room table while we ate dinner, the large black phone placed on the table like an ominous centerpiece, awaiting a call from Marie-Jean. I tried to call the overseas operator, but the lines remained busy all evening.

I was concerned about my family, but not like Marie-Jean's parents, who stayed glued to the television with the phone nearby, pressing me for more information. Now, as a parent with daughters far from home, I understand their fear that night, not being able to contact or help their daughter in a foreign land. They said they trusted she was unharmed, but the furrowed brow, the trembling hand, and the catch in their voices spoke otherwise.

The next day after school, I rode my Solex over to their house to let Madame know my family was fine and to offer to call their daughter again. This time, Marie-Jean answered and dismissed the fact she was ever in danger. In fact, she said she had found the earthquake exciting. She told me she loved everything about Venice Beach, "even the smog makes the sunsets more beautiful." No matter how much her mother pleaded, Marie-Jean had no intention of moving back home any time soon.

Madame hung up the receiver, calling me her American daughter: "Merci, Peggy, tu es ma fille Américaine." That evening, Chantaille set a place for me at the table next to Pierrot, which remained my place for the rest of the time I was in Bordeaux.

Often I stopped by the Delannes' in the early afternoons, hoping to have some time before dinner with friends, especially wanting to see Pierrot. If I arrived in the early afternoon, I made a point to sit with Marie-Paule's partially blind grandmother as she quietly crocheted small flowers in lavender, blues, reds, and yellows, connecting them into necklaces or embroidering them onto the children's clothes. She taught me how to crochet the tiny flowers, her nimble fingers hooking the fine threads, her gentle touch holding my hands, making sure I didn't lose a stitch. The afternoons were always longer in her presence. Her slow, deliberate, and patient movements slowed me down, heightening my anticipation for when I could join my friends above the garage in the evenings.

One day, while Marie-Paule and I were crocheting flowers and sewing them onto our jeans, she paused and asked, "Peggy, what happened last weekend with Pierrot?" She had a funny look on her face as if she knew more than I did. I feared she liked Pierrot too

Marie-Paule had gone on yet another family ski trip. Jacques and Pierrot had stayed behind and invited me to a chic Moroccan costume party at Jacques's parents' home.

His sister took advantage of the parents being out of town to avail herself of the servants and sumptuous surroundings. Entering the house, I scanned the guests who gathered in clusters, holding their iced mint tea and champagne flutes high in the air, feigning importance and snubbing me. The young men wore djellabas and Middle Eastern garb, and the ladies wore elaborate belly dancing costumes. As usual, my clothes didn't meet French standards. My "Arabian" costume consisted of a leather skirt, beads intertwined in my braided hair, and kohl lining my eyes.

Lynette kissed her brother Jacques and Pierrot perfunctorily on each cheek and embraced me as a friend, or so I thought, but in front of everyone she derided me, saying, "Voila, une Indienne Amèricane!" The others laughed, and I was on edge for the rest of the evening.

At dinner, the servants, in Aladdin costumes, ladled couscous into bowls and poured wine into colorful goblets. We sat on cushions around a low table, the conversation lively and fun, until I again became the butt of the jokes.

At the head of the table, a cigarette-sucking French asshole called out, "Hey, American, do you smoke hashish?"

"Non, je ne fume pas," I replied as tartly as I could in French.

"Oh, you no smoke?" He baited me, pretending to take a toke on his cigarette.

"Hey, arrête. Laisse-elle tranquille." Pierrot told them to leave me alone. Then he took out a small pipe, tapped some kief into the bowl, lit it, and passed it around the table.

"A peace pipe from the Indian." The guys laughed; the girls twittered, light-headed from drinking. Unbeknownst to me, Pierrot and Jacques had been invited to get the guests stoned, many for the first time. The virgin dopers took hit after hit, not knowing how strong the powdered Moroccan cannabis was. The contagious laughter circled the table as they got more and more wasted. A particularly large man dressed as a belly dancer, his face caked in makeup and kohl around his eyes, stood up as if he wanted say something. Then he blacked out, falling right onto the table. Cries erupted, two guys flipped him over, and his girlfriend listened for a heartbeat.

"Vîte! Un docteur!"

Pierrot and I slipped out the door unseen.

* * *

"Last weekend?" I played dumb. Marie-Paule kept her head down, sewing the little flowers on the back pockets of her jeans.

"You went to Jacques's house with Pierrot, non?"

"Yes, but nothing happened. Everyone got stoned and a guy passed out, but I found out later he was okay."

"I'm asking about Pierrot. Anything happen?"

"No, why?" *I wish something had happened.*

"It's okay, Peggy; you're my sister. You have my sister's place at the table, now her boyfriend. No problem, she has another boyfriend in California and one in Australia."

I began to understand the French a little better. There was something Zen about their romances. As Billy Preston said, "If you can't be with the one you love, love the one you're with." Perhaps I had a chance with Pierrot after all.

Carcassonne

Chapter Twenty

Winter Break

February 20, 1971
Dear Mom and family,

I haven't written because I have been taking tests and writing papers. It's over now 'til the big ones come at the end of May. Now we get two weeks for ski break! The French are always taking vacations.

Marsha, my roommate, her friend Leslie, and I are going to meet Claire in Aix-en-Provence then on to Nice for Mardi Gras. Maybe I'll get to visit Claire's relatives in the Alps this time—don't know for sure but I'll drop you a card on my journey.

Marsha, Leslie, and I knew that hitchhiking would be difficult with three, so we hid Leslie, all four foot ten inches of her, behind a bush. Blond Marsha and I, tall and lanky, stood with our thumbs out, our arms wrapped around each other to fight off the icy winds. Within minutes, a big, comfy Citroen stopped.

"Vîte! Entrez, c'est froid mes filles!" A nice-looking man dressed in the typical gray business suit rolled down his window, imploring us to get out of the cold. Leslie emerged from behind the bush and climbed in the backseat with us, our thighs pressing against each other, our packs securely between our legs.

The man looked over the front seat, his arm stretched out, his fingers tapping, and accused her of hiding: "Elle se cache?"

"Elle est petite, non?" Leslie's eyes showed above her pack. Marsha and I exaggerated her tininess by pushing her head even lower.

"Bof! Pas de problème." He shrugged, expelling air out of his cheek with a laugh, and said, "Allons-y, let's go." He put the key in the ignition and the Citroen magically eased up on its hydraulics for the cushiony ride.

He asked the usual questions: *What are you doing in France? Where are you from? Where are you going?* These were the same questions I had been asking myself and I still didn't have the answers.

"Nous sommes étudiantes." Marsha.

"Nous venons de Santa Barbara." Leslie.

"Nous allons à Aix-en-Provence." Peggy.

We had the script down pat, and by the end of our journey we threatened to have the words emblazoned on our foreheads.

Monsieur L'Heureux rattled on about his family, warned us of the dangers of hitchhiking, and lectured us on French history. About an hour later, he veered off the main road and insisted we visit the famous monastery of Moissac, even though we said we were pressed for time to get across the south of France in two days.

Once inside the cloister, the air grew still and smelled of fresh cut grass and roses. A monk glided under the carved colonnade saying his vespers and fingering his rosary. The Angelus tolled from the bell tower as the religious gathered in the chapel, and Gregorian chants filled the vaulted ceilings, drawing our eyes heavenward upon entering.

Oil paintings in dark burnt colors hung on the flaking walls, silently telling stories: Abraham, his sword above his son's head and God's voice echoing in sunrays; Saint George plunging a spear into a dragon; archangels jabbing swords into naked lost souls trying to climb out of hell. The macabre art was familiar and comforting to me in an odd way. We walked down the musty aisle and stopped in front of Saint Sebastian, wearing a loincloth revealing his defined muscles. Blood dripped down Sebastian's torso.

"What's that all about?' Marsha and Leslie didn't know any of the allegories.

"The Romans tied him to a tree and shot him with arrows because he believed in Jesus Christ." I knew all of the saints, as if they were family. "This is Saint Veronica. She wiped the face of Jesus, and he left the bloody image of his crown of thorns and face on her veil, like a thank-you miracle for being kind. Some people think she was Jesus's mistress."

"How do you know all this stuff?"

"After twelve years of Catholic school, it's hard to forget this shit."

* * *

I had been obsessed with religious icons and rituals as a child, praying for a vocation to be a nun, wanting to be Christ's bride. Most preteens spent hours in the bathroom putting on makeup, but I wrapped my head in towels, mimicking the nun's habit, going for the saintly look, like Audrey Hepburn in *The Nun's Story*. My friends perused the fashions in *Seventeen* magazine while I thumbed through *Habits and Holy Garb*.

At twelve years old, I'd leave home on my bike at seven in the morning, arriving at church with frost on my hair, my fingers blue with cold. Alone in the sacristy, I laid out the priest's garments before mass. Opening the wide set of drawers, I carefully placed the vestments on the dressing table and lingered until the priest rushed in to put on the garments, kissing each article and incanting a prayer for each item. "May the white alb keep me pure, the purple manipule remind me of Christ's suffering, the yellow amice to honor His Holiness..." As he cinched the braided belt tight, the priest repeated his vow of chastity. I was entranced with the ritual.

"Hurry on along," Father O'Brien would say in his deep Irish brogue, spittle flying. "The altar boys will be coming anytime; can't have ye here." I had wanted to be an altar girl, but only boys had that privilege. Girls weren't as important in the Catholic Church.

Religion was my refuge from an alcoholic father and a distraught mother. Church dogma provided a stable situation, security in knowing what I had to do to be saved. I said novenas and sought the intercession of Mary and the saints to rescue my father from addiction and to protect my mother, my siblings, and me from his wrath. Dad's rage was no less than an archangel descending on the poor souls in hell, but Dad's love was also as giving as the Sacred Heart of Jesus.

My parents praised my religious fanaticism, telling me I was the "good child," but my brothers made fun of me and called me a lesbo religious freak.

When I was in eighth grade, the nuns chose me to crown the Blessed Mother on May Day, further proof of my goodness. I wore Shereen's wedding veil, but had to borrow a wedding gown, since she had been buried in hers a few months back. My entourage of altar boys led me to the steps, where the young Father Fred, handsomely dressed in his black cassock, waited to escort me to the Virgin's altar. He grasped my hand as I climbed the short ladder behind the statue of Mary. Holding my breath, my arms outstretched, I held the crown of flowers above Mary's head, the congregation in rapt silence, the choir voices singing, "Oh, Mary, we crown you with blossoms today, Queen of the Angels, Queen of the May..." On cue, I placed the wreath of flowers gently on Mary's head. Then, holding my hem in one hand, I reached for support from an altar boy and tripped getting off the ladder, knocking the crown to the floor. I recovered my balance, gathered up the skirt of my dress, and retreated back to my seat, mortified. An altar boy scurried up the ladder and placed the crown squarely on the statue. As I slipped past her in the pew, Sister Eileen uttered, "I always wanted a boy to crown the Virgin." But at that moment, I went blank, unable see past my embarrassment. I knelt with my head down in prayer and shame, shaking. Then I noticed a strange sensation between my legs and thought I was peeing, only to realize I was unprepared for my first period.

During adolescence, religion and sex crossed boundaries. My obsession with Christ turned into an infatuation for priests, the young, good-looking ones, who tantalized me with their power and holiness, bestowing grace in the confessional and blessing my crystal rosaries and holy statues. I had a crush on Father Fred, as many of the girls did, but he chose me and wrote me letters, signing them, *In Christ's name.*

One afternoon, Father Fred came to visit me in my living room. He kissed me on the cheek in a fatherly way, but I tingled inside with an unknown passion. My sister had recently died, and he may have known of our family's struggles, but for whatever reason, he doted on me and gave me a statue of the Virgin Mary, telling me I was special.

My brothers found one of his letters tucked in the back of my underwear drawer, with a photo of Father Fred in his black cassock and starched white collar, his arm around me at the altar on May Day. "It's your wedding photo," Larry taunted, holding the photo high and running to show my other brothers and Mom. Distressed and confused, I kept my longings a secret, ashamed of my feelings for him.

It never occurred to me that I was having sexual fantasies. Boys didn't like me, so I didn't feel sexy. I thought my love and joy was all about Christ—a mystical experience, like the ecstasy of Saint Theresa of Avila. In tenth grade religion class Sister Mary Helen had talked about spontaneous climax. "I am Christ's bride, and when I pray, I get as much pleasure from him as a wife does from her husband." My friends and I laughed about having an orgasm while praying, but it does happen.

During the senior class weekend retreat, Father McQueen (a nickname my girlfriends and I gave the priest because he looked like Steve McQueen) became friendly with my group, telling jokes and hanging out with us after evening meals. Saturday night, after he had changed into his blue jeans (and by all standards, looked hot), he suggested *walking confessions*. Each girl took a spin in the garden with him alone, confessing her most private sins. I confessed my usual three: "I talked back to my mother, fought with my brothers, and"—I blushed—"I have impure thoughts." He chuckled, telling me he did too.

The last one to walk with him was Camilla, but her walking confession continued after the ten o'clock curfew. When she snuck back to the dorm late that night, she bragged,

"I let Father get to second base." Camilla bragged all the time about what boys did to her, so I tried to let it go, but I couldn't stop thinking about it.

The next morning during Sunday mass, the first consecration bell rang and Father McQueen intoned, "The body of Christ." Waves of pleasure flooded my muscles as I imagined it was me last night, not Camilla. My thoughts returned to Jesus. The second bell rang. "The blood of Christ." I switched back to my fantasy of *night walking confessions*. The sensation in my groin peaked, and I held my breath silencing a small cry. The tingling between my legs subsided, and the moisture left an uncomfortable itching. I received Holy Communion from his hands. Three bells rang, *mea culpa, mea culpa, mea maxima culpa*. I prayed for forgiveness, but I wanted him.

* * *

We left the monastery around noon, stopped for a trucker's lunch in a Routier, and were back on the road by two with our thumbs out. Resting against our packs in a ditch at the side of the road, we took turns jumping up when we heard a car coming. One young girl on a deserted back road had a pretty good chance of getting a ride. Bingo! A truck came to a slow, grinding halt in front of Leslie.

"Où va tu?" The trucker threw open the door with a trunk of an arm and asked where she was going.

"Aix-en-Provence," she cried back over the noise of the running engine.

"Allez-oop!" he exclaimed. Hearing this, Marsha and I jumped up from the embankment, and all three of us grabbed our packs and mounted the high steps, giving Leslie a boost.

Seeing us, he laughed, showing a missing front tooth. "Plus on est de fous, plus on rit!"

Laughing, Leslie interpreted, "The more the merrier!"

But we weren't that merry. Drowsy from the long day and from drinking wine at lunch, we didn't provide the conversation the trucker desired; rather we mumbled a few words and fell into a light sleep, leaning against each other like children after a long outing in the sun.

Leslie awakened me. "He's groping me," she whispered. "Change places with me."

I reluctantly agreed, knowing I could fend off his unwanted advances better than little Leslie. She scrambled over me and snuggled close to Marsha. I remained vigilant, my arms folded protectively over my yet to be developed breasts, unlike those of the voluptuous Leslie. He scowled, swearing under his breath, "Merde putains, et alors." His breath reeked of garlic and red wine.

The miffed trucker rolled to the side of the road, his brakes grinding to a stop. "Allez," he ordered curtly, telling us to go. Within seconds of us jumping out, the engine revved and a cloud of exhaust spit out of the rusted tailpipe, leaving us coughing and perplexed about where to go next.

Arrows pointed south to Spain, east to Perpignan, and straight ahead to Carcassonne, a silhouette of a castle beneath the name.

Marsha pulled out her guidebook. "Carcassonne, a medieval French town. Sounds cool." We trudged along the highway in the direction of the castle when a family took pity on us and stopped to ask if we needed help. We piled into their old car, the children on their mother's lap. They dropped us off at the walled city of Carcassonne and returned to the main highway.

I felt like Dorothy at the emerald gates as we waved goodbye to the family and walked across the drawbridge into the medieval city. It was late afternoon. The shopkeepers had already shuttered their windows, and a few people walked the narrow cobblestone streets carrying home long loaves of bread. We had stepped back in time. The youth hostel was in an old section of the massive castle, replete with a tower and dungeon. We pulled the cord to ring the tarnished brass bell above the portal. An old woman wrapped in a black woolen shawl let us in, took our passports, and showed us to the dorm room. We each found a bunk, dropped our packs to claim our spot, and went out to explore the ancient fortress. We found an open café where we shared a small evening meal.

The next day, church bells woke us at dawn and the smell of freshly baked bread enticed us downstairs. After *petit déjeuner,* we packed up for another day on the road to Aix, hoping not to have any more truck drivers to deal with.

By late afternoon, we arrived in Aix-en-Provence, a quaint college town, its streets lined with overgrown trees and its red tiled roofs slanting in delightful angles, making a storybook impression.

We caught a local bus to the university and found the dorms and Claire waiting for us. I dropped my pack, opened my arms, and she ran toward me, arms outstretched, crying "Pegee, Pegee!" just like in the movies. We all squeezed into Claire's dorm for the night.

Marsha and Leslie left early the next morning, taping a note to the door that said, "See you at the youth hostel in Nice." I didn't see them again until I returned to Bordeaux two weeks later. Mardi Gras festivities had gotten out of hand, so they turned back and went south to Spain.

Marianne, the symbol of the French Republic

CHAPTER TWENTY-ONE

On Our Way to Carnaval

Le 22 fevrier
Hola familia,
    Leslie, Marsha, and I met Claire in Aix after a night in
Carcasonne, a fortified city from the XII century and a night near
the Pont d'Avignon across from the Pope's castle—been seeing a
lot of impressive things. We split up and Claire and I are in a
little hotel on the Cote d'Azur. Pictures on the front of card show
St. Tropez where we stopped for lunch. No Bardot spottings.

CLAIRE AND I GOT a late start but kept our plans to take
the longer route south along the coast to St. Tropez, hoping
to get a glance of Brigitte Bardot, the epitome of French
beauty and glamour. France was buzzing about the recent scandal at the unveiling of the bust of Marianne,
the national symbol of the French Republic. The sculptor
had used Brigitte Bardot as his model. It was like putting
Marilyn Monroe on the US dollar bill. Since the late fifties,
I had cut out photos of Brigitte Bardot from *Life* magazine,
putting them in scrapbooks along with my saint cards.

I yearned to meet her almost as much as I wanted the Virgin Mary to appear to me. I thought for sure we could be friends if we happened to meet in St. Tropez and hoped she would find me more alluring and interesting than her rich, snobby friends. As do most starstruck fans, I had an inflated idea of our friendship.

Standing on a corner in Toulon, a seaside resort on the edge of the Riviera, we watched sleek convertibles whiz by with fancy people in furs, their woolen scarves buffeting in the icy wind. After an hour had passed with no luck getting picked up, Claire and I ducked inside a bistro to warm up with a café au lait and to discuss a different approach to autostop. In the bathroom, we put our hair up in French twists, dabbed on a little makeup, threw scarves around our necks, and practiced our best Bardot lips, painting them in glistening red lipstick.

Striving for a classy approach to hitchhiking, we stepped out onto the street, hid our backpacks behind a wall, and tried out various sexy stances, each of us attempting to outdo the other. Claire stood with one leg cocked, leaning up against a telephone pole, her jeans tucked into her boots, her beret pulled low over one eye, her scarf rakishly tied, and a cigarette dangling from her pouty lips, quoting Mae West: "Is that a pickle in your pocket or are you just glad to see me?"

Whether it was our jovial demeanor or Claire's seductive stance, I don't know, but it worked like a charm. After doing a double take, a gentleman in a slick red sports car made a sharp U-turn and pulled over to the side of the road a few meters in front of us.

Claire ran up to the car and asked where he was going: "Bonjour! Où allez-vous?"

"Où allez-vous?" he responded, wanting to know where she was going.

Breaking rule number one in autostop—never tell them where you're going first—Claire gave him our final destination. "Nous allons a Nice!"

"Moi aussi!" He feigned surprise to be going to the same place. Leaping out of the car, he gallantly grabbed our backpacks, put them in the trunk, and indicated for Claire to get in the front seat, holding the door open for her and gently placing his hand on her head as she ducked in. He gave me a cheesy smile.

I guardedly watched him as he looked into Claire's eyes, ignoring my existence in the backseat. He crooned, "Je m'appelle Michel. Et votre nom, ma belle?"

There is a universal sound to a male's voice—in any language—when he wants sex, a sound that can make your skin crawl. Claire may not have noticed, or perhaps she liked getting all the attention.

"Je m'appelle Claire," she coyly responded.

Michel handled his sporty car as an extension of his ego, stepping on the gas as he rounded the curves, keeping the engine revved at a high pitch on the straightaway. He leaned over, brushing across Claire's breasts as he pointed out the sights, one hand on the steering wheel. I started to feel carsick. Or was it his disgusting behavior that was making me want to vomit?

Michel made a quick turn, jarring me to the other side of the seat, and exited onto Boulevard de Corniche, winding through the wooded hills of the Cote d'Azur. I caught glimpses of the deep blue water, sparkling in the sunshine through the branches of the trees, making me dizzy and irritable.

"Please, slow down!" I pleaded.

"Arrêtez! C'est une surprise pour Claire," Michel snapped at me.

As if to make up for his harsh words, he stopped at an overlook of the picturesque harbor of St. Tropez. Standing on a rock at the side of the car, he put his arm over my shoulder and pointed out Brigitte Bardot's mansion atop an island in the bay. I glanced across the open water, my hopes dashed. Unless we had a helicopter, there was no chance of spotting Brigitte, let alone talking to her.

We walked along the marina, the fresh air easing my queasiness, until Michel clutched Claire's hands, kissing them and whispering private jokes. She giggled, emitting a high, nervous laugh, but played along with his farce.

"What are you doing, Claire? This guy's a creep," I hissed in her ear. "He's so skinny, short, weird—not your type."

Michel interrupted me midsentence. "On y va," he barked and sprinted back to the car, again opening the door for her and letting me fend for myself. As he skipped around to the driver's side, Claire looked back and said, "Don't worry, we'll lose this guy after lunch."

We arrived around noon in San Rafael and stopped at a secluded *auberge,* a small hotel and restaurant amid the cypress above the sapphire sea. Michel was civil to me during lunch, almost delightful. I couldn't keep up with their conversation, so I just nodded periodically while the meal absorbed all of my attention: bouillabaisse with succulent fish and seafood floating in a clam broth and seasoned with saffron, garlic, and fresh tomatoes. Michel explained how to use the white mustardy sauce and the brown *rouille* as garnish for our freshly baked bread. "Dip the bread in the broth and suck it." He demonstrated the technique, slurping and sucking the soft white bread tinged in red and brown. Michel was a pervert. His beady eyes narrowed, his furry brows twisted absurdly, and his mouth contorted like a lizard's. "Je t'aime, Claire." He fell onto her lap, kissing her arm like a dog licks his owner, rhythmically, seductively, begging her to go upstairs with him.

Thinking quickly, Claire lifted his head off her chest and complained of stomach cramps and needed to go to a drugstore. "J'ai mal au ventre. Je dois aller au pharmacie."

Claire batted her eyelashes, imploring him to get help for her *mal au ventre*, careful not to anger him, since everything we owned was in the trunk of his car. She coyly suggested he take me to a hotel in town before taking her to the drugstore, so they could be alone. Little beads of sweat appeared on his upper lip "Ah oui, ma chèrie."

Arriving in front of a modest hotel in town, Michel alighted and opened the trunk for me to get my pack. As if reciting a line from a movie he said, "Tu connais pas l'amour; moi, je connais l'amour," telling me that unlike him I didn't know a thing about love. I almost gagged, but I kept my cool, sneered, and grabbed both bags Claire jumped out of the car, and before he realized what had happened, we were running down the street. We dashed into another hotel farther away and pounded the desk bell impatiently, all the while looking over our shoulders to the street. His car rolled into view. A young clerk emerged from the back, wiping his face with a napkin.

"Nous avons des problèmes avec le monsieur dans la voiture rouge." We pointed to Michel's car, which had stopped outside the window. "Il faut nous cacher!" Claire's voice lifted an octave telling him we must hide. Noting the urgency, the young clerk spirited us to the back room where his wife and young child were finishing lunch.

"Restez là," he whispered in hushed tones and went back to the front desk. He returned a few minutes later. The red car was gone.

Having dodged an ugly situation, we decided to register at the little hotel and stay in our room for the evening. We pushed the dresser against the door, hung our rosaries on the hook as a talisman, and went to sleep early.

Looking back, I wish I could say that we'd learned our lesson, but the next day we were back on the road hitching rides, although perhaps a bit more discerning...at least for a while.

Claire at Carnaval

Chapter Twenty-Two

Mardi Gras

Le 22 fevrer

We made it to Nice and stayed with a nice French family and saw Carnaval. There were millions of people in the streets stuffing confetti down your throat literally. (And floats like in the ole Rose Parade, reminded me of Dad and New Years.) The crowds got to us so we went on to Monaco and spent the day with some French kids discussing the Revolution while we sipped our aperitifs on the villa patio overlooking the Mediterranean Sea. (All students here are revolutionaries and against Capitalism.) I'll write from Chamonix, Love, Me

IT WAS THE MONDAY before Mardi Gras, and the roads getting into Nice were gridlocked, horns honking, brakes screeching and tempers rising. Our driver shrugged his shoulders, explaining he could go no farther.

"Pas de problème." It was easier to walk anyway. Following the signs to the old town, we found the youth hostel. It was full. The halls had bags pushed against doors and stacked behind the manager's desk.

The overwhelmed clerk took one look at us and shook his head and said, "Full! Complet!"

"S'il vous plait. Marsha Tiedy est ici?" I'd hoped we could find our friends and share their beds.

Taking his finger, he ran it along the list of names in his ledger.

"Non! Elle n'est pas là." He slammed the brown leather book shut.

Upon leaving the hostel, we serendipitously ran into Clifford, Chris, and some other compatriots along the parade route and asked if they had seen Marsha and Leslie.

"Yeah, but they left earlier today. Couldn't take any more drunks puking."

"Too bad for them," I said out loud, but again I felt ditched. We joined arms with the tall American boys and continued from one street party to the next, singing and drinking, swept up in the moment until we got separated from the group. Strange bodies rubbed against us, old men in masks with long noses grabbed our butts, and absurd-looking clowns tweaked our breasts.

As night fell, the dense crowd got scary, moving along the parade route like a boa constrictor that might crush us in its path. Claire tugged on my coat and grabbed ahold of my arm. "Let's get out of here." Gargantuan papier-mâché heads bobbed and wobbled above us. Maneuvering away from the serpentine line, we slipped under a rope to watch the parade from the curb, landing next to a family with small children.

"Vous êtes Américaines?" the mother asked.

"Oui, nous sommes étudiantes," we yelled over the noise of the crowd. The young woman moved over to make room for us on their blanket and offered us bread and cheese; her husband handed us each a glass of red wine.

After the parade, the couple invited us to stay at their modest apartment. Robert, a clean-cut man around thirty, was a grad student finishing his dissertation on Karl Marx. Cécile, his waiflike wife, worked for the government. She seemed proud to support Robert while he studied and took care of their children, not atypical for a modern French family.

Robert excused himself, left the room to make a phone call, and returned with a smile. "I'm busy tomorrow, but you can have lunch with some of my friends in the program."

"But we leave tomorrow for the Alps."

"No problem. Girard lives in Monaco and is going to Italy in the afternoon. He can take you to a good road for hitchhiking."

The next morning, Cécile had already left for work, the children were at the École maternelle (Infant School), and Robert was having what appeared to be a serious talk with his friend, Girard, a good-looking, wiry, dark Frenchman, casually dressed in jeans and a T-shirt but wearing a Rolex watch, which was not characteristic of a graduate student. From the tone of their conversation, we intuited that something was obviously wrong. After a quick good-bye, we left with Girard. Putting on his Vuarnets, he motioned for us to get in his red Ferrari, which was parked on the sidewalk in front of the apartment. He smiled insincerely and drove in silence. I wondered if his curtness was due to his concentration on driving, as he changed gears and increased his speed along the winding Corniche, or if he just didn't find us interesting or attractive enough to waste his time talking to.

Exiting the main thoroughfare, we sped along narrow streets and hairpin curves, climbing above the Mediterranean. He turned into a long driveway and stopped in front of a palatial residence. A butler greeted him, took the keys, and parked the car.

"This is my parents' home. Not mine," he apologized with disdain in his voice.

We entered the home and crossed the parlor to the garden patio, which overlooked the sea. The palace and casino below looked like a miniature toy city.

A group of long-haired guys in jeans and work shirts sat around an outdoor table, the tablecloth stained with red wine, the ashtrays filled with cigarette butts and roaches. In the corner, a thin, Goyaesque body lay on a chaise lounge. She was barefoot, wearing a carmine peasant blouse and a long, shabby skirt bunched between her shapely legs. The girl twirled her scraggly black hair with her long, bony fingers, her red nails bitten to nubs. Her puffy lips appeared bruised or chapped. I tried to avoid looking at her, but she fascinated me. Her brown eyes caught me staring. She cursed in a guttural, animal-like growl, calling us pieces of shit. "Qu'est-ce que c'est cette merde?"

"Ignore her." Girard dismissed her and introduced us as American friends of Robert.

Something didn't jibe. How could these people be friends with clean-cut Robert? They grunted, "Enchanté," and turned back to a heated conversation. Girard pulled up a couple of chairs for us to sit down at the table.

The male servant brought two more glasses and another bottle of Lafitte red. Claire and I drank water; they continued to drink more wine and chain-smoke, arguing and gesticulating with their arms.

"What are they saying, Claire?"

She leaned over my shoulder, cupping her hand to cover her mouth, and spoke into my ear. "They're planning to blow up a government building in Italy."

I studied the group and listened more attentively. They dressed and talked like the university radicals I knew in

Bordeaux, but the disparity of having an anarchist meeting in opulent surroundings confounded me. I thought Marxists and Communists were the proletariat, not the rich.

Bits and pieces of their conversation—*revolution, down with the establishment, emancipation, capitalist pigs*—reminded me of the speech that ignited the students to burn the Bank of America during the Isla Vista riots. I noted the similarity with SDS meetings I had gone to on campus. The UCSB students lived the good life in a paradise on the ocean with plenty of food, nice homes, and a good education, just like these revolutionaries.

If students in Isla Vista could burn the bank, then I believed these guys could carry off their plan to blow up a building in Italy. They had the means to make it happen.

The brooding, dark-haired girl got up and went into the house. She returned a few minutes later to the chaise lounge and curled up in a fetal position with a ragged baby blanket in one hand and a pacifier protruding from her swollen lips. The whole thing was so very Fellini, but I wished it were a movie and not actually happening.

"Américaine!" the apparent leader shouted to get my attention. He spoke slowly, in halting English. "You." He pointed at me. "You are rich, spend so much money, a capitalist pig like all Americans."

I filled with rage at his accusation. *How dare these spoiled, rich brats, playing anarchists, criticize my country and me? Money? I had no money, no family supporting me, no mansion on the Riviera. I earned my money and paid for my education.* My mind raced at the injustice. *They're the enemy of the people, fuckin' bourgeoisie. Go ahead and blow up your fancy cars, destroy your home, splatter your fine china. I don't give a shit about you! You have more to lose than I do.*

I shouted back, "You're such hypocrites! You use your daddy's money sitting around playing anarchist. Why don't you do something to help the world rather than destroy it and sit self-satisfied? *You're* the bourgeois pigs."

Shocked, Claire grabbed my arm. "We should go, Peggy."

The guys remained cool. Goya Girl sat up, her interest piqued by the fact that I had raised my voice to the men.

The group's silence frightened me more than their harsh words. Calmly, Claire spoke in French, easing the pressure and letting them know we were only students, not rich.

A dinner bell rang.

"On mange." Girard motioned us to go inside.

A table had been set in the atrium with a simple feast of vegetable salad, freshly baked bread, and a steaming pot of bouillabaisse. Girard poured wine from crystal decanters, and Goya Girl served the soup as we passed our plates family style.

The Mont Blanc Tunnel

Chapter Twenty-Three

The Road to Chamonix

Le 28 février
Ciao Bella. We're in Italy! The roads were closed on the French side due to snow so we took the long way around through this amazing new tunnel that connects Italy with France. Have to go through customs again! Write more later.

AFTER LUNCH, WE HAD no choice but to catch a ride with a few of the anarchists as they headed to Italy in a converted bread truck with bench seats in the back. We insisted they drop us off in the French border town of Menton.

"Non, it's the wrong way in winter. Cross with us to Italy. C'est mieux."

We lied and said we were meeting friends: "Nous avons des amies ici."

Once safely out of the little van, I blew air from my lungs, my legs woobly. "What freaks! Scared the shit out of me."

"Then why did you fight back?" Claire was pissed about my outburst before lunch.

"I couldn't help myself." I offered no excuse. "I'm glad we didn't take the ride to Italy."

"Yeah," Claire agreed. "There must be a shorter route through the Alps."

I took the map out of my pack and sure enough found a direct route through the mountain passes to Chamonix. "It's about six hours of driving. Let's just stay at the youth hostel here and get an early start tomorrow."

The next morning, the weather had turned cold and windy. After a few short rides, we came to the foot of the Alps. Digging into our bags, we pulled out our sweaters, jackets, scarves, and hats and bundled up. A delivery truck stopped and we hopped in. Slowly, he climbed the mountainous road, the engine laboring. After about twenty kilometers, the truck stopped, unable to make it any farther due to ice on the road. The driver told us to get out: "Descendez vous. Je ne peux pas continuer." We got out on the side of the road.

He backed slowly down the hill, made a U-turn, and rumbled out of sight.

"What are we going to do now?"

"Let's keep walking with our thumbs out. It's too cold to stand still."

We walked past a row of houses shuttered against the weather. We trudged up a gradual hill, following the sign to Chamonix until we came to the end of the road. A barrier of snow blocked our passage. On a closed gate was a sign: *Fermé pendant l'hiver. L'interdit d'entrée!*

"The road's closed for winter. Why didn't the fuckin' trucker tell us, the bastard!" I cried.

"What a moron!" Claire screamed.

Anger gripped us, followed closely by fear; we had no idea how we'd get back to a town. The cold air stung our faces and numbed our feet and hands. A light snow began to fall, covering our clothes. We clung to each other, shivering and jumping up and down, trying to stay warm.

"We've got to get out of here, Claire. No one's coming this way in winter."

Claire's eyes looked spacy. She quoted from a John Lennon poem that had once made us laugh. "I have a little budgie, he is my very pal…"

"Stop it!" I grabbed her arm as she faltered in her fashionable black boots. My construction boots gripped the slick pavement as we stumbled and slipped on the icy pavement, retracing our steps to the crossroads.

A car approached and we ran into the street, waving our arms. A middle-aged woman dressed in a jacket with a fur collar and matching hat skidded to a stop, her eyes bulging in surprise.

"S'il vous plait, Madame," we pleaded.

"Entrez! Entrez!" We climbed into the backseat, rescued from an uncertain fate.

That night we slept in a little hotel room above a bar in a nearby village, grateful for the noise below and the heat in our room. At breakfast the next morning, the local truckers laughed at our stupidity for taking the wrong road in winter. "Oh la la, les Américaines, quelle bêtise!"

We hitched a ride to the heavily guarded border, or *frontier* in French, like in the Wild West, a more apt name for unknown territory. The patrolman rifled through our bags and checked our student ID photos, matching them to our faces and passports. We waited warily for our next ride.

"Do you think those students are really going to blow up a government office?" I speculated aloud once we were out of earshot of the soldiers standing guard.

"Don't know. Maybe they're just blowhards." Claire smirked.

"Bad pun, Claire."

Before long, a sporty yellow Alpha Romeo pulled up in front of us. "Ciao, bella!" a smartly dressed young Italian shouted over the noise of the traffic.

Like parrots we replied, "Ciao!"

He got out, opened our doors, and bowed, introducing himself as Luigi. "Dove stai andando?"

"We're going to Chamonix," I said, guessing he wanted to know where we were going.

"Non, non, non. No speak de English. Speaka Italiano." He enunciated clearly, "Vado a Chamonix."

Catching on, I repeated, "Vado a Chamonix."

"Molto buono. Si parla Italiano." He laughed at my prowess in speaking Italian, a compliment the French had yet to give me.

We sparred back and forth, sharing words we knew in each other's language. Luigi sang, "When the moon hits you eyes like a big pizza pie…"

"That's amore!" Claire and I chimed.

"Amore," he teased us. "Do you like to make-a-love?" He pretended to slur his words, raising his thick eyebrows, imitating Dean Martin doing his drunken monologue. "I know American girlzz, zey like to make-a-love, but they're like bunny rabbits." He stopped to make sure he had our attention. Panting as if having a tremendous orgasm, he blurted out, "Hurry, hurry, hurry, pleeeeeese, hurry, hurry, hurry, hurry."

At first we didn't know if we should laugh, get mad, or ignore him. Unable to contain ourselves, we chuckled, which only encouraged him. With exaggerated movements, he thrust his hips with a suggestive rhythm of lovemaking, squealing in a falsetto voice.

"Spanish girlz aren't so easy to get in bed as zee Americans They pretend not to want me, but the more they say *non, non,* the more they mean *si, si.*" He put his fingers to his lips making a kissing noise. "So grateful, they pray, thanking the Virgin Mary."

His eyes gleamed. We shook our heads but still didn't object to his humorous soliloquy.

"The German girls, so strong. I'm so small, my height, not my you-knowa-whatta. Zey take over. *Achtung!* You vill do zis, and you vill do zat." He mimicked the straight upper body of a Nazi soldier, his arms stiff and swinging as in a goose step while managing to drive.

Claire's high-pitched giggle got me laughing so hard my side hurt.

"Ahhh, but the Italian women. They're soooo nice. Beeeg breasts to cuddle. I go sooo crazy. Mmmm, I luvva Italian women."

Luigi settled down and looked directly into my eyes, his sparkling. "Do you wanta make-a-love with me?" He turned to Claire. "Ah, and you too?"

He was so charming that his proposition didn't insult us, but we declined anyway.

"That's okay, I'm going home to zee most beautiful Italian woman, my wife. I love her so much."

After Luigi, the rest of our rides seemed boring as we made our way to the entrance of the Mont Blanc tunnel, an architectural and structural feat.

The smell of diesel on the damp asphalt permeated the cold midmorning air. My blue jeans stuck to my legs, the moisture conducting cold chills up my spine. Cars and trucks lined up, waiting their turn at customs before entering the tunnel. Claire and I paced the line trying to thumb a ride.

"Are you sure your cousins are expecting us?" I worried that we might be stranded in the Alps with a meager amount of clothing and not much money left.

Claire unfolded her letter for the umpteenth time and read aloud, "Nous vous attendons avec plaisir pour les vacances d'hiver." She looked at me. "They're waiting for us with pleasure for our winter break."

"But they don't say when or where to meet them." As much as I longed for the comfort of family and a free place to stay, I didn't believe they still expected us a week late.

"Stop worrying. We'll find them. The Balmats are well known," Claire said with both pride and exasperation.

A long horn blast sounded, and a truck pulled to the side. The driver leaned out of his window, "Où allez-vous?"

We cried above the din of the engines, "Nous allons a Chamonix!"

"Allons-y," he called back.

Pushing our bags in front of us, we climbed up and settled on the bench seat next to the driver. His breath smelled of strong coffee. In thick Marseillaise patois, he chatted, his words ending in a twang with an inflection. "Le tunnel du Mont Blanc est le plus longue du monde! Onze kilometres." He told us the tunnel we were about to enter was the longest tunnel in Europe, eleven kilometers under the Alps from Italy to France. Shaking his head, he expelled air from his rosy cheeks. "Incroyable!"

I found this interesting but troubling as well.

He proceeded to tell us about last week's collision inside the tunnel that wound up shutting it down for six hours. The interior lanes were too narrow for a car to pass, and the emergency vehicles couldn't rescue the victims! Now he really had me worried.

"I can't do this, Claire. I'm claustrophobic! I'll freak out. Ask him if we can go around."

Claire questioned the truck driver about an alternate route.

"Eh, eh? Peut-etre en printemps!" he chuckled. Maybe in spring, but in February it would be over one hundred kilometers to go around the mountain.

The mouth of the tunnel loomed ahead. I gasped, imagining the cold tomb if the heavy snow fell and blocked the exit. Claire took hold of my hand as we entered a darkness punctuated by low-emitting blue lights every hundred meters. My fear compounded. *Thousands of tons of rock and snow are above us. What if the ceiling fell in? We could die!* I squeezed my dry eyes shut, blinking occasionally to see the oncoming headlights flash on and off the convex walls of hewn rock secreting droplets of water. The stifling heat, the echoing noise, and the rancid smell of gasoline sickened me as the cars and trucks lumbered through the narrow hallway.

"Tell me when it's over," I murmured and repeated the Hail Mary under my breath and tried to remember the Apostles' Creed, touching each finger as if they were rosary beads.

"I see the light at the end of the tunnel," Claire whispered after an interminable fifteen minutes, "and there're no angels!"

My eyelids flickered open. The light in the near distance got brighter, the tunnel opening grew bigger and bigger, and finally the truck punched through.

A snow globe view of sharply defined frosted mountains emerged against a cerulean sky, framed on either side by evergreens, as we rolled out of the tunnel and into France. My shoulders relaxed. The serpentine road led to a fairytale village of quaint chalets and crystallized rivers. In the distance, a train wound its way up the valley, blowing its whistle at each bend, and steam puffing from its smokestack.

View from panoramic station L'Aguille du Midi

Chapter Twenty-Four

Chamonix Mont-Blanc

Bonjour Maman!

You won't believe the stories I have to tell about Chamonix. Claire's relatives have lived here from the time the village was found- ed. Her great-great-uncle was the first to climb Mont Blanc, and there's a monument to him in the village center. I've skied a couple of days and watched the races. "Grandpa," really Claire's great-uncle, Charles Balmat, took us to the top of the mountain on a gondola to Station Panoramic sur L'Aguelle du Midi, right across from Mont Blanc. I'm having so much fun that I might not leave.

THE TRUCKER DROPPED US off in the village square next to a bronze statue of a young man pointing toward Mont Blanc. People passed by carrying skis, boots dangling over their shoulders, and children dragged sleds through the mushy snow left on the sidewalks from last night's storm. On the slopes, skiers glided through the trees, kicking up powdery white snow in their wake. Caught in the moment, we hadn't noticed an old man staring at us.

"Qu'est-ce que vous cherchez?" He looked like a caricature of a mountain man with his white whiskers, plaid flannel shirt, and winter overalls.

Claire reached into her pocket and brought out the wrinkled letter, unfolded it, and handed it to him. "Mon oncle est Charles Balmat."

"Oh la la, c'est les Balmats! Cette une famille très connue!" He pointed to the statue. "C'est Jacques Balmat, Alpinist, le premiere de faire l'ascension de Mont Blanc." The bronze statue was Claire's distant relative, the first to climb Mont Blanc.

The gentleman proudly offered to take us to the Balmats' home. We followed him, weaving in and out of back streets along the river until we came to the edge of town. A pigtailed girl, bundled up in a bulky quilted jacket and pantsuit, sat on the doorstep of a storybook chalet, a stream of smoke circling above the chimney. Spying us, she shouted, "Maman! Maman! Ma cousine Américaine!"

Hélène, the young mother, opened the door and waved her arms in a welcoming gesture. "Entrez! Entrez!"

Her husband, Arnaud, stopped chopping wood in mid-swing, setting his ax on a tree stump, and hustled over the snow to greet us and take our bags. Shaking hands with the old man, he thanked him for accompanying us.

Inside, the table had been set for *le petit dejeuner*—large cups on saucers, baguettes, jams, and butter. Hélène pulled a plate of ham from the fridge, saying they had expected us on an earlier train, maybe a few days ago. I glanced at Claire, curious how she would explain our tardiness. Over steaming café au lait, we recounted our journey, leaving out parts we knew would upset any mother.

A rush of cold air entered the room. Grandpa Charles came in from the woodshed, shaking off bits of sawdust and carrying a bundle of wood, looking as if he had stepped out of the book *Heidi*. He had gray hair, a scraggly beard, and a pipe protruding from his mouth.

"Bonjour. Bonjour!" He embraced Claire before sitting down for his midmorning tea, smiling at me and nodding. "Famille d'Amérique!" In an old-person reverie, he talked about deceased relatives and climbing Mont Blanc. His deep-blue eyes twinkled. "Demain nous faisons du ski." He promised to take us skiing tomorrow but rest today. "Vous devez être fatigué." He sensed our weariness, left the table, and took little Marion to her ski lesson.

Hélène showed us to our room. "Faîtes comme chez vous!" She insisted we make ourselves at home. The door closed.

The welcoming beds had eiderdown covers and clean towels at the foot.

"I haven't showered in a week," Claire sighed in anticipation of a bath.

"You first."

We took turns bathing in a tub of hot water with a handheld showerhead, not like the communal showers we had shared with strangers in cheap hotels and hostels. We dried ourselves with clean white towels instead of our dirty T-shirts turned inside out.

Afterward we wrapped ourselves in warm blankets and lay down on the feathery mattresses. The dormer window framed Mont Blanc, its craggy glory crowned with snow and ice, sunlight dancing across its crevasses.

"This is unreal, Claire. Thanks for inviting me. Sorry for being bitchy about finding your relatives."

"It's okay. I couldn't think of a better friend to share this with."

"Remember Tiny Naylor's Coffee Shop, where we pretended to be French?" I reminisced.

"Bien sûr, ma chèrie," she imitated our fake French. "Zee ham sand-wheech, s'il vous plait."

* * *

Claire and I had been best friends in high school, bonded by common troubles at home. My mother needed me to wash, clean, cook, and care for the younger siblings while she recovered from health issues. She was bedridden each month for ten days with uncontrollable bleeding. Dad was unreliable and prone to drinking binges, which meant that my older brothers were in charge of the parking lot business and weren't much help to me around the house.

At fifteen, I wasn't allowed to go on dates, hang out at the local Bob's Big Boy, or drive with another teen. A parent had to drive to school functions, dances, basketball games, and club meetings. When it was my parents' turn to drive, my brother Larry drove us with his learner's permit, because Mom didn't know how to drive and Dad was too drunk or passed out in the front seat. The one exception Mom made was that Claire could drive me places.

"She comes from a good family," Mom would say, which meant she had money and a Catholic upbringing.

Two toots of the horn, and I flew out of the house Saturday night to meet Claire. The first thing she said was, "Peggy, my aunt the Carmelite nun is visiting. I've got two of her habits in the backseat. Do you want to wear them and cruise Taco Bell?" She knew I had a crush on Brian, who worked there. The twinkle in Claire's eyes and her nervous laughter were like forbidden fruit.

"Count me in," I said, knowing that if we were caught, this could get us expelled. I also worried if it was a sin to wear a nun's habit.

Sister Eileen had preached, "The garments I wear are sacred." She brushed her hands down the brown rectangular scapular that hung over her large breasts and rested them on her generous hips, posing like a top model. "If I die wearing the scapular, I will go straight to heaven." I imagined her wearing her habit to bed as security for eternal happiness.

Looking at the habits in the backseat, I wondered if the magical powers of the nuns' garments worked in reverse if stolen or borrowed. If I died wearing them, would I go straight to hell? I didn't want to believe Sister Eileen that her silly garments had special powers, but the belief stuck like a crumb caught in my throat, irritating even after it'd been removed.

I remembered the day Sister Eileen had gotten in the face of a young student and yelled, "I'm going to slap you, but I can't with my holy garments on." Slowly, she removed her scapular, set it over a chair, pulled off the sacred half of her sleeves, and slapped the poor girl across the face, leaving the stinging red imprint of her hand on her left cheek. Calmly, she put the holy vestments back on and continued to teach English as if nothing had happened. I hated Sister Eileen and her hypocrisy.

To justify the nun habit stunt we were about to commit, I promised God that I would not hit anyone while wearing the holy garb. We drove to a side street, climbed in the backseat, and changed into her aunt's habits, wimple and all.

Back in the driver's seat, Claire blasted the radio, threw me her pack of cigarettes, and punched in the lighter. Catching the pack of ciggies, I shook two out, lit both on the red-hot glowing lighter, and handed one to Claire. Turning the corner onto Colorado Boulevard, we rolled to a stop at the red light. I stuck my head out the window, my veil flying, a cigarette dangling from my hands, and yelled, "Hey, buddy do you want to race?" The Mexican lowrider in his souped-up Camaro looked annoyed and then did a double take. Claire gunned her fifty-horsepower engine and turned up the radio full blast, and we took off, singing along with Sam the Sham and the Pharaohs: "Little Red Riding Hood, you sure are looking good." Screeching down Colorado Boulevard like Mr. Magoo, Claire made a quick left turn, stalled the car, turned the key to rev the engine, and entered the one-way parking lot of Bob's Big Boy the wrong way. I saw my older brother's car parked in the corner and didn't want him to rat on me. "Claire! Let's get out of here—that's Larry's car."

"Larry? Your brother? I can't see him like this!" Claire made a U-ee and skidded out of the lot, blurting out that she had a crush on him, which was news to me.

Next we cruised our girlfriends' boyfriends' homes so we could report back on Monday if they had been home on Saturday night. The fuel gauge slipped below the red reserve line, so we stopped and got gas at the Mobil station on the corner of Huntington Drive and Rosemead Boulevard. Getting out, we wiggled our bums seductively, watching the gas station attendant's reactions as we went inside to the bathroom. Looking in the mirror, we were unrecognizable. "Looking good."

Our last stop was the drive-up window at Taco Bell, where Brian—my heartthrob—worked the night shift. Claire eased the car forward to the take-out window and laid it on heavy, blowing smoke in his face and asking for a nun's discount on tacos.

Brian attended public school and didn't know what to make of the two nuns cruising in a red VW Bug. Visibly confused and flustered, he stuttered, "Um…we don't have nun discounts."

Feeling bad for him, I leaned over Claire and said, "Brian, it's me, Peggy, and this is my friend, Claire."

"You guys better get out of here before I lose my job!"

We laughed and turned back onto Rosemead Boulevard just as "The Hullabalooer," our favorite DJ, announced, "All right, all you partygoers, it's time to head home." He played the ten-minute version of the Rolling Stones song, "Going Home," signaling ten minutes to midnight, the teenage city curfew. "Spendin' too much time away, I can't stand another day…" Claire and I belted out the chorus, "I'm goin' home, home, home, going home, back home…Yes, I ammmm!"

⚹ ✳ ✳

Looking out at the Alps, we realized how far away from home we were—no longer pretending to speak French in a funky Pasadena restaurant, we were speaking French and living in France with no curfews, no parents, and no responsibility.

"Going home…when are you going home, Peggy?"

"Don't know. I like the freedom here. How 'bout you?"

Claire spoke softly. "My mother wrote. I have to go home. She doesn't want me to stay in France; she wants me to help out at home as soon as school's out."

In high school, Claire had had to take care of her siblings after school while her mother sobered up. Her father worked late. It was hard to believe. They lived in a big Spanish-style home in posh San Marino, where the families are supposed to be like those on *Leave It to Beaver*. I lived on the other side of the tracks, the county strip, and everyone knew my father drank and we were poor. I never would have guessed the sorrow Claire suffered having to keep up the image that everything was fine. She hid it so well.

Over the next day few days, Grandpa took us skiing and to watch the downhill races. The last day we rode to the top of the observation gondola and he pointed out the route where he ascended Mont Blanc in his youth. Neither of us wanted to leave the idyllic valley, but we had to get back to school. I would not see Claire again for two years.

My father on Smokey, 1935 Iowa farm

CHAPTER TWENTY-FIVE

Fathers

Le 18 mars

Happy St. Patrick's Day! Thought of you all drinking green milk and bitching about green mashed potatoes. Not a custom here. I made Irish bread and brought over some to the Delannes who've taken me in as part of the family. I feel really indebted to the French, they've been so hospitable. Contrary to common belief, they're friendly, warm and open.

I tried to make a cassette tape—spent hours on it—then played it back and it sounded like I was talking underwater. I can't remember what I said in my last letter and what was on the tape. My roommate's dad died last week. Marsha is handling it well and staying in France.

Pat, please send me tapes of the top ten from the "hit parade," (I'm really behind times with music and happenings) and record the sweet melodious voices of my brothers who don't write me!

WINTER BREAK HAD ENDED, and I was in my room studying "Le Chanson de Roland" from the *Lagarde et Richard* textbook when Madame Assemat knocked on my door.

"Excusez-moi, Mademoiselle Peggy," she began with her usual formality, her face flushed from climbing three flights of stairs. She caught her breath and asked me to come to the parlor. "Le Director Monsieur Carter est sur le télèphone."

"Oui, Madame, je descend." I followed behind her as she held the rail and eased her heavy body down each step with a click of her black old-lady shoes. *Why is Mr. Carter calling me?* I wondered.

I entered the normally off-limits parlor and picked up the phone, Madam hovering over me. "Hello, Mr. Carter, this is Peggy."

"Dear"—he paused—"I have some bad news."

My heart sank. Not another death in my family! Unexpected phone calls always meant death, the crackling words over a pay phone, "Dad died," the nighttime ringing and ringing, the click and crying, "Grandpa died...your sister died...your cousin died."

Mr. Carter continued, "I know your father died recently."

My breath caught. I gasped, "Is it my mother?"

"No, no, sorry," he bumbled. "Marsha's father died this morning of a heart attack." He said it bluntly, like a dull knife cutting.

"Oh, I'm so sorry," I replied automatically, not quite understanding why he was telling me and not Marsha. "Should I tell her?" I asked, not knowing how to handle death secondhand.

"No, her mother wants to tell her. Just say that I need to see both of you. It will be better if you're here, because you know what it's like to lose a father."

Did I know what it was like to lose a father? I had blocked his death from my mind. He was gone, not dead. He remained near, more so than those I had left at home. He seemed to follow me through Europe. I wrote home: *Mom, I always feel close to Dad when I'm at the beach or in some port in the world or doing something stupid and fun.* It wouldn't be until seven years after his death, alone and lonely in a mountain cabin, that I finally cried for my father.

I put the phone back in its cradle and pondered what I was going to tell Marsha. She always talked about how funny her dad was, which made me miss my own father. Both of our dads were from the Midwest, jovial guys with corny sayings and jokes. Marsha used her father's good ole boy sayings with a cartoonlike chortle. "Madame Ass-mat is as broad as a barn," and about her skinny sister, "Ya can't see her if she turns sideways." The weather was "so hot you can fry eggs on the asphalt" or "colder than a crapper." But at the mention of her mother, Marsha's mood would change like a cloud crossing her face, worried that her mother's cancer had taken a turn for the worse. *She was supposed to die, not her father.*

Madame waited uncomfortably until I came out of my trance. She gave me a stiff hug, an uncharacteristic show of sentiment. "Let me know if I can help." *Maybe a bottle of wine from your cellar?* I had the sense not to say it aloud, but making light of a bad situation had always helped me cope with tough times.

Marsha was upstairs in her room reading in bed with her afternoon cup of tea balanced on her lap. "Bonjour, Peggy! Do you want a cup of tea?"

"No, but thanks. Mr. Carter called. He wants to see us. Don't know what for; he just said to hurry over." I forced a smile, and Marsha knew immediately.

"Is it my mom?" she looked at me intently, not really wanting an answer.

"I don't know," I lied.

Marsha jumped from her bed, grabbed her coat, and ran out the door with me right behind her. Chris, her stalwart male friend, was waiting outside for us.

All the way over to Mr. Carter's apartment, she kept repeating, "I knew my mother was going to die while I was away."

Elderly Mrs. Carter, with her curly gray hair, opened the door and led us into the living room, where Mr. Carter waited by the phone. "Your mother wants you to call her. You can use our phone."

Marsha looked at him quizzically.

Mr. Carter and his wife didn't understand Marsha's bewildered look. They stood silently holding the phone, with the compassionate look of a minister and his wife. Mr. Carter wrapped an arm around her shoulder as she dialed. No one but Chris and I knew that she had thought her mother must have passed away and had no idea it was her father. I had no time to tell the Carters of the misunderstanding.

I watched Marsha's face grow ashen as the distant ring of the phone sounded in the quiet of the room. "Hello? Mom? Are you okay?" A long silence ensued.

I imagined her mother's words. "Daddy died at work. He had a heart attack and didn't suffer. The hospital pronounced him dead before your sisters and I got there."

Marsha trembled as if cold. "Mama, it's not true."

Minutes later, she handed the receiver back to Mr. Carter. "My father died."

"We're so sorry, dear. If you need time off, we will arrange for makeup classes…don't worry, you're a good student and we'll make sure you get credit. Are you going home for the funeral?" His voice trailed off, kind but insensitive to her confusion. The Carters had funny, old people habits, clicking their dentures, rubbing their hands nervously, talking to us like little children. They reminded me of my grand-parents, all love and honey. Marsha collapsed in the old man's arms, her shoulders shaking without sound or tears.

Marsha's mother and sisters told her not to come home for the funeral, so she stayed to finish her classes, shortening her stay abroad to return home in early summer to care for her mother, who died the following year.

The three of us walked back home in silence from the Carters' that day. I felt inadequate, unable to find words to comfort Marsha. She never spoke of her father's death the rest of the school year, but we shared the bond of losing a father and the stoic trait of not showing emotion.

Bill in Hawaii

CHAPTER TWENTY-SIX

Stood Up

Le 27 mars, 1971
Dear Mom,

When Bill comes to see me, if he does, (he's staying longer in Hawaii with some friends on Maui), how about sending a care package with him? With spring and beach days coming I'd love to have some of my shifts and Mexican blouses and cut-offs. I miss them.

I was planning on going to Morocco for Easter break but that's pretty far from Bordeaux and my schoolwork is piling up. I received a letter from Bill saying he might come before Easter and I don't want to miss him, so maybe I'll stay home. I might go skiing in the Pyrenees with Marie-Paule and her family or maybe to London cuz I know some kids who're going there or maybe Normandy or maybe...Mom, I've got a chronic case of indecision, which sure has broken out bad.

I'm pretty happy in Bordeaux. I have some friends, split to the beach easy enough, and I feel at home with the Delannes. So, I guess I've settled. Wish you could meet them, they're bitchin people. Drop me a line this week.

BILL HAD WRITTEN IN February saying he moved to the infamous Banana Patch commune on Maui, assuring me he'd leave in time to be in France by Easter break. I knew what went on in communes. I'd spent the summer of '68 bumming around Hawaii, camping on beaches, and staying with draft-dodging friends in a rent-free shack on a sugar plantation. Long-haired utopians had stormed the islands, disappearing into the back country to live off the land, build homes in trees like big kids, grow pot, harvest wild psilocybin mushrooms from cow pies, and *make love not war.* Why was I waiting for him?

Bill had chosen the Banana Patch over me. I simmered, wondering when he was coming to France, if at all. Finally, reality hit me. I'd been stood up! My imagination conjured up images of his tanned Adonis body swimming freely with naked ladies in cool freshwater ponds, waterfalls trickling over his blond curls while he ate passion fruit.

Too much time had passed, and I no longer loved Bill. But French wisdom expressed my feelings: "Jealousy lingers long after love has passed." If he wasn't with me, I didn't want him to be with anyone else.

Marsha's boyfriend, Rex, a Tom Sawyer type with sandy hair and freckles, had arrived before spring break and bought two Peugeot bikes, one for him and one for her. By the time I figured out I'd be alone over break, they'd already left on a bike trip. Marie-Paule told me I had waited too long to make up my mind, and the family camper at the ski resort in the Pyrenees was full.

I asked Leslie what she was doing.

"I'm going to London to see my aunt." She didn't invite me. "Why don't you go to Morocco with Sarah? She can't find anybody to go with either."

Dull, boring Sarah.

I wanted to be with my French friends. I began to think maybe if I stayed in Bordeaux I might have a chance with Pierrot. I had taken a few yoga classes with him in the downtown gym, and I could feel things heating up between us, especially last weekend.

Pierrot, Marie-Paule, and I had piled into Jacques's Deux Chevaux and headed south on a surf trip with the lure of a big swell. A few miles north of Biarritz, Jacques turned onto a dirt road to check out the surf and drove across the bluffs in a torrential downpour.

Getting out of the car, we stepped in the gooey mud, our sandals like plungers as we walked to the edge of the cliff. The mighty waves crashed silvery white against the rocks, and the full moon peeked through ominous black clouds. Epic surf. Shivering and wet, we climbed back into the car, Jacques and Marie-Paule in the front seat, Pierrot and me in the back. Jacques turned the key, the engine sputtered, and the wheels spun uncontrollably, digging into the muck. The boys got out to push the car, while Marie-Paule gunned the engine, flooding the carburetor. The engine cranked but didn't catch, and all the while, the mud was oozing up to the doors. There was no choice but to spend the night in the cramped quarters of the Deux Chevaux.

I tried to sleep upright, avoiding physical contact with Pierrot, who had yet to make an advance. He had fallen asleep leaning against the window, the rain pounding on the tin roof. Sometime in the night, our bodies touched.

The next morning, the sun rose over the Basque hills, waking us to a brilliant day after a devastating storm. Upon inspection, we found the wheels encased in mud like a boot lock.

Straggly-haired Jacques stretched his arms across Marie-Paule to open his glove compartment and, like a wizard, produced a few bars of chocolate and a tab of mescaline. He grinned. *A perfect day for pyschedelics!*

Within an hour, we were running across the grassy field, which glistened with dewdrops like diamonds, and down to the sandy beach, frolicking in the icy waves and rolling in the warm sand. The high wore off around noon. The guys chipped the mud away from the wheels, the car started, and we rolled into Biarritz hungry and tired. On the way down the stairs to the Grand Plage, we stopped at the tea shop and bought warm baguettes and soft cheese. Pierrot spread the gooey mess onto the loaf, broke it, and passed a half to me. We fell asleep in the warm sand side by side.

I had expected to see Pierrot during the week, but he vanished with the rest of the students. Without any other option, I resigned myself to going to Morocco with Sarah.

On Friday night, I rode my Solex motorbike over to Marie-Paule's house to store it in their garage over vacation. Bumping over cobblestone streets and weaving around parked cars, I pulled up to the back gate and buzzed the doorbell. As I had thought, no one was home. Balancing my bike in one hand, I pushed on the vine-covered walk gate and lifted my bike over the threshold. Once inside the garden, I heard voices and music coming from Marie-Paule's room. I parked my motorbike in the corner of the garage alongside the myriad bicycles, motor scooters, lawn mowers, and anything that had wheels. As I was leaving, the lights went off upstairs, and the door opened. Marco, Pierrot, and Jacques came out, trailed by a halo of blue smoke.

Marco and Jacques threw air-kisses, too preoccupied to stop, but Pierrot lingered in the garden, igniting butterflies in my stomach in anticipation. He embraced me. Was it more than the light touch of the friendly bise? His kiss lingered on each cheek with a murmur barely audible in my ear. My face burned as I awkwardly stood there.

He asked, "Où vas-tu?"

Where was I going? What did he really mean? Was he asking me to go out with him tonight? Or was he just curious where I was going? Or did he want to know if I was going somewhere for vacation?

"Nowhere." I left an opening for him to invite me… *somewhere. I* would have changed my plans in a heartbeat if he had asked me to stay.

I'd fallen hopelessly in love with him.

"Pourquoi tu laisses ton Solex ici?" He wanted to know why I was leaving my bike there if I wasn't going somewhere.

My mind whirled as I tried to find the right response. The femme fatale, *Je ne sais pas quoi faire,* emphasizing I didn't know what to do. Or the direct approach, *Je vais avec toi n'importe où* ("I'll follow you to the end of the earth"). Instead, I answered truthfully, with as much nonchalance as I could muster. "Je vais au Moroc avec Sarah."

"Ah, Peggy, c'est très dangereux pour une femme au Moroc!" Dangerous? I figured he was talking about the white slave trade in North Africa.

"Ça va, Pierrot," I assured him. "We're staying with her family friend."

"Sois sage," he counseled, like an older brother. He held me again and whispered, "Quand tu reviens, viens me voir." I flushed thinking about my return to his arms, or at least I thought he had said that. *He must like me if he's concerned for my safety and wants me to come see him as soon as I get back.* I magnified the situation in my mind to a Humphrey Bogart and Ingrid Bergman moment.

"Bien sûr, Pierrot, tu vas me manquer." I took the chance to tell him I was going to miss him. I felt so brave to use those words—*tu me manques*—an idiom in the French language that trips up many English-speakers because it reverses the subject with the object. Translating in my head, it sounded as if I were saying, "You will miss me," which I hoped was the case, but the awkward phrase translates literally to "You will be missed by me."

Peggy hitchhiking in Spain

CHAPTER TWENTY-SEVEN

Journey across Spain

Le 5 avril
Dear Eileen and Kathleen (the only ones who write to me),
Did you get the cheese I sent? I think you'll like the processed one, le vache-qui-rit, it means the laughing cow. The little round ones are goat cheese which are great when you acquire the taste. Tell Mom, she doesn't have to save them if nobody eats them.
I hope your plans for Easter vacation are better than mine. Bill never showed up. Bummer, but I'm going with a friend to Morocco. Tell Mom she's the kind of girl she'd like me to travel with: nerdy and safe.

THE NEXT MORNING I pulled my rucksack out from under the armoire, threw in clean underwear and some lightweight shirts and added shorts, jeans, and a bathing suit. *Don't forget your toothbrush and rosary. Mind your p's and q's.* No matter how many miles were between us, I always heard Mom's voice.

Mousy Sarah waited outside my door, nervously glancing at her watch. Unremarkable in all ways, she had squinty gray eyes, brown hair, and faded freckles across the bridge of her nose. She was far from a cheap girl who would attract too much male attention.

"Sorry I'm late. I had to pack."

"It's okay," Sarah said with docile acceptance of my rudeness. Neatly unfolding her map, I saw that she had highlighted a route that cut through the center of Spain, jumped across the Strait of Gibraltar, and made a beeline down the coast of Morocco. The days of the week dotted the route in neatly penned red ink. "If we don't stop 'cept to sleep, we can get to my aunt's friend's house in five days."

"Cool. Where's that?

"Casablanca. It's her second home. She's French."

I agreed to her plan: no sightseeing, no side trips, no dilly-dallying along the way—just head straight to the port of Algeciras, catch the ferry to Tangier, take a train to Casablanca, and stay a week for free. Sarah had it planned down to the minute.

What she hadn't planned on was spending long hours on the side of dusty roads, hoofing it through dirty industrial cities, and getting lost searching for the way out of towns. Neither of us spoke Spanish. Once we had crossed the border from France into Spain, we were tongue-tied. The safety of familiarity vanished, and the verdant rolling pastures dried out, replaced by desert plateaus. Old cars and rusty trucks moved sluggishly along rutted highways, the air hung gray and heavy, reflecting the dismal life in Northern Spain under Franco's Fascist government.

"What a stinkin' place. Fucking Franco raped the land and doesn't give a shit about the North." Stewing in my own misery, I ranted about the evil of bad governance and praised socialism, ending my diatribe with "Franco's a Fascist pig."

Sarah blinked and shook her head in disbelief. "What are you talking about?" I took it to be a rhetorical question and shut up.

On the fringes of Bilbao, high-rise apartments sprouted like weeds. Brightly colored garments whipped in the wind on clotheslines, some catching on the balconies, others falling to the ground. Trash blew across the vacant lots and gathered in the ditch behind us. Smokestacks from a nearby factory spewed gray clouds, adding to the diesel fumes trapped in traffic. We covered our faces with our shirts, our eyes watering.

A dilapidated truck, its open bed full of potatoes, rambled to a stop, kicking up pebbles and dirt. An old man in overalls leaned out the window. "Dondé vas?"

"Morocco." We dusted ourselves off, smiling expectantly.

"Ai yi yi, es muy lejos, hijas." The old man shook his head contemplating the distance, scratching the stubble on his chin. Shoving his shoulder against the dented door, he pitched forward and stepped stiffly to the ground. His overalls were caked in muc, his brown leather shoes curled at the toes, his undershirt yellowed from sweat. He must have been in his sixties, judging by his gait as he walked around to the passenger side and opened the door for us.

"Mi nombre es Pedro. Vamanos." He took our bags and secured them on top of the potatoes under a burlap tarp. The sun hung low in the sky. This would be our last ride of the day.

The truck painfully chugged up and over arid hills as huge sixteen-wheelers passed us and zippy cars sped by in a constant stream, blasting their horns. Large, black-silhouetted bulls punctuated the peaks of the rolling hills with red letters spelling out *Veterano*, ads for the famous sherry of Jerez. Pedro joked about *los cuernos*, "the horns," making the universal sign with his pinky and pointer fingers. I found myself hoping that *los cuernos* didn't carry the same frat boy connotation of *horny*.

We bumped along in silence.

It was pitch black when the farmer veered off the main thoroughfare onto a desolate road. Fearing we'd be mugged, raped, or at the very least, inconvenienced by a longer route, I begged him to take us back to the highway. "Por favor, stop! Finito!"

But he kept driving.

An hour later, he stopped at a gas station to fill up his tank. He bought some candy and sweet sugary bread from a vendor sitting next to the pumps to share with us.

We drove late into the night.

Lulled into an altered state, ours eyes focused on the road ahead. We willed ourselves to stay alert, hoping not to crash. Our heads nodded. Sarah slumped against my shoulder first, and then my eyes fluttered shut, my head flopping forward.

The sound of grinding brakes and gravel in the wheel wells startled me. My eyes popped open.

"Estoy muy consado." Pedro's baggy, half-closed eyes stared past me like a blind man. He climbed out of the truck, the door swinging closed behind him.

"He's not leaving, is he?" gasped Sarah.

"No, he's tired and we're stuck out here in the boonies. No cars passing at this hour."

"What's he doing?"

We turned to watch him.

In hushed voices, we speculated about what might happen to us on that deserted road. My skin crawled as if I was watching a Hitchcock movie.

He futzed with the tarp at the back of the truck, unhooking a corner and pulling out a dust-bound wool blanket.

Then he walked around to the passenger window and tapped. We rolled down the window only halfway, and a blast of cold desert air whipped against our faces. Reaching out, we took the blanket and rolled the window back up. He dropped the tarp on the ground, lay down on it, and rolled under the truck to sleep.

Sarah locked the passenger door, and I reached over and locked the driver's door.

"What about our packs?" she asked.

"He can have them," I answered.

Pulling the blanket over us, we curled up on the seat together and fell into a restless sleep.

At dawn, we awoke to Pedro tapping on the window. I unlocked his door. In daylight, everything looked less menacing, and my mind cleared of the cobwebs and fear from the night before. The sun peeked over the distant hills, illuminating the vast expanse of road ahead. Cactus dotted the countryside, and I took in the smell of a desert dawn, cooling and fresh.

By eight in the morning, we had arrived at the foot of the Sierra Morena mountain range. Despite the low elevation, there was no chance the old truck could get over the pass. Pedro pulled to the side of the road and pointed south. "Este es el camino." It was our road. "Vaya con Dios." He pointed back from where we came and said, "Mercado." He had to get the potatoes to market.

"Gracias, Pedro." I had expected the worst from the old man, and in the end he was kind enough to take us out of his way. We unloaded our packs, which had become buried under the potatoes and were now covered in earthy grit. The truck backed up and turned around, sputtering and stalling, and then it disappeared behind a ball of dust.

I pitied him and yet, I felt lucky not to have to work so hard. I had always noted people worse off than me. It made me feel grateful and sometimes even superior. In grade school, I wasn't the poorest child—not like Judy who wore dirty clothes to school and smelled. I had two legs—not like the old legless man who sold newspapers on Colorado Boulevard. I had a roof over my head—not like the hobos who slept in our front yard bushes. I wasn't retarded—like Jerry, the neighbor boy who never went to school.

In the distance, two cars approached.

We put our thumbs out. The second car stopped down the road and backed up. Or was it a car?

"It sounds like a sewing machine," I observed.

"It's a ride, Peggy. Let's go." Sarah took the lead and I followed, packs in tow.

A bespectacled man grabbed a door handle on the dashboard and lifted the entire front of the car open. His compact, wiry body unfolded like a clown getting out of a toy car. Standing a foot taller than his car, he wore a gray three-piece suit, his unbuttoned coat flapping in the wind and his shoulders thrust back, poised like a magician ready to cut a woman in half.

"Dondé va?" his voice squeaked.

"Morocco."

He smiled, gesturing to get in. "Andale!"

We examined the car, uncertain how all three of us could fit in the tiny space with our rucksacks.

He repeated forcefully, "Andale, andale! Yo trabajo!" Apparently he was in a hurry to get to work.

Dutifully, we put our packs in the backseat, which doubled as the trunk and was about the size of a coffin. Sarah squeezed in the back, her knees up to her chest, and insisted, "I'm fine, I'm fine, just get in."

The little Spaniard gallantly whisked his hand aside, indicating for me to climb in the front seat next to him. I ducked under the car door that looked like a broken wing and scrunched my legs against the dashboard. The driver squeezed in next to me, reached for the door handle above his head, and with a *whoosh*, hermetically sealed us in.

The engine whirred as the car eased back onto the rural highway heading toward the pass over the mountains. The Spaniard spoke rapidly, trilling his *r*'s and waving his hands for emphasis, pausing only for us to nod in agreement. His minicar chugged steadily up the narrow, serpentine road. Trucks passed and blared their horns, their fumes seeping into this poor excuse of an automobile.

The agitated Spaniard swore, "Puta madre!" pounding the dashboard and shaking his steering wheel, as if that would make the machine move faster.

Paralyzed with fear, I avoided looking to the right, where a sheer drop-off threatened disaster. My eyes held the road; my body tensed at every hairpin turn.

"Esta todo bien?" the Spaniard turned his head to ask Sarah how she was doing.

In a split second, he lost control of the car. Slamming on his brakes, we skidded into the path of an oncoming truck. Swerving, he missed the truck, but our car spun out of control like a top, crossing the centerline and hitting the side of the interior cliff. Pebbles and rocks streamed onto the road as we ping-ponged off the wall and headed toward the precipitous edge.

This can't be happening. I can't die. My mother can't lose another daughter. Please, God, don't let me die.

I didn't black out, but to this day I don't know how our car came to a stop. In silence and slow motion, I remember other cars and trucks zigzagging to miss us. A mishmash of vehicles came to a standstill, blocking the road like bumper cars in a jam. A few men got out of their cars, lifted our little car off a boulder, and pushed it back onto the road. A moment of unsettling calm turned to calamity—cars honking, people screaming. The ashen Spaniard mumbled incoherently in a weepy voice and turned the ignition over and over until it spurted and started.

We drove to the crest of the hill and stopped at an auberge perched on a crag overlooking the valley. "Café?" the spent driver asked.

"Si, por favor." Anything to get out of this death trap!

Our legs unfolded like pipe cleaners, only we had no wires to support our weakened knees. At the side of the road, our bodies shivered from the cold mountain air and jangled nerves.

Inside the café, red-checked cloths covered the tables, plastic flower garlands framed the large windows, and a wooden cross with a bronze body of Christ hung above the entry.

The Spaniard ordered coffees. His hands trembling, his voice quivering, he apologized, "Discúlpame, discúlpame." Five minutes later, having barely touched his coffee, he pushed back his chair and said, "Vamos prisa."

Hurry up and go? Was he serious? No way were we getting back in that piece of shit car. We said we were hungry and wanted to stay and eat. Appearing miffed, he shrugged his slight frame, straightened his jacket, and lisped like a Castillano, "Como quierath." He told us to get our things out of the car, that he was in a hurry to get to work. He was like the main character in Kafka's *Metamorphosis,* who was more concerned about being late for work than about having turned into a giant bug overnight, unable to get out of bed.

Outside, the Spaniard lifted the front door up and over the top of the car. The backpacks lay like tiny bodies in the coffin-like space where Sarah had been sitting.

Why didn't we die that morning? Was it just not our time? Or was it divine intervention that saved us? In either case, I blessed myself and said a prayer to Dad and Shereen, my personal angels who were guiding me on my journey.

Lifting our packs out of the back, I passed Sarah hers, slung mine over my shoulder, and wished the Spaniard well. In a very businesslike manner, he shook our hands as if settling a deal, climbed into the driver's seat, and enclosed himself in the machine.

Back inside the auberge, I sat down, exhaled deeply, and gazed out the window to the steep valley walls descending into the brush below.

"Do you think we would've survived the fall?" I asked. Worry lines creased my forehead as I thought of my father's body, hidden in the fields, dead for days, and my sister's body, crushed in her VW bug from the impact of a train.

"Put it behind you," Sarah advised. She rarely showed any emotions, leaving me to wonder what she was thinking and making it hard to develop a friendship, but she was a good traveling partner. Avoiding the topic of the crash, she opened her map and traced her finger along our route. "It's not even noon yet. We should be able to get a ride at least as far as Seville today and Algeciras by Tuesday to catch the ferry." She folded the red map along the creases: *Espagne* in bold green letters on the front and the Michelin man smiling on the back.

We made it to Seville as the vendors lifted the metal grates, opening their doors for business after siesta. Church bells tolled, people milled around the plaza, and life returned to the streets. Tired from the bad night's sleep in the truck and emotionally wrought from our near-death experience, we decided to get a hotel rather than continuing on.

We happened upon what we thought was a funeral procession, with donkey carts and villagers dressed in black. A long-haired, bearded man in white robes, wearing a crown of thorns on his head and sandals on his feet, carried a large wooden cross. He was followed by black-hooded men who reminded me of the Ku Klux Klan, except for the color of their robes. We stopped to watch. A statue of the Madonna in a tortuous stance, her arms outstretched, her face contorted, rode on a donkey cart lined in purple satin and pulled by several young men in somber grays and blacks. Crowds gathered behind a life-sized statue of Jesus nailed to the cross, depicting him bleeding and bruised, with blue veins bulging on his crossed feet and translucent flesh.

Santa Semana, the first day of Holy Week! How could I forget?

"This creeps me out," Sarah complained. She had grown up in a secular home; her father was a professor and her mother a psychologist. She had little interest in churches or religion.

I watched the faithful crawling on their hands and knees, self-flagellating and praying as if in a trance. At one time, I would have joined them, but I had done enough Lenten penance as a child—going forty days without candy or gum, not sleeping with a pillow, and giving my allowance (a nickel each week) to the poor. I had spent hours praying novenas to the Blessed Mother and saying the Stations of the Cross. That little girl lived inside me, but I ignored her and kept walking to the hotel.

The ferry to Tangiers

Chapter Twenty-Eight

Ferry to Morocco

Postcard
Le 7 avril 1971
Peace ba-beee,
    *Happy Easter family—I'm leaving Spain today and I'm on
my way to Morocco with my friend Sarah who has some friends
in Casablanca. Probably we'll stay a week, maybe more. It's going
to be quite a culture change but I think I can get behind being in
the sun among a bunch of hooded Arabs. Don't worry, I'm taking
caution and the place is full of tourists now.*

A LONG BLAST OF the horn signaled that the ferry was about
to leave the harbor. Deckhands dashed to pull the moor-
ing lines aboard, and the vessel rolled into the open sea. A
salty spray splashed over the bow, sending the passengers
scurrying inside as water sloshed to and fro on the deck,
emptying down the scuppers and cascading back into the
sea. Sarah and I preferred to stand on the deck rather than
crowd onto the wooden benches below in the stuffy cabin.

A man in his late forties walked up and stood next to us, uncomfortably close by American standards. He wore a heavy coat that partially covered his ill-fitting suit, and his trousers were too short to hide his shabby shoes.

"Excusez-moi, Mademoiselle, are you traveling for vacation?"

"Yes, we're on spring break." I wrapped my scarf tighter around my ears.

"Vous parlez français?" he continued.

"Oui, nous sommes étudiantes en France," I answered, grateful to speak French again after the long journey across Spain.

The fellow made small talk about his family in Rabat and his important job with the Moroccan Railroad Company and how he got to live above the train station because he knew important people in the government. We nodded politely.

Sarah moved away, annoyed that the stranger had now physically moved between us, interrupting our conversation. He glanced dismissively at Sarah, turned, and gave me his full attention. "Je m'appelle Monsieur Abadi." To detain me further, he reached into his pocket, took out his tattered wallet, and pulled out old photos of his family.

"C'est ma famille." He proudly pointed to each family member, saying their names: "Ma fille Amina avec la petite Yasmin, et Laila, les jumeaux Yassine et Zahra. Les garçons Ali, Jalal, Hassan, Mouhammed, et Karim."

In the center of the photo I recognized him, dressed in what looked like a military uniform but could have been his work uniform. Next to him sat a large woman in flowing robes, her somber face peering out from beneath her headdress.

"C'est comme ma famille." I too came from a family of ten, five girls and five boys.

"Incroyable!" Visibly thrilled, he beamed and patted me on the back like an old friend. People who come from large families often share an immediate bond, an unspoken understanding that in the morning everyone must wait to take a turn in the bathroom, bedrooms and beds are shared, fights break out spontaneously over food at the table, and hand-me-downs are as prized as store-bought clothes.

"Venez chez moi, ma fille." Calling me his daughter, he invited us to his home and handed me a wrinkled business card with the emblem of the Royal Railroad on one side and his address and phone number scribbled on the back. He insisted we call him when we got to Rabat, the capital, and he said he would send his son to pick us up.

"Oui, merci." I took his card, thanking him.

He beamed as if he had won an award and patted me on the back again, repeating, "Ma fille."

Sarah wasn't impressed with the invitation, but I kept the card in my pocket—rainy day insurance in case we needed a place to stay.

Three long blasts of the ship's horn announced our arrival into the port of Tangier. People emerged from the cabin below, bundles slung over their shoulders, lugging overstuffed suitcases with their children in tow.

Disembarking, we felt the pulse of the crowd as we were pushed and jostled down the gangplank and out into the street. The smells of open barbecues and mule dung drifted in the intense heat. Hooded men and veiled women bustled through the narrow alleyways, their heads down, weaving between donkeys struggling under huge burlap bags tied on their backs. Vendors cried in singsong voices selling their vegetables, pots and pans, and sundries. Inside the shady courtyard of a mosque, men prostrated themselves on rugs, praying in unison, lifting their bodies and arms and returning to their mats while soul-piercing wailing emanated from mosque towers. We navigated our way into the city, all so raw and human.

"Madame, voulez-vous une guide?" A ragged boy approached us, his loud voice attracting more little urchins. Like Pied Pipers, we plodded through town with a line of children trailing behind us.

"Pleeese, misses, I'm a good guide," a child of ten or so pleaded. His pants were in shreds, displaying his skinny legs and scabby knees, and he wore two different-sized sandals that made him trip.

"Guten tag, ich bin ein gutter leiter," he tried again in German. "Por favor, soy una guida."

I was impressed. He spoke so many languages for such a dirty little fellow. "How many languages do you speak?"

Pleased with himself, he rattled off the numbers one to ten in several languages; then he got carried away and said all the bad words he knew in just as many languages.

I couldn't help but laugh, which only encouraged the entourage of ragamuffin kids to pursue us, begging for money, cigarettes, and candy and offering to help carry our luggage or take us to a hotel.

We clutched our bags and packs even tighter and held our purses above our heads. Seeing our distress, two older boys rushed over and gave the youngsters a verbal thrashing in their guttural Arab language. The kids fled.

Our rescuers apologized for the street children. "They're pests and no one cares for them."

I had never been to a country where poverty was so apparent. Women sat in doorways begging while nursing dirty, naked babies, and dogs scurried and fought for scraps of food that floated down the open gutters of the streets.

Children sat on old carpets and blankets with cups for offerings set out, their legs bent in ungodly positions, the result of being broken as infants to make them better beggars.

In contrast, our young saviors were neatly dressed in typical Western teenage clothes, blue jeans, white button-up shirts, and sneakers. The older one acted as our guide, pointing out mosques, Moorish buildings, and other landmarks of a vibrant, old culture. The younger boy, Ahmed, had a Cheshire smile and an impish hop in his walk as he tried to keep up with his older brother, who occasionally elbowed him to keep him from interrupting. They took us to their home and told us to wait outside.

A few minutes later, a small girl opened the front door to let us in. A tall, stately woman followed close behind her. With a harsh tone, she dismissed the young maid.

"Vous êtes Américaines?" she asked us, as if being American was an accusation.

"Oui," we replied, put off by her strict demeanor and unwelcoming introduction. She led us into the parlor, where tea had been set up. Her two daughters, in their midtwenties, sat on a midnight purple divan, their deep brown eyes highlighted with heavy kohl and their thick lips accentuated with red lipstick.

"Tea?" one girl asked in English.

"Yes, thank you."

"I am Azra and this is my sister, Haifa, and you met my mother, Kayla. What are your names?"

"I'm Peggy and this is Sarah. We met your brothers getting off the boat today."

She laughed. "They're always bringing home strangers. My mother is quite used to it but also a little fed up." The mother's face remained stern. "Please excuse her. She doesn't speak English. I go to the university and am happy to practice my English with you."

The painfully subdued maid returned with more tea and cookies, her eyes downcast. "Don't mind her," Azra explained. "She's my cousin from the desert. She's deaf and doesn't speak. My mother took pity on her and gave her a place to live." It was customary to take in poor children from the country, not to educate them but to have as indentured slaves. My impulse was to rescue the child.

After we all drank mint tea and ate sugared breads, Azra and Haifa left the room. Layla offered more tea. In a few minutes, the girls returned with an array of djellabas, embroidered caftans, and finery.

"Can we dress you?"

Sarah and I laughed at the idea of playing dress-up but agreed. We must have looked mannish in pants, baggy shirts, and old boots, especially compared to them in flowing gowns, hoop earrings, and arm bangles. The sisters put the flowing robes over our heads and gracefully covered our hair and faces with veils, and then they stood us in front of the full-length mirror.

"Do you like the way you look?"

My robe hit midcalf, exposing my jeans and clunky construction boots, but from the waist up I looked feminine and exotic.

"The robes are beautiful, but I'm too tall. And my boots look so big."

Looking back, I wonder if they were embarrassed for us since we didn't have proper clothing. Or was this a warning we didn't heed that women in Morocco shouldn't wear pants and are obliged to cover their arms? It came as a surprise that they were proud of their traditional garments and headscarves, not oppressed by them. I had held the belief Arab women were prisoners under veils, not free to express themselves like Westerners.

Late in the afternoon, we left with promises to write, which we never did. I wonder what became of Azra and her family and if they have felt the oppression of fundamentalists.

The mother showed us to the door and insisted her two sons escort us to the youth hostel. Once outside the house, the boys suggested we walk by way of the beach. We nodded in agreement, happy to be in the fresh air and eager to see the Moroccan beaches. But once we got to the shore, we saw a different side of the Arab male hospitality.

"Don't you want to take off your clothes at the beach?" Jamaal asked.

"No," we responded.

"I mean to swim. Don't you have bikinis?" He pointed to our packs.

"No, we don't want to swim."

"But we brought you to the beach. You must swim."

Looking around, we noticed only men in trousers and long robes—no women under umbrellas or children frolicking in the water. The brothers paraded us along the boardwalk, as if we were trophies, greeting the men in Arabic, drawing attention to us. The men took license to ogle and comment with gurgling voices as we passed. One man stopped and waved money in our faces and then haggled with the boys as if we were chattel. Frightened, we demanded to leave the beach.

"No, just stay awhile; we'll go swimming too," Jamaal said, unbuttoning his shirt.

Afraid to flee and be chased by the pack of men, we kept walking at a steady pace ignoring the illicit offers and gaining distance. Haifa ran up to grab us. "I'll get in trouble from my mother if you're found alone." The absurdity stunned me. He would sell us but not let us walk alone in town?

"We won't tell your mother or anyone what happened on the beach. Just leave us alone!" Sarah screamed at him. He ran back to report to Jamaal and we got away.

The next morning, we took the train to Rabat to look up the nice man we had met on the boat.

My new djellaba

CHAPTER TWENTY-NINE

Rabat

Salaam alaikum Mom!
We met a nice man with ten children and he invited us to stay
with him and took us on a tour of Rabat. I told him that you had
ten children. He said he loves you—he wants 20. We visited a school
where the little girls, almost like slaves, learn embroidery. I bought
a few little things, a man's djellaba because the blouses and kaftans
are muy expersivo. It's amazing all the work is done by hand in
Morocco. I'll write more later.

EYES FOLLOWED OUR EVERY move as we bought tickets and
found a place to sit on the wooden benches in the waiting
room at the train station in Tangier. Eyes behind translucent
veils, single eyes peering from black holes, bright blue eyes
beneath white turbans, and condemning dark eyes of listless
males. I felt naked in my shorts and tank top. I put on my
sweater, even though the temperature was already eighty
degrees by eight in the morning. I stared right back. The
women averted their curious eyes, but the men continued
to glower.

Sarah had worn long pants with a short sleeve shirt. She covered her shoulders with a shawl. "Let's not bring any more attention to us than we already have. Cover up."

"I can't hide my legs." I took my pack and set it in front of me, wishing the man next to me would stop looking at my crotch. Arab men stared, brushed too close when they passed by, and emitted low, growling sexual noises.

The train pulled into the station. No one queued in lines. Everyone shoved, moving us along. A hand felt my butt. I turned around to slap the culprit, but he slithered into the throng of people.

On board the train, I changed my clothes in the dirty bathroom, straddling the hole in the floor trying to keep my pant legs from getting wet.

We got off at the Centre Ville train station in Rabat, found a café nearby, and ordered iced mint tea, which was syrupy sweet and refreshing. I asked the waiter if he would mind calling Monsieur Abadi's number and handed him his card. I could trust Monsieur Abadi, the father of ten and a businessman.

"Je connais Monsieur Abadi," the waiter said, recognizing his name. He shouted at a young boy, who was huddled in a circle of friends playing a game with stones, and ordered him with a swat to the head to find Monsieur Abadi. Yelling and the back of a hand fell too often on the children here, but no one seemed to mind, not even the little ragamuffin who took off running.

Sarah took out her guidebook and unfolded her unwieldy map. "You know, we can't stay in Rabat more than a single night if we're going to get to Casablanca."

"That's fine with me. I don't like cities." I sipped the tea. A mint leaf caught on my tongue, leaving an acrid taste in my mouth. "Maybe we can find Jill when we get to the coast."

Jill was legendary among the EAP students. She had gone to Morocco at Christmas break and never returned. It was rumored she was staying in Agadir getting loaded with other hippies, living on the beach and surviving on oranges. The lure of the Saharan beach and a carefree life beckoned, my mind imagining sand dunes, lush palm oases, eating dates and oranges, and bathing in warm ocean water, all for free. The inches on the map made it look possible. Sarah etched a line passing through Marrakesh to Casablanca down to Agadir, the edge of the great desert.

A half hour had passed. We gave up waiting, paid our bill, and left.

Within minutes, our waiter came running after us. "Attendez! Vous ne pouvez pas aller toute seule." He warned us not to go alone and promised Monsieur Abadi was coming.

We followed him back to the restaurant, and he led us past the kitchen to a darkened room in the back. As my eyes adjusted to the dim light, I saw three Arab men, two dressed in robes and headdresses and one in a suit and tie, reclining on Persian rugs propped up against red leather cushions with gold stars. Monsieur Abadi wasn't there. The light from intricately cut lanterns danced across the room, sending flickering shadows over our faces. The Arabian night atmosphere both scared and excited me; my arms tingled, my throat clenched, and my stomach dropped, but that didn't deter me from joining the men. I had confidence I could befriend them. They reminded me of the motley group who hung around my father's parking lot, older men smoking cigars, drinking out of brown bags, wagering bets on the races, and playing blackjack and liar's poker. These Arabs weren't going to harm anyone, at least not in broad daylight, so I sat down. Sarah was less sure of the situation and remained by the door.

"So, you are friends of Monsieur Abadi?" the elder one asked. He ordered tea and freshly baked cookies and motioned to Sarah to sit at the low table. The waiter set down the tea and cookies.

"Vous aimez le hashish?" The Arab in western clothes spoke in a deep resonant voice as if asking, "Do you like Coca-Cola?"

"Non, je ne fume pas le hashish." I didn't smoke hash, at least not in Morocco. If caught the punishment was life in prison, if not death.

He laughed. "No smoke. You eat hashish cookie. You're American...you like kief?" he laughed, assuming all Americans liked drugs.

I hadn't expected to be offered hash in a cookie, especially from a guy in a suit. My impression was kids did that stuff and hid it from authority. I'd first seen hashish at Marie-Paule's house, little brown clumps of kief, wrapped like chocolates in foil, small pieces we put in a pipe and smoked. I knew better than to take a laced cookie. These guys may have been undercover cops for the Moroccan government, luring us into their dens to arrest us and throw us in jail.

"You like a beer?" offered the third gentleman, leaning in close.

"No, thank you, the tea's fine." I was concerned. Things weren't as I had expected. Muslims don't drink alcohol, but here at midday three Muslim men were drinking beer, smoking hash, and cavorting with us, women without veils!

Luckily, or maybe not, Monsieur Abadi appeared in the doorway, not in his shabby suit but in full Arab regalia. He greeted the men as friends—a handshake, an arm around the shoulder, and a kiss on each cheek.

Beaming, he introduced us as his "American daughters" who had come to visit. I don't know what he said in Arabic, but it made the men argue. Once on the street, Monsieur Abadi reprimanded us for being alone with men. "You stay with me. They're not good people."

Whom could we trust? At this point we felt obligated to go with Monsieur Abadi to tour Rabat. I had an inkling something wasn't right.

Our first stop was the King's Palace. The police had cordoned off the entire square mile block, and tourists were being turned away.

Monsieur Abadi looked about furtively and whispered, "The king is coming back to Rabat soon—maybe to my train station. No one knows where or when. There was an attempt on his life." He took his two fingers and ran them across his throat, bulging his eyes. "Don t say a word, or else!" I didn't really believe him; he was so dramatic and made everything sound so grandiose, inflating himself with importance. We followed him into the Medina. He gave yet another warning: "Stay close by or you'll be lost.'

Twisting through the labyrinth of shops, we ducked down an alley and climbed stairs to an attic above a small factory. In stifling heat, little girls, ten and eleven years old, sat at rows of tables embroidering designs on fabric and clothing. Outside in the courtyard, young boys with batons swirled hot vats of dye—reds, purples, oranges, and blues—while others lifted the scarves and material from the boiling water with boat hooks attached to long rods and hung them to dry.

Clearly this was child labor, so I questioned Monsieur Abadi. He shrugged. "They're poor and need to earn money for their families. Their life is not like yours."

Later that afternoon we arrived at Monsieur Abadi's home above the train station at the edge of town. Females of every size and shape came running to greet us, talking at the same time, taking our packs, offering us tea, and touching our hair and clothes in a friendly manner. The oldest daughter, Amina, showed us to our room with two small beds draped in pink flowered coverlets. The younger brothers carried our packs, and the little girls peeked around the corner.

"I guess we're spending the night." I sheepishly looked at Sarah, knowing she wanted to get to Casablanca.

"One night and that's it. We'll leave in the morning."

In the morning, we awoke to the chatter of women. Hurriedly we dressed, prepared our bags, and left our room. At the door, we thanked the women for their hospitality, but before we could open it, the matriarch stopped us.

"Vous restez ici," Jamina insisted, her mother barring our way.

"Non, merci, il faut partir." We explained we had to go.

"Non, c'est pas possible." Another woman waved her apron, as if shooing chicken, backing us into the kitchen. They shoved sweet sticky buns in front of us, giggling light-heartedly and jabbering in Arabic, while putting their chubby hands around our thin arms and pointing to our large packs. The festive atmosphere piqued our discomfort. Monsieur Abadi had already gone to work, and we couldn't leave the house without a male escort.

In the cramped apartment, the women bustled about doing daily chores, yelling at the children, gabbing to each other in Arabic, ignoring the fact we wanted to leave and acting as if nothing was wrong with holding two Americans captive against their will as they waited for an able-bodied male relative to escort them into town.

"Let's just leave," I told Sarah. "We don't have to follow their crazy rules about women."

"What do you want to do? Rush the doorway?"

"It's that or wait till who knows when. And we don't know what they're planning to do to us."

The matriarch stuck another plate of gooey baklava in front of our faces and insisted we eat. "Mange, mange." A young servant girl placed a silver tea service in the center of the kitchen table. Everyone stopped working, sat down, and chattered across the rectangular table.

The bizarre morning had turned into a mad hatter tea party.

We elicited the help of oldest daughter, Amina, who spoke French. "Nous devons partir."

She knitted her eyebrows, walked to the window, peered out the curtain, and came back to the table. "C'est pas possible."

"Pourquoi?"

As if to answer our question, we heard a thunderous knock on the door. A disquieting lull in the chatter ensued. Abadi's wife got up to open the door. A gruff male voice boomed. Peeking around the corner, we saw three soldiers enter the house. Amina's almond eyes darted between the soldiers and us.

"Allons-y," she whispered. The young woman shepherded us into the back and down the hall to the little girls' bedroom. The flowery coverlets and lacy curtains were incongruous with the sound of boots echoing in the hall. Who were they looking for? By the tone of their voices, the soldiers seemed to be scolding the women. *The hashish cookie! They're looking for us.*

The door opened, and a soldier entered the room, walked past us straight to the window, and closed the shades. The room fell dark.

"Allez-vous," he commanded, marching us out to join the others gathered in the living room. He gave terse orders to the women and left.

"Qu'est-ce qui ce passe?" I muttered, trying to make sense of what had just happened.

"N'ouvrez pas les rideaux." The other daughter, Laila, told us not to open the curtains.

I felt helpless and confused in a culture where women had no rights.

Sitting in the dark silence, time passed slowly. After what seemed like an hour, the door burst open and light flooded in. Monsieur Abadi, silhouetted in the doorway, cried excitedly, "Hassan II va arriver ici! Dans ma station du gare!" The king was coming to his train station! The women broke out in a high penetrating call, talking jubilantly in staccato voices. They ran hither and thither, putting on their slipper-like shoes, donning veils and finery. With their heads covered, faces down, they filed out the door behind Monsieur Abadi.

In the shuffle, Sarah and I were left alone in the apartment. Afraid to move, we waited until we heard the boots again. Armed guards stormed up the stairs, flung the door wide open, and yelled furiously, "Get out! Get out!" At gunpoint, they escorted us out of the station and into the open space.

The desert glistened in a sunshine made brighter by the hours we'd spent in the darkened apartment. The dry, hot air hit our faces with a sweet, pungent smell of desert flowers.

Stretched out across the sand, for as far as the eye could see, horsemen in billowing white robes corralled a sea of people, intimidating them with their shimmering swords pulled out of the scabbards. Their horses, reined in tightly, danced along an invisible barrier. The women's ululating pierced the air, their voices ascending in high pitches and then diminishing, like katydids on a warm summer night. The undulating roar of the men carried like a wave through the crowd, which continued to grow by the hundreds.

The soldiers accompanied us to the edge of the crowd and returned to their post along with other armed guards who encircled the entire station. I realized then that they weren't interested in us at all. Their mission was to protect the king.

We melted into the crowd, jostling for position, while people shoved, lifting their children onto their shoulders, pushing to the front in hopes of catching a glimpse of their king, Hassan II.

The horsemen galloped through the crowd clearing a swath to the train station like the parting of the Red Sea. A distant hum of engines heralded a fleet of black limousines snaking across the desert, rolling to a stop in a semicircle in front of the train tracks. I was confused by the drama unfolding; it appeared the king was arriving by limousine, but I turned around in time to see the sleek silver Royal Moroccan train glide to a stop at the quay. The doors opened.

More than fifty women, faceless and dressed head-to-toe in black clothing, descended from the railcars, one after another, their robes swishing, shoulders stooped, and heads down. Bodyguards whisked them into the waiting limousines.

"The king's concubines!" Sarah cried.

The people's cries intensified, electrifying the air; trumpets blared, and gunshots reverberated off the walls. I stood on my tiptoes above the crowd, and caught a glimpse of King Hassan II, his eyes hidden behind dark glasses, his brown face framed by a white and gold turban. He didn't stop or wave to his subjects. The special police surrounded him in a swirling cocoon as he ducked into the first limousine, the door shut, and the vehicle pulled away, kicking up sand and dust, followed by his motorcade.

The next morning, the women didn't want us to leave. They offered more food and more tea and gave us gifts of bracelets and scarves. Their eyes pleaded, *Stay*. After three days together we had grown fond of them too, laughing at our misunderstanding, grateful for their hospitality, but eager to leave.

Did they realize their bondage? Did we represent freedom? I'll never know. The cheerful older women appeared content, even happy. Jamina and Laila, who were smart, young, and beautiful, had potential for a bigger life. They asked us to write, to come back. I extended an invitation to visit me, but sorrowfully, I realized they were destined to follow in the other women's footsteps.

As promised, Ali, the oldest son, arrived to take us to Centre Ville train station to catch the Marrakesh Express. We waved good-bye to the women standing outside on the staircase. They cupped their hands over their mouths and warbled a haunting, piercing farewell. *Yewyewyewyewyew.*

Outside of the walled city

CHAPTER THIRTY

Marrakesh Express

Le 21 avril
Hi kids,
This train to Marrakesh is just like the song! Please send some new
tunes from the hit list. And write me!

> Traveling the train through clear Moroccan skies,
> Ducks and pigs and chickens call
> Animal carpet wall to wall
> American ladies five-foot (ten) tall in blue...

Graham Nash, 1969

WE BOARDED THE MARRAKESH Express, an open-air train
with slatted wooden seats and a porous roof that allowed
the sun to sprinkle in. Warm, dry winds blew gently on our
faces as we rolled out of the city and into the desert dappled
in purple, orange, and sage-gray plants against oyster-pink
sand. I extended my arms out the window, and my hands
played with the air currents—I felt childlike and grown up
at the same time.

I poked Sarah in a friendly way and said, "This is wonderful!" but she just glared at me. "Is something wrong?" I asked.

"What do you think? We're missing Casablanca, and my aunt's friends expected us yesterday."

"We'll send a telegraph when we get to Marrakesh." Sarah would have to do the explaining later.

Traveling with Sarah was like being with a kid sister. She did whatever I wanted but blamed me if things went wrong. I liked being in control, but I didn't want the bad feelings of having screwed up.

"Sorry. I didn't know we'd be stuck in Rabat for three days." I offered her a piece of baklava wrapped in sticky wax paper.

"No, thanks." She turned away. "It's not your fault."

An hour later, the train stopped near a desolate village of red mud houses built into the cliffs. In a dried riverbed next to the tracks, men unloaded their goods off donkeys' backs and out of rusted truck beds, shoving crates of dates, oranges, and figs through the open windows to the women who had already boarded the train with cages of screeching hens. Young men climbed to the top of the train using our windowsill as a step, their footsteps pattering above us. The farmers threw large bundles up on top of the train, shouting back and forth, until all their goods were loaded and tied down tightly.

The train jolted forward, and the women and children scurried to find an open bench in our car. The men jumped on the slow-moving train in the open cars in front and huddled together drinking hot tea from thermoses and smoking brown cigarette butts, the fumes wafting into our section. The women cared for the children and livestock. The inequality reminded me of living at home with five brothers.

* ⁂ *

I was twelve years old when I revolted against the unfair division of labor. The boys shared the work outside while I did all the housework. My older sisters had already left home, and the younger sisters weren't old enough to help.

"Why can't Larry do the dishes? It's not fair," I complained.

Mom shook her head. "That's women's work. The boys do the yard work."

"Let's trade jobs for a week," Larry interjected, with a cocky attitude and a devious smirk.

"Okay, it's a deal. Shake."

Larry had to do my jobs: fold the clothes, dust the furniture, set the table, serve the food, and wash the dishes. I had to do his jobs: pick up trash outside and sweep the patio.

The next day after school, I found Mom folding the laundry.

She made an excuse for him—"Larry has baseball practice"—and kept folding, with a toddler crying in the other room.

Ted ran by with his mitt and bat. "Peggy, don't forget to pull the weeds. It's Larry's turn."

Throughout the week, the outdoor jobs multiplied, each brother passing his job to me. Larry had yet to do a dish. Finally, I called off the deal. Life wasn't fair to women.

* * *

At the next stop, more people loaded onto the train, squeezing Sarah and me into a corner, our sticky arms touching each other while chicken cages, goats, and pigs filled the aisles.

The woman across from us smiled, her face cracked with age and her front teeth missing. I smiled back. Out of the corner of my eye, I saw an indistinguishable movement under her garment. I looked again and, clearly, one of her large breasts moved involuntarily under her black robe. I pretended not to notice, but the children did and began to laugh. A ruffled head popped from the opening in her robe and gave a loud *squawk!* One chicken flew out of her robe and then a second one emerged. Feathers flew as the children chased the old woman's chickens down the aisle, caught them, and proudly returned them to her. She tucked them back into her robes, wiped her nose on her sleeve, and crossed her arms tightly below her chest.

The train stopped on the outskirts of Marrakesh at an expansive open market, almost village-like, with a white-washed wall enclosing the grounds, stalls lining uneven paths, open cafés, and a tall, narrow tower in the middle. The women disembarked, carrying cages, children, and baskets and leaving behind feathers and a farmyard stench. A loudspeaker crackled and emitted a long static noise followed by a wailing chant. The men descended from the train, unfurled their prayer rugs, and reverentially went down on their knees, prostrating themselves, reciting the midday prayer. Reflexively, I bowed my head in respect. It wasn't so different from us genuflecting and saying the Hail Mary on the playground at parochial school when the Angelus bells rang at noon recess.

The ancient scene of the market, the farmers, the stretch of desolate sand, the camels, the mangy dogs and pigs called to mind the concept of the *noble savage*: people unencumbered by modern civilization, natural in a wild environment.

"Isn't this beautiful?"

"Not really, Peggy. I'm hot, I'm tired, and this train stinks!"

The train resumed, picking up steam as the sun reflected off the corrugated metal roofs of the tenement houses built along the edge of the tracks. Raggedy boys ran gleefully alongside the train, throwing rocks and competing for our attention.

"Cute, huh?" I peered at the children running and waving.

"No. They're malnourished and dirty."

This was true, but in my mind I wanted to keep the image of an idyllic life here, as I had imagined while reading *One Thousand and One Nights*. I wanted to believe they had magic lanterns, flying carpets, and beautiful princesses so I wouldn't have to see their life as it really was.

Blue-eyed Arab outside the Souk

CHAPTER THIRTY-ONE

Blue-Eyed Arab

Dear Kathleen and Eileen,
Tell Mom not to worry. I'm taking caution and this place is full
of tourists now.
PS. Weird, I ran into a friend of Larry's in the Souk.

WE ARRIVED IN MARRAKESH in the early afternoon, dropped our bags at the youth hostel, and headed to the Diemaa el Fina, the largest *souk* in Morocco, a mysterious and medieval marketplace, a crossroad between Africa and Asia, where Blue-eyed Nomads sold their wares.

"Pierrot told me you can get anything you want here cheap. You just have to bargain."

"I want to get a hash pipe," Sarah said casually.

"Sarah, you don't smoke hash. What are you thinking? I don't want to get busted down here."

"It's for Chris. He couldn't come with me, so he asked if I'd get him a hash pipe...well, a hookah, but that's too big to carry."

"Okay, a small pipe, not used, or at least cleaned out so we don't get busted for residual drugs." Stories had been circulating in the youth hostels about foreigners thrown in jail and left to rot for minor possession.

We crossed the plaza, stopping to watch acrobats, magicians, fire-eaters, snake charmers, and even an organ grinder whose monkey jumped on my shoulders, begging for money, his hat tipped. Laughing, I dumped a few worthless coins in the hat and continued on to the rows of barbecues at the entrance to the souk. My stomach began to growl.

Stubble-faced men sat on their haunches around low tables eating the freshly cooked meats. The smell, both nauseating and alluring, increased my hunger pains. A tall, thin man with hairless arms turned slabs of meat on a large grill while a heavyset woman, her sleeves rolled up, stirred a deep pot of couscous. A man in a bloodied apron wielded a saber, chopping the mutton legs and goat meat into cubes on a large cutting board. He slid the meat into the brewing pots, the red-spiced grease bubbling over.

"Mange, mange," the big woman cried, thrusting a platter of couscous and spicy meats in front of me.

"Non, merci," I replied, but my stomach said, *Eat!*

She smiled her gold-toothed grin, holding the plate of couscous in front of me and putting her other hand out for money. I dug into my fringed leather purse and brought out five dirhams, less than fifty cents, and took the plate.

"Are you going to eat that?" Sarah asked.

"Sure, why not? Do you want some?"

"No, thanks!"

I sat down on a little stool, bending my long legs, like a camel lowering itself. The men laughed but also stared dreamily, as if I were a sun-kissed goddess.

264

More men joined us, some standing and staring, others buying food. The big woman dished me another platter of food, this time refusing my money.

Sarah shook her head. "Don't you know women don't eat with the men? Those guys are leering at you."

"So what? I'd rather eat here than some fancy restaurant I can't afford. You're missing out."

I loved eating, drinking, and talking to the local people in my pidgin French. Sarah stuck by me, even if disapprovingly.

After lunch, we left the bright sunlit square and entered the dark alleys created by tents and awnings covering a maze of crumbling buildings and dirt streets. The souk had a life of its own—the vendors lived in their stalls, sleeping in lofts, on stacks of carpets, or on the ground. The smells of nighttime life lingered and mixed with the sweet scents of perfumes and incense.

We took note of our starting place, having been warned that it was easy to get lost in the labyrinth. Holding on to each other's arms, we dodged carts filled with woven textiles and rugs and ducked under brass pots and pans hanging from hooks. The tapping of hammers on metal, the humming of sewing machines, the bantering of vendors, and the barking dogs all echoed in the dark hallways. The reek of tanned hides and the pong of greasy food in the stifling heat made me regret having eaten the street vendor's food.

I spotted a gold charm with Arabic writing in a small jewelry shop window. I entered.

"What does that mean?" I asked the clerk.

"It means *Allah*. Wear it, and you're protected." He placed the necklace in my hand. It felt warm and comforting.

"How much?"

"It's real gold." He weighed the piece and came back with a price I couldn't afford. I bargained, and he cut the price in half.

"I'll buy it." I hooked the gold necklace around my neck and tucked my cross inside my shirt. I was a religious chameleon; I figured the Allah charm should work in a Muslim country.

The sun sank lower, casting shadows across the narrow alleys.

"Let's find a pipe and get out of here."

We found the paraphernalia shop selling hookahs, hash pipes, and curvy wooden vessels for kief. A bearded man in white robes sat in front of the store, his head wrapped in a blue shesh. He had the most piercing blue eyes. *Is he a legendary blue-eyed Arab from the desert?*

"Do you want to buy some hash?"

Stunned by his American accent, I looked at him again. He looked familiar! I blurted, "Are you Dan Weinstein?"

He looked at me quizzically, his eyes glazed over. "Huh?"

"I'm sorry; I thought I knew you." I pushed Sarah to move on. "I know that guy. No one has eyes like those except the Weinsteins. He's the brother of a friend of mine." I was sure of it but didn't want to talk to him. The idiot was selling hash in the open.

"That's crazy, Peggy. You know a guy in the souk getting stoned outside the pipe shop?"

During the seventies, dropouts and druggies from the Western world traveled in third-world countries where life was cheap and drugs were easy to come by, like modern-day Siddharthas, eschewing materialism in order to find meaning in their life. But Dan Weinstein didn't fit that type. He was such a geek in high school: the kid with the high forehead, greasy hair, and pimples. Dan was the stereotypical nerd with a pocket protector. He was also my first date.

*** * ***

My older brother, Larry, didn't want me dating fast guys or his cool friends. He ruled over me like an Arab father, rating guys as to whether they were good enough for "O'Toole's little sister" or not. He had assumed the role of father when my dad was mentally absent from too much drinking.

When Larry acted chummy and sweet, I knew he was up to no good. "Peggy, I got a date for you." I didn't trust him, but I needed a date to the *American Bandstand* TV show the following Saturday. All my friends had dates. "My buddy Dan said he'll take you to the dance. Of course I had to slip him some money."

I took the insult and reluctantly accepted the date.

Getting ready Saturday afternoon, I looked in the bathroom mirror and saw a beautiful face, a nearly perfect oval, according to the *Seventeen* magazine beauty checklist. My eyes were set equally apart, lashes long enough to be curled, arching eyebrows, nose perfectly centered, rosebud lips, and high cheekbones. I sucked in my cheeks and applied a dark peach blush. I lined my eyes in navy blue, colored my eyebrows with Maybelline cocoa pencil, and brushed white gloss on my lips. My face didn't have a blemish. Looking deep into my clear blue eyes, I wondered why boys never asked me out. Was it my flat chest? Was I too tall? Was my face too pretty? Dark thoughts entered my mind: *Maybe I should take a knife and cut a scar across my perfect cheeks. Would that make boys find me interesting? Or at least not intimidating?* There was a knock on the bathroom door.

"Hurry up. Your date's here," Larry bellowed.

I looked at my watch. "He's early! Tell him to go away," I shouted back. At sixteen years old, I had idealized how my perfect date would be. I had imagined being whisked away in a sports car by a big, handsome guy who could stand up to my brother in all categories of cool. I wanted my date to come into my home, sit down, talk with my mom, and joke with my dad, maybe play a round of liar's poker while I finished getting ready. I wanted my little brothers to be in awe of him and my younger sisters to giggle because he was so cute. I wanted to match my older sisters' dates, the one who had been captain of the football team or the guy with cool turquoise-blue peg pants who drove a slick car. Rather, I had settled for the nerdiest, most intellectual, and boring guy at La Salle High School.

Dan showed up wearing a bow tie, buttoned-up starched shirt, and skinny-legged purple dress pants. He had shaved, scraping off the tops of his pimples, and put pieces of tissue on them to soak up the blood.

"Let's go, Peggy-O." We got in the car with his sister and her near fiancé and left for Hollywood to be on the American Bandstand TV show, a teenage dream.

Dan danced like a crazy man, falling to the floor, spinning, and sweating while he lip-synched to "Summer in the City." At the end of the show, Dick Clark awarded us "best dance couple" in front of millions of viewers. I was mortified.

* * *

Sarah convinced me he wasn't who I thought he was, and we returned to the head shop and bought a small pipe. As we walked out, the stoner called, "Hey, aren't you O'Toole's little sister?" The blue-eyed guy stared right at me.

"Yeah. I have a name—Peggy."

"I know. We were on *American Bandstand* together."

"Dan? What are you doing here?"

"Traveling...on a journey." He chuckled, his eyes twitching and his hands trembling as he reached into his robes and pulled out a pipe. He lit it, sucking in deeply so the ash burned red, and tried to pass it to me.

Backing away, I said, "No, thanks. Good to see you. Can I say hi to anyone at home for you?"

It saddened me to see him so messed up. The last I had heard he was studying to be a doctor, like his father. Now he was lost in the souk of Marrakesh.

Inside the walled city

CHAPTER THIRTY-TWO

Night in Fès

Le 21 avril
Morocco is really a different culture, except now the kids my age are
pretty westernized. Give my love to everyone.

IT WAS OUR FIRST evening in Fès, and Sarah and I were
sitting in a little café outside the old city's wall, drinking
mint tea and chatting about our boyfriends, when two young
Moroccans in 501 jeans and collared paisley shirts asked to
join us. With a glance, we nodded in agreement. The boys
sat down.

"Do you like zee Grateful Dead?" Ahmed spoke slowly.

"Bien sûr!" we echoed, letting them know we could speak
French.

The conversation jumped around as we talked about
college, rock and roll, and pastimes. Both of them worked
at their father's gas station while attending university. What
a relief it was to meet normal kids our own age.

"Nous vous invitons au Holiday Inn pour boire une bière. Ça va?" asked Jamaal, the less talkative but equally good-looking brother.

The Holiday Inn for a beer? Not our idea of an authentic Moroccan experience, but we liked these guys.

The boys paid our bill and escorted us outside to a new Camaro.

"Cool car," I said, shocked to see such an expensive car.

"Our father lent it to us for the night."

We drove to the Holiday Inn on a hillside with views of the Medina, the old walled city. Heads turned to stare at us as we walked through the lobby and entered the wood-paneled bar, dimly lit by small lanterns and blinking white lights on palm trees that ringed the room. Men dressed in long white robes and turbans lounged on divans and pillows, and a few western businessmen stood at the bar. The bartender wore the universal starched white shirt and dark pants. We were the only women in the room.

We sat down at a small table and Jamaal ordered alcoholic drinks.

"Why can you get alcohol here and not in town?" I asked.

"It's an American bar." He leaned in closer. "See that man in the corner with those businessmen?" Ahmed pointed to a private area where a particularly thin-faced, wrinkled Arab reclined, surrounded by attendants and men in suits. "He controls the oil business in Morocco—even my father's gas station."

Shortly after our drinks arrived, the waiter brought over a note and handed it to Ahmed, who read it, scribbled something on it, and returned it to the waiter.

Ahmed looked at us with a satisfied smirk. "Nous avons la chance. The sheikh invited us to dinner. Of course, I accepted."

I glanced at Sarah, but this time our eyes did not see things equally.

"Bien sûr, on y va," I said, indicating that we would go.

Sarah looked startled and whispered in my ear, "It's not a good idea. We don't even know them." I ignored her plea.

The boys left money on the table and sent for the car. The sheikh and his entourage filed into the waiting limousines in front of the hotel.

Sarah acquiesced. We climbed into the backseat of the Camaro. Jamaal sat shotgun and Ahmed drove, following the black limos up a winding, dark country road that led into the foothills of the Atlas Mountains north of Fès. The boys engaged in a rapid-fire conversation in Arabic, leaving us to wonder what they were saying.

About twenty minutes later, we took a sharp right, drove a few hundred feet, and stopped at a guard station. Jamaal passed a note through the window. The guard looked at it and made a phone call. An interminable few minutes passed and the guard returned, stamped the note, and handed it back, waving us through the opened gate into an oasis of palms, ferns, birds of paradise, rolling lawns, and fountains. The driveway led to an opulent old palace. Beautiful tiles framed the arching wooden doors, and a jeweled chandelier showered dancing lights above our heads as we entered a great hall.

A butler escorted us to the main dining room. The sheik and his entourage had already been seated at a long table, which was lavishly set with fine china, candelabras, silver serving dishes, and crystal wineglasses. Again, we were the only women. Conspicuously underdressed for the occasion, I rounded my shoulders, buttoned my gray sweater, and yanked at my jeans, trying to hide my construction boots.

The maître d' seated Sarah across the wide table so we couldn't really talk. Our eyes met through a large floral centerpiece.

"Don't worry," I mouthed, but I was concerned. We were far outside of town and dependent on Ahmed and Jamaal, who sat at the opposite end of the table.

A balding gentleman, perhaps in his early forties, sat to my right. He wore a polished gray pinstriped suit, scuffed brown shoes, and argyle socks. His clothes defined him as less important than the finely dressed Westerners surrounding the sheikh. He appeared friendly and approachable, so I struck up a conversation.

"I'm Peggy. What're you doing here?"

"I'm Alain. Enchanté." He spoke both English and French. "I work for the Moroccan Oil Company as an interpreter."

"American?"

"Yes. My father was an American diplomat, now retired, and my mother is French, a Pied Noir, born here." Pointing to the head of the table, Alain confirmed what the boys had told us. "That man, he's Sheikh Sayyid, friend to the king. He controls Moroccan oil refineries."

The servers filled the goblets with wine and set decanters of deep amber whiskey around the table. Unlike most Moroccan Muslims, these Arabs drank liquor and lots of it. Throughout the evening, the waiters topped my glass with wine. I let down my guard and conversed freely, the men on both sides of me vying for my attention.

Sarah sat stoically, refusing the wine and barely touching her dinner. Ahmed and Jamaal appeared to be having a good time by their raucous behavior—drinking, smoking, and laughing loudly at jokes that could have been ribald, for all I knew.

At the end of the meal, the sheikh loudly called out in Arabic, slurring his words and waving his arms as if batting flies. He tried to get up and then slumped over to the side of the table, his arm dangling, the chair wobbling beneath him. There was a collective gasp, and an attendant quickly righted his chair and motioned to Alain to come. The old man, his skin taut on a bony face, said something to Alain and gestured toward me. Alain returned to his seat and slipped a fifty-dollar bill under my plate. "Sheikh Sayyid would like to see you after dinner."

I pushed the money away. "No way."

Alain lowered his voice. "Don't insult him. Take the money." He tucked the fifty-dollar bill into the sleeve of my sweater and left.

The party broke up. Two large men, probably bodyguards, escorted the sheikh, holding him firmly under each arm. Sarah and I found the boys waiting outside. Gratefully, we jumped into the car and asked them to take us back to our youth hostel. The boys raved about the dinner party and how the sheikh liked us. I made light of the comment, joking about the sheikh propositioning me.

The tone changed.

"You have the sheik's money? We have to take you to him." Jamaal sounded serious.

We laughed nervously. I explained, "I didn't take the money; it was forced on me." My heart raced. I felt helpless, sinking into despair.

Ahmed emphasized, "You kept the sheikh's money; we're taking you to him." He gunned the engine and screeched around the curves to catch up with the sheik's limousine.

We could see the lights of Fès below. Whispering feverishly, Sarah and I devised a plan to jump from the car. The boys could tell by our low voices that we had no intention of going to the sheikh.

"We'll lose our jobs if we don't take you to him. My father will lose his gas station. Don't you know who he is?" Jamaal, now agitated, yelled at Ahmed to drive faster.

"Pas de problème," I said calmly, taking hold of Sarah's hand. Once in town, the car slowed and came to a stop at an intersection.

"Quick, jump!" I flung the door open pulling Sarah with me.

Ahmed and Jamaal yelled through the open car window, "Stop! Thief!"

I turned back, flung the fifty-dollar bill through the window, and shouted, "Keep the filthy money!"

We ran down dark streets, their car following us slowly. Jamaal leaned out the window and taunted us with curses and threats. Crossing a large open square, we ran into the walled city.

It was after midnight when we arrived at the hostel, which had been closed since eleven o'clock. We rattled the doorknob and knocked loudly, hoping the night guard would let us in. Moments passed.

The unshaven guard unlocked the door, looked down at us, and sneered, "Putains, les Américaines." He followed us to our room and unlocked our door with his skeleton key. Once we were inside, we heard the lock click behind us. This may have been standard procedure in Moroccan hostels, but we felt like prisoners. We pushed an old dresser against the door, got onto our straw-filled mattresses, wrapped the dirty wool blankets around us, and sat in silence, only falling asleep at dawn to the plaintive cry of morning prayer and roosters crowing.

At ten o'clock, the guard pounded on the door and yelled, "You must leave!" The click of his key unlocked the door. His tired eyes glared. 'The hostel is closed until six this evening. Get out."

Still in our clothes from the night before, we snatched our packs and left under the watchful eyes of the scowling caretaker. He smirked as we passed him and walked into the bright sunlight, only to discover the Camaro waiting outside in the sweltering streets. We ran. The car slowly followed us. Hanging his head out of the window, Ahmed derided us, saying we were stupid girls not to go with them last night.

"The sheikh is angry, and our father will suffer because of you whores."

Ignoring his insults, Sarah and I hooked arms and kept going toward the train station. We would be in Spain by nightfall.

Pierrot

CHAPTER THIRTY-THREE

May Day

Hi Kathleen and Eileen,
I'm just getting back to France and glad to be home. Tell Mom,
I'm safe and ask her to write and ask if Fred got my tax return forms.
Give everyone my love. Peace, your big sis, Peggy

RAGGED FROM TRAVELING ACROSS Spain for more than twenty hours, we got off the train in Irun, went through customs, then walked across the border to the French train. Euphoria hit me as I crossed into France, as if I were crossing from Tijuana to California. France had become my home, and I kissed the ground when I safely returned to my attic room in the mansion on Rue de l'Abbé de l'Epée.

The next day, I met up with my friends at Le New York Bar. After a beer and a game of baby-foot, I noticed Pierrot looking at me. He suggested we go somewhere else to talk, so we went to Marsha Le Brun's slummy apartment. We buzzed a neighbor to let us into the building and then walked up the twisting staircase, passed the communal WC, and found the hidden key under the frog doorstop. Opening the door, we plopped down on the bed in the entry and rolled around like two wrestling puppies.

After an awkward pause, I breathed. "Je suis heureux de te voir." Unable to restrain myself, I kissed him on the lips. He pulled back.

"Dis-moi, how was your trip?"

He'd rather hear about what I did in Morocco than make out with me?

I tried not to show my disappointment and embellished my stories to impress him, exaggerating the danger. "I was held captive at gunpoint...propositioned by an oil sheik...came near to death on a mountain road." Surely my stories would entice him to hold me tight. Instead he sat up and reprimanded me. "C'etait folle!"

Crazy? I was crazy in love and delusional. The danger wasn't falling off a cliff; the danger was falling in love with him. *I should never have told Pierrot my boyfriend was coming. That's why he didn't want to make love to me. He thought I was taken.*

Bill's impending arrival had made me more desperate to consummate my relationship with Pierrot. I wrapped my arms around him, tousled his black hair and murmured, "I'm happy to be back."

Footsteps and loud laughter echoed in the stairwell. The door opened. Marsha Le Brun and her roommates burst in with a bunch of guys from the bar. Marco lifted Marsha across the threshhold, her dark hair flying, and threw her down on the bed next to us, tickling her and pushing us off. Body heat rose in the room. Some skinny, drugged-out French guy put a Doors album on the turntable, singing along in a heavy accent, "Show me the way to the next whiskey bar." Others joined in dancing and miming Jim Morrison, ruining a favorite song. Another straggly longhair lit multiple joints and passed them around. As the late spring sun set, the room dimmed and the mood changed. One of the roommates, Rosa, sat in her bedroom doorway, her below-the-waist hair falling across her bare breasts. She eyed Pierrot, purring, growling, her arms on the floor, extending and arching her back like a cat. She lifted a single finger, curled it in and then out, enticing him to enter her room. I left and Pierrot stayed.

I didn't see Pierrot at the Delanne's the rest of the week. Marie-Paule told me he was organizing students and workers to march in the May Day *manifestation* in Paris.

The following Wednesday evening, I attended the Communist Workers meeting and signed up as a demonstrator, putting myself on the ride list. I looked around the room, filled with blue-collar workers sitting on folding chairs, and spied Pierrot talking to a group of men in overalls. I crossed the room, waited for a break in the conversation, and told him I was going to the May Day march. "Can I go with you?"

His demeanor had changed—he was no longer gentle; rather he was businesslike. "Okay," he said, and he turned back to the men, heatedly discussing another issue.

Friday before dawn, I walked across town to the fairgrounds along the river and made my way past the derelict bums to meet up with the protestors milling around buses. Pierrot stood by the bus with a clipboard.

He greeted me like any other demonstrator, checked my name off the list, and turned to the next in line. I sat alone on the bus. When we arrived in Paris, Pierrot asked where I was staying. I had no place to stay. "Avec toi?" I thought I could stay with him.

"C'est pas possible." He had always been so nice to me, but now he acted annoyed.

I pleaded, "Je ne connais personne à Paris. Une nuit?" I knew no one in Paris and had nowhere to go.

"Okay," he reluctantly said. I grabbed my bag and followed him to the metro.

We arrived at his friend's apartment in the Seventeenth Arrondissement, a nice part of Paris. The building was old but clean, with a black marble floor in the entry and a polished wooden staircase with a wrought iron banister. We circled up to the fifth floor. Pierrot buzzed and the door opened.

A beautiful young Air France stewardess answered and invited us in. She gave Pierrot a peck on each cheek and extended me her hand, as he introduced me as a friend from California.

"Nice to meet you. I'm Christine. I just flew in from LA! I love California. Look what I brought back!" She handed me a bouquet of sagebrush, juniper, and wildflowers wrapped in a copy of the LA Times. "Smell this."

I had been gone ten months, and the fragrance transported me home. "They're beautiful." I breathed deeply and passed the bouquet to Pierrot. "It smells like the Santa Barbara foothills."

I brushed back tears, thinking of the warm Santa Ana winds in the canyons, the scent of lavender and sage wafting over my body as I lay in the sun, cooling off in streams, being in love with life.

Christine in her Air France uniform looked a lot like my sister Shereen in her airline photos, both tall and slender, both drop-dead gorgeous.

Touched by the similarity, I blurted out, "My sister flew for Western Airlines. She was Miss Wings Over the World in 1963."

Christine smiled, a dimple gracing her lower right cheek. At that moment, she embodied my sister.

* * *

I'd had dreams that Shereen never died, just moved somewhere else. When I would find her in my dreams, she was lovely and welcoming but wouldn't come back home. *I can't, Peggy. I have another life.*

* * *

The three of us had a simple late dinner of tossed salad, pâté, and a baguette. After dinner, Christine excused herself for the night and went into her bedroom. Pierrot followed and brought out some blankets and put them on the couch. I had the mistaken notion he was inviting me to sleep with him.

"Bonne nuit," he said as he kissed me on both cheeks and walked into Christine's bedroom.

I lay awake most of the night, imagining what I didn't want to know.

The next morning, Pierrot and I took the metro to Quartier Latin. Coming up from the urine-stained stairwell of the underground, we saw gendarmes stationed along the wide Boulevard Saint Michel, tear gas canisters hanging on their belts and machine guns positioned against their shoulders. Two years earlier, students had ripped up the cobblestones to make barricades along Boul Mich to protect themselves from the CRS riot police, which had been called to quell the student and worker demonstrations against the De Gaulle government.

The May Day parade could prove to be volatile. If I were to be arrested, it would mean deportation.

"C'est trop dangereux. Je te l'avais dis!" he cried out, angry that I had not listened to him. Pierrot turned to the right, away from the crowd. He led me through the student section, slipped into an alley near the Sorbonne, and climbed the back stairs to a dingy apartment. He knocked. The splintered door looked as if someone had tried to break in. A dark woman with gypsy earrings opened the door.

"Pierrot, comment ça va?" She grabbed him in a bear hug, her marked arms sliding off him.

"Ça va." They spoke quickly, using l'argot I couldn't understand. He pointed to me and asked if I could wait there until after the demonstration.

"Pas de problème."

He left. The single room flat had towels stuffed in broken windows, a filthy, lumpy mattress on the floor, and a small bathroom with a missing doorknob, which created a peephole that spotlighted a dripping faucet. A bearded stoner looked up from reading his paper. No one spoke. I sat down on a chair in the corner and waited.

Someone from outside pounded on the door. "Let me in. Now!" a high-pitched American voice shrieked.

The skeletal man got up from the table, his Trotskyite newspaper, La Lutte, falling to the floor.

Leaning against the doorframe, he rasped, "Go away. You're alrrrreadeee fuckt up."

"Please, please, just one more. I promise I'll pay," the voice pleaded.

"Shaddup. You'll alarm zee police." He reluctantly opened the door, and a young, disheveled blond pushed her way past the skinny Frenchman and sat down on the bed.

Methodically, he picked up a needle off the table, got a vile from below the bathroom sink, and returned to the side of the bed.

"Thank you, thank you so much." She was American, typical of the groupies who hung around Isla Vista, trading sex for drugs, traveling with musicians for the high, doing anything to stay stoned. He rolled up her long sleeve revealing red lines up and down her arm. The man took a rubber tourniquet, roughly tied it around her arm, and pumped with his thumb to find a vein

"You can't have anymore, no more veins."

"Give me the goddam shit now or I'll scream till the police come." Her eyes were wild and crazy, and her evocative beauty clashed with her anger and despair. She lifted her long voile skirt exposing her legs. "Find a vein."

I huddled in the corner, unable to avert my eyes, and watched the needle go in. She faded, her arms went limp, her eyes closed. He pulled the needle out, wrapped his own arm, and shot up with the same needle. He pushed her aside and lay down.

I have a foggy memory of Pierrot at the door and a silent walk back to Christine's apartment.

Line out the door of the boulangerie

Chapter Thirty-Four

Sunday Morning in Paris

May 9, 1971
Dear Mom,

   I went to Paris last weekend but didn't stay long and now I'm tired and bummed cuz everyone seems to have plans for summer except me. Don't worry, things usually work out for the best. I'll be thinking of you on Mother's Day—unfortunately I don't know where you'll be. For a gift I'd like to call you so give me a time, place, and a number in the near future where I can reach you. Maybe I'll catch more of the family at home. Where is everybody? I have to call collect so my landlady doesn't have to hassle with the bill. (She can be such a bitch.) I'll send a check to pay for the call. It'll be great to talk to you again.

EARLY SUNDAY MORNING, I woke up on the couch, quickly pulled on my jeans, threw on my shirt and jacket, and left a note on the table next to the bouquet of juniper and sage.

   *Thank you Christine for your hospitality...*I stopped writing. Should I tell Pierrot that I went back to Bordeaux?

He might worry, so I added: *I took the train back to Bordeaux. Merci, Peggy*

I reread the note hoping for two effects: I wanted Christine to like me, even though she was sleeping with the man I loved, and I wanted Pierrot to think I didn't care. I didn't want his romantic interlude to be a deal breaker. We weren't officially a couple until we slept together, so I shouldn't mind. Besides, I was geographically more desirable than Christine because I lived in Bordeaux, not Paris. I had one up on Christine…aside from the fact that she already had slept with Pierrot.

Truthfully, I was devastated and embarrassed that I had followed him to Paris, only to be jilted. I didn't want to see his tousled hair when he came out of the bedroom or the glow on Christine's face over breakfast. My heart ached and my stomach churned. I held back my tears as I gingerly opened the front door so as not to wake them, descended the stairs, and walked into the vacant streets of Paris. Wrapping my scarf around my neck, I braced myself for the brisk walk to Gare du Montparnasse. I hurried past shops shuttered with iron grates and corrugated steel doors. No one made deliveries on Sundays or picked up the trash; an isolated drunk slept on a stoop, and a cat rummaged through garbage left in the gutters. The sun had barely cast its first shade of pink across the tops of the buildings, slivers of light shining on the glass dome roof of the grand station. I checked the boards for the next train to Bordeaux. The flaps on the monitor twitched and flashed the current departures and arrivals, the times and the quays. *Ah bon! The train to Bordeaux leaves in an hour.*

Inside the cavernous terminal, I sat down on a metal bench and watched the pigeons pecking at tiny crumbs of bread and croissants dropped by the harried travelers. My stomach growled. I opened my pack, pulled out a piece of baguette wrapped in a folded napkin, and looked at the miserable piece of stale bread. It reminded me of *Les Miserables*. Crumbling the lousy morsel, I tossed the crumbs to the pigeons. A gray mass of fluttering birds rushed over to fight over the pieces of bread. A few dozen more descended from the high rafters, dive-bombing the flock and splattering my shoes with muck. Passersby stopped to watch as I wiped my shoes with the napkin. I glared back, picked up my pack, and walked outside.

Not far from the train station, I found an open *boulangerie* and went in. The bell over the threshold sounded pleasantly. A rosy-faced woman came out of the kitchen, parting the beaded curtain.

"Bonjour, Mademoiselle."

"Bonjour, Madame," I replied in my best singsong French. "Un croissant et un pain de raisin, s'il vous plait."

She picked up the warm pastries from the glass case and put them in a little bag. "Et voilà. Six francs."

The bell rang again, and an elderly couple walked in.

"Bonjour, messieurs-dames. Comment allez-vous?" she greeted her customers. I stood holding the coins in my hand, waiting for their conversation to end. In France when someone asks how you are, you are obliged to give a detailed account of your ailments.

"Bonjour, Madame. J'ai un crise de fois..." The old gentleman had indigestion.

The bell rang again and more people filed in to get their fresh baguettes before the boulangerie closed at noon.

"Bonjour messieurs-dames," the proprietor called out, acknowledging her patrons.

The line of customers ran out the door, but the old gentleman continued to list the details of what ailed him and his wife. While the baker listened with appropriate nods and consolations, I placed my six francs on the counter saying, "Merci, Madame."

She looked up and replied, "Au revoir, mademoiselle." As I left, each person greeted me and said good-bye.

It amazed me how concerned the French can be about their ailments and how willing they are to speak openly about bodily functions in public. No one objected to the wait, because when it was their turn they would be happy to let everyone know about their *rhume* or *mal au dos*. Maybe I should have told them about my *crise d'amour*.

Outside, the sun had peaked over the buildings. I crossed to the sunny side of the street, found a park bench, and ate my breakfast, reassuring myself that I would be okay.

Bill and Peggy on Rue de l'Abbé de l'Epée

CHAPTER THIRTY-FIVE

My Boyfriend's Back

May 9 (continued)

Bill hasn't called or come by has he?

I finish school May 29th and as soon as possible will be travel-ing, but will keep Bordeaux as a base. No definite plans.

I haven't heard from Bill. If he doesn't come I'll maybe stay in France and probably work. Yesterday I was offered a job near Paris taking care of two children, ten and eleven. It's a good offer and good pay for France, $190 a month, with all my meals and a day off once a week. Guess what family? The Rothschilds, who own the Rothschild Bank. He's the winemaker's brother and a friend of my landlady. Don't know how long I'd like to be stuck in that posi-tion—but a month would be fun and the wine good.

I'm still thinking about traveling with Bill. If he calls or comes by could you give him my two shortie blouses for summer and some cut-offs? Thanks, hopefully I'll see him this summer, but you never know about boys.

Want to get this off in the mail. Give everyone my love— 'specially Grandma on her birthday.

Less than three weeks until summer vacation, and I hadn't heard from Bill. In his last letter he had told me he was back on the mainland, having left the Banana Patch— *hippie haven for free love*—and still wanted to travel together. What a screw job! I'd told everyone my boyfriend was coming at Easter and now a month later, he still hadn't shown up.

With my summer plans up in the air, I didn't know if I should take the job babysitting the Rothschild children. Monsieur Carter, our director, encouraged me. "You can make good connections that could benefit you in the future. Your French will improve immensely." His thick, old-man glasses reflected my disillusioned face. "For heaven's sake, Peggy, it's the Rothschilds! Please, consider this opportunity."

I had no desire to connect with bankers during my summer vacation. I wanted adventure and a real boyfriend, not Bill. I wanted Pierrot, though he'd made it clear he wasn't interested. In my double reflection in the old man's bifocals, I saw the responsible girl who should take the job and the other one who wanted to escape.

"I'll think about it."

Late Friday afternoon on the bus ride back from campus, I replayed the weekend fiasco in Paris and daydreamed. *What if Pierrot chooses me over Christine? If he did I would stay with him this summer, go to the beach together, swim and surf and take side trips on weekends. I'd get a job in town, even babysitting.* I pined to have someone love me and only me. It hurt deeply knowing that Pierrot was with another girl, even though he wasn't my boyfriend. We hadn't even *done it* yet, so it wasn't like he'd cheated on me. I imagined our first time would be romantic, on the beach, maybe Chambre d'Amour, the lover's cove in Biarritz, or in a campground beneath the trees overlooking the ocean. The last person I wanted to be with was Bill, the cheating son-of-a-bitch.

Getting off the bus at Place Gambetta, I noticed the flower beds, freshly planted with begonias, azaleas, and poppies. The barren trees had new leaves sprouting on the knuckles of the branches. In spite of my dismal love life, I was excited to finish the school year and travel. The sun's rays played with the shadows, casting long geometric angles down Rue Judaique. I turned right and walked up my block.

I stopped and took a double take. Panic raced down my legs. I jumped onto a stoop, hiding myself behind a wall, and peeked down the street. A big, blond, hairy American guy, wearing blue jeans and a Hawaiian shirt, sat on my front steps, leaning against a huge fatigue-green backpack. His legs were stretched out, blocking the sidewalk.

Bill had arrived.

I bent down, pretending to tie my boot and giving myself time to think of what to say before he saw me. Should I start out pissed off and give him hell for not writing and not showing up when he said he was going to? Or should I feign delight to see him and act nonchalant about the Banana Patch and schtooping hippie girls?

I stood up, turned toward him, and marched right up to my doorstep.

Deeply engrossed in his book, *The Fellowship of the Ring*, Bill didn't even look up as I approached. Last year, he had been into the *Hobbit*, speaking of the Middle World as if it were a real place, calling himself Bilbo and his pet hawk Gandalf. The guy loved all books, especially history books about wars,—the Spanish conquest, Greeks and Romans, and the World Wars. When we were in love, we had talked about going to the Greek Isles to see the Roman ruins and to Germany to see the World War II sites. He spoke Spanish and German and I spoke French, so wherever we would travel we could communicate with the locals, avoid the tourist routes, and melt into each culture, as long as our money held out. And although we hadn't discussed it, I had hoped to marry him, find a home in the world, and raise our babies.

I kicked his heel to get his attention. "Hey, whatcha doing here?"

He jumped up, dropping his book. "Hey, you're looking great!" He seemed almost shy, which, in that great big body of his, appeared odd. "You're not mad at me, are you?"

"No," I lied. "Well, you didn't write much after you left for Hawaii, and you didn't tell me when you were coming." There, I said it. But the words came out of my mouth so amiably, I didn't sound angry at all, even though I'd been seething for months.

"Yeah, well, sorry. I'm here now. How about a squeeze?" He opened his big bear arms, giving me no choice but to lean into him.

Make this fast and don't let anyone see us, I prayed, embarrassed to be embraced in public by someone so obviously American.

He wrapped his arms around me and swayed back and forth, saying, "Oooh, you feel soo goooood." I should've known what was coming next.

* * *

Sophomore year, Bill had introduced me to his dope-smoking-bad-guy fraternity, Kappa Sigma, infamous for wild parties and losing its charter in 1969. I liked the bad boys, and they loved shocking me with crazy antics involving nudity, racy comments, and practical jokes, like "the sandwich." One Thursday night at the FUBAR, the local college hangout, Bill walked up to me and offered me a mug of beer, while his fraternity brother grabbed me from behind for the ritual sandwiching. They bounced me back and forth with strong pelvic thrusts.

My dad had taught my brothers and me how to box, wrestle, and bring a guy down. I jabbed the frat guy right in his solar plexus with my elbow and brought my knee up to Bill's groin. Then I doused them both with my beer. I went home alone that night, angry as a hornet, but was back partying for the rest of the year with the bad-boy frat.

* * *

On my front doorstep, the swaying turned into a rhythmic thrust as Bill pretended to dry hump me, in daylight, in a foreign country. I didn't knee him, but I gave him a strong push. "Don't do that; you know I hate it."

"Ah, come on, Peggy. Loosen up. I was just kidding for old times' sake."

That was the problem. I didn't want to go back to old times. I liked my life in France. I didn't want to be the person I had left behind. I liked the person I had become. Besides, I was in love with Pierrot.

"Where are you staying?" I asked icily.

"Can't I stay here?"

"My landlady won't let any boy past the foyer, let alone into my bedroom. You can stay in the youth hostel."

"I guess you don't need a chastity belt."

"You know, you can really be an asshole."

He looked visibly hurt. 'Sorry. When did you become so touchy?"

In spite of his rude behavior and comment, I felt bad for him. After all, he'd come all the way to France to see me, and I'd made it obvious I was less than thrilled to see him.

"I need to go inside and put my stuff away." I left him standing on the stoop.

When I returned downstairs, I heard noise from the kitchen. Marsha had found Bill waiting outside and invited him to meet Rex, her boyfriend, and the other Americans, Valerie, Leslie, Chris, and Sarah.

Popping open a bottle of champagne, Marsha handed me a glass and toasted, "Cheers! Your boyfriend's back!" The girls improvised the chorus, "and there's gonna be trouble."

I laughed, thinking, *Yep, there's going to be trouble.*

Marsha held up her glass a second time. "And, here's to Madam Ass-mat! She's gone for the weekend. The house is ours." Marsha clinked her glass against mine.

"Great," I said halfheartedly, not happy to have my boyfriend here, but glad the Wicked Witch was gone.

Bill wasted no time becoming the center of attention. He pulled albums and magazines from his pack and told us the latest news, from current events to rock stars. After nine months in France, we craved information from California: music, film, the hip stuff. The French were so far behind in pop culture. By the end of the evening, Bill had bonded with my American friends. Rex invited him to go on a surf trip while Marsha and I finished the school year. Valerie offered to take my babysitting job in Paris so Bill and I could travel together. After a few glasses of champagne, Bill didn't seem out of place, at least not among Americans.

Still, I didn't want him to meet my French friends. He was way too politically conservative, loud, and uncouth.

I'd tried hard to fit into the French culture, rolling my *r*'s, wearing a scarf around my neck, and pouting when I spoke. Bill talked like Daffy Duck, his words slurred and sloppy, his language dotted with yeah man, cool, and groovy. And he spouted inane information about sports teams and surfing.

I'd been around French students who talked about politics, philosophy, and literature. Bill would be aghast at my newfound interest in Communism. He had been in ROTC since high school, his father was a colonel in the US Marine Corps, and his stay-at-home mother cooked, cleaned, and grew orchids for a hobby. What I once thought important in life had changed. We had grown apart. Nevertheless, I needed him in order to travel, so I played along as his girlfriend.

At the end of the evening, Marsha announced that she and Rex were going to stay in his camper, and, as a surprise, Bill and I could have the big bed in her bedroom.

"Hey, man, groovy, that's really cool of you."

"Are you sure, Marsha? Bill was going to stay at the youth hostel." Silently, I implored her to take it back, hoping to send a message telepathically that I didn't want to sleep with him.

She assured us it was perfectly all right. "See ya in the morning for coffee and croissants." They left.

Bill grabbed his pack and looked expectantly into my eyes. I hoped he was too drunk to do anything. We dragged ourselves up the stairs to the third floor to Marsha's room.

"I'm a little tired," I said.

"Oh no you're not," Bill replied, dropping his pack on the floor and tackling me onto the bed.

Stunned, I laughed, hoping he was joking around. "Come on, Bill, let's just go to bed."

I got up and went to my room to change into my pajamas. When I came back, he was passed out naked on top of the bed. Relieved that I didn't have to face sex, I climbed in on the other side of the bed, slipped under the covers, and switched off the light.

He rolled over, pulled the covers off me, and started to fondle me under my shirt.

"Stop, Bill, I don't want to."

"Come on, just a little hug."

Believing him, I consented to a hug, but he wouldn't let go of me, wrapping his legs around my waist and rolling on top. I wriggled away and started to get up when he pulled me back onto the bed. Did he think he had a right to screw me just because I said I was his girlfriend? Couldn't he tell I wasn't into him?

I didn't yell—not that it would have done any good in the empty house. I lay there stiffly, wanting to get it over with, blaming myself for inviting him to France and playing along that he was my boyfriend.

Why had I gotten into bed with him? Did I feel I owed it to him, that it was my duty as a girlfriend? I had yet to develop the sense that my body was my own.

After it was over, Bill commented on how good it was, rolled to his side of the bed, and fell asleep. I waited until I heard his steady breathing before I got up, went to my room, and washed myself in the bidet.

The next morning, Bill acted as if nothing had happened. He whistled merrily, chirping about coffee and croissants, when he noticed my sullenness.

He looked surprised. "What's the matter, Peggy?"

"Just leave me alone. You were gone too long, and I wasn't ready last night."

"Listen, I'm sorry. I got a little drunk and couldn't help myself. It's been a long time for me too." He put his arms out to hug me. I turned away. "Even if you don't believe me, I was faithful to you."

Not saying a word, I kept my head turned, unable to look at him or believe him.

"Okay. I'm leaving. Rex and I are going to Spain." Bill put a few things in his pack. "I'd still like to travel with you when I get back. Can I leave some stuff here?"

"Sure." A cloud of doubt swirled inside my head. Maybe he had waited for me, and I was the unfaithful one. But it was no longer a question of faithfulness. I had lost interest in Bill months ago. I loved Pierrot, although it was unrequited.

Marie-Paule's room above the garage

CHAPTER THIRTY-SIX

Last Days

May 30, 1971
Dear Mom and family,

I'm glad I got a hold of you last week. I had to call late at night from my house downstairs, and even though I woke up the household and upset Madame Assemat (she deserved being woken up cuz she's a real bitch), it was worth it. It eased my conscience to know that staying in France to next Christmas didn't upset you or change any of your plans. Bill finally arrived so we'll be traveling together. PS. Oh, I did okay on my tests. I got my scholarship papers and hope that the money comes through for winter quarter since I won't be coming back to UCSB in the fall.

IT WAS NOTHING LESS than a miracle: I turned in my papers on time, passed my exams, and finished the year with enough credits to get my scholarship money for the next year. The last few weeks of school flew by as we American students tried to cram in as much of French life as possible. The Faculté d'Étrangères invited us to a five-course farewell dinner with paired wine in an elegant hotel ball-room in the center of town. No one screamed this time when the Ortolan was served; we had learned to appreci-ate the delicate birds and the small portions of rare beef, the fried potato dumplings, the blanched French green beans, the moldy cheeses, and the decadent desserts. Each bite was bittersweet. We were leaving a country we had grown to love.

The evening after the dinner party, I went straight to Marie-Paule's room above the garage. Entering the garden gate, I heard Led Zeppelin's latest album blasting through the windows, a gift to Marie-Paule from Bill as a thank you for introducing him to her friends in Biarritz.

Marie-Paule opened the door and a plume of smoke exited the room and swirled down the stairs. "Beeeg Beeel is here, Peggee! He's so funny." I walked in and there he was, Big Bill, taking a hit off the hash pipe and laughing at his own stories.

"Yeah, he's really funny," I replied sarcastically.

In the few weeks Bill had been in Europe, he'd made friends not only with the Americans but also with my French friends. It rankled me to see him having a good time sitting between Marco and Jacques. It had taken me five months to meet any French friends and another four to gel my relation-ships. I was jealous that he fell right into my close-knit group and got all of their attention by being a cool, dope-smoking surfer from California. Worse, he came into my world and ruined any chance I had with Pierrot.

The glow from the lava lamp and black light gave the room an eerie feel. Posters of Jim Morrison, Bob Dylan, Joan Baez, and Jimi Hendrix hung alongside photos of Einstein and Che Guevara. Indian batik bedspreads covered the couches, and muslin curtains blocked out the garden below. Bill fit right in.

As I crossed the room, I stopped and gave everyone the customary kiss on both cheeks, "Ça va?"

"Salut, Peggee." Bill stood up and gave me *une bise*. How had he picked up the French habit of kissing so quickly?

I hadn't spent any time with Bill since his first night in Bordeaux. I was still upset that he had arrived unannounced and expected me to sleep with him. Fortunately, he had left me alone after forcing himself on me the first night, and surprisingly he returned three weeks later, confident, eager to be with my friends, and happy to see me.

During Bill's absence, I had cemented a lasting friendship with Pierrot along with Marie-Paule, her brother Marco, and Jacques. We had spent lazy afternoons at a friend's neglected chateau, pureeing vegetables from the garden to make a pot of hot soup. We dipped our bread in the cracked bowls to get the last taste. After lunch we would lay out the old tablecloth on the grass and lie there, watching the billowy clouds float by, stopping time. In the sand dunes of Arcahon, I rolled down the sandy hills in Pierrot's arms, splashing in the ocean and eating mussels and sea snails with tiny forks at a local fish market, licking our fingers and laughing. I never wanted to leave the sand dunes or the magic times with friends in a place that just nine months earlier had seemed so lonely and foreign.

It was my last night in Bordeaux, and I had to say goodbye. I didn't want to hurry the night. I sat close to Pierrot and ignored Bill, blocking out him and my American life. I wanted to linger in Marie-Paule's room.

Jacques passed the hash pipe. I took a hit, passed it to Pierrot, and whispered close to his ear, "Tu va me manquer."

"Moi aussi. Je te revois en Septembre." He would miss me too and see me in September.

Even though Bill didn't understand French, our body language spoke loudly enough for him to stop talking and stare at us. Pierrot leaned over and gave me a quick kiss good-bye, stood up, and shook Bill's hand. Then he got his jacket. "On y va?" He looked at Marco, Jacques, and Marie-Paule. It was time to go.

We hugged and kissed good-bye, with promises to keep in touch. The guys filed out first. Marie-Paule waited until I started down the stairs, and then she turned off the lights. It was the end of my French experience as a student. The movie had ended, and all my favorite actors climbed into the Deux Chevaux. I would miss handsome Marco's cutting remarks and aloof manners, Marie-Paule's generous spirit, Pierrot's gentle touch and kind words, and Jacques's crazy manner. Bill and I stood on the sidewalk waving good-bye. Just as my friends and I had done so many times before while driving through the streets of Bordeaux, they made the old car look as if it were falling apart. First Marco, the driver, opened his door, then Pierrot opened the front passenger door, Marie-Paule opened and closed the back door, and Jacques followed suit. With all four doors flying open and shut, the old car looked like a keystone cop car as they drove down the darkening street, flew around the corner on two wheels, and disappeared out of sight.

PART TWO

The Long Road Ahead

Bill hitchhiking

Chapter Thirty-Seven

The Long Road Ahead

June 10, 1971
Dear Mom,

I left Bordeaux today—I was really sad to leave my friends but I'll be going back to Bordeaux in September. Probably to work, picking grapes during the vendange, or else I'll live with Marie-Paule. I'll be in touch with them all summer, so if something comes up that you need to get a hold of me, (or to send money) here's their address: c/o Delanne-172 boulevard Wilson-33 Bordeaux

I'll be heading for Algiers to visit Marie-Paule's sister and brother-in-law. Right now I'm in the Pyrenees heading for Andorra and Spain. We stopped in Lourdes. I bathed in the water (kidding, just dipped my hands) and said a prayer for the family. Will keep you posted.

THE STREETS OF BORDEAUX were empty at seven in the morning when Bill and I started our journey across Europe, North Africa, and Asia Minor. My heart ached to leave France and my friends after nine months at the university. I stashed some of my winter clothes in Marie-Paule's room and sent a box of clothes and books home. Everything else I owned I jammed into my pack: my blue jeans, cutoff denim shorts, a sundress, two peasant blouses, a long-sleeve green shirt, my old purple poncho, a corduroy coat, and my clogs, along with minimal toiletries, underwear, and my rosary. I had three hundred dollars in traveler's checks and some odd change in francs. Bill carried a larger pack filled with his stuff plus our camping gear and double-zipped sleeping bags.

Passing Le New York Bar, I looked in and saw the waiter sweeping the floor; the smell of old beer and Gauloise cigarettes lingered in the air around the door. A sudden burst of laughter brought me back to the first night I'd met Pierrot and Marie-Paule in the back room of the bar. A stab of nostalgia hit me, but I didn't say a word; there was nothing I wanted to share with Bill. Walking on in silence, my mind churned, angry that Bill had gone to Hawaii last spring instead of coming to visit me as promised. I stewed over his likely infidelities and was miffed that he had shown up unannounced on my doorstep after not having written me for three months. He had no right intruding on my life in France, regardless of the fact we had made plans a year ago to travel in the summer. It was different now.

So much had changed during my year abroad. I didn't recognize who I'd become until Bill arrived, reminding me of the Isla Vista days, the frat parties, and being Bill's girlfriend. I wasn't "his girl" anymore. Bill was the same person I remembered: the big, blond, hairy American surfer I had fallen in love with during Spanish history class in Campbell Hall. Back then I had adored his surfer mannerisms, like tossing his hair back and answering in monosyllables. But looking at him now, with his baggy jeans and Hawaiian shirt in the middle of the city, turned me off. He didn't fit my image of the man I wanted to share my life with. I wanted Pierrot, and I wanted to melt into Europe and become part of it.

I walked a few feet in front of him.

"Hey, do ya wanna get a cup of joe?" Bill called loudly in his American voice.

Slowing down, I turned and nodded. "Sure."

At the corner café on Rue St. Catherine, we sipped our café au lait standing at the bar, watching the Frenchmen in suits and ties and the women in tight pencil skirts and heels, their voices humming in a songlike melody. The bustle and pushing at the coffee bar had been my daily ritual: grab my espresso, chug it, and run to catch the bus to the university.

"Can't we get breakfast with this?" Bill asked, polishing off his coffee.

He wanted to sit down and have bacon and eggs and a bottomless cup of coffee, not stand eating croissants and pain au chocolat.

"Not here. This isn't a restaurant. Can you wait till lunch?"

"Okay, but I'll need something to eat before then."

Tension between us vibrated and hung in the air like static on a radio. He was hungry and kept talking about food, and I only heard the blood rushing in my ears. I didn't want to be with him. My heart was with someone else. I had fallen deeply in love with Pierrot, who had no interest in me sexually, but his kindness and attention bound me in an emotional tie. I could only hope to kindle a true relationship with him when I returned to Bordeaux in the fall.

At the outskirts of town, Bill and I stuck out our thumbs, but getting a ride proved more difficult than it had been with my girlfriends. Around ten o'clock we hitched a ride with one of the many truckers and slowly made our way southeast.

We arrived in the Pyrenees before noon and took a detour to see the shrine of Our Lady of Lourdes.

* * *

As a child I had prayed to the Virgin Mary, hoping she would appear to me. As if setting a trap, I built a shrine to Mary in my backyard, hidden in the safety of the oleander bushes next to the lathe house, surrounded by camellias. I unearthed red bricks from the garden walk, mossy green on top and crawling with earthworms on the bottom, and stacked them in tiers, setting little vases on the brick ledges. On the top of the altar, I gingerly placed a white porcelain statue of the Blessed Mother. Around her feet I wrapped my plastic glow rosary beads, and on her head I adorned her with a crown of dandelions. Every day in May, I placed fresh flowers on the altar and said the rosary, beseeching Mary to visit me, digging in the dirt with my bare hands, like St. Bernadette, hoping a spring would burst forth with curative waters.

When I was ten, a family friend, Roseanne, fell ill with multiple sclerosis, and all the parishioners collected enough money to send her to Lourdes. Upon her return, I remember I held her bony hand and looked into her eyes, trying to see her soul, now a pure soul. She died within hours of our visit. It was my first contact with death. My dad said she went straight to heaven because she had suffered so much and had received enough grace from bathing in the waters at Lourdes to get in. Her husband, Al, had brought back a statue of Mary for my mom and some holy water in a plastic bottle with the image of Our Lady of Lourdes for my dad. When life got tough, I remember Dad sprinkling the holy water all over the living room. One day he found the statue broken in two and yelled, "Who the hell broke Mom's statue?

Were those knucklehead boys throwing the baseball in the living room? God damn son of a bitch!" All of us kids knew to get out of his way when he got angry. Mom went silent, and Dad fixed the statue by plastering it in a painted china cup Grandma had made. I can't explain the confusion of love, anger, and redemption locked in my body.

* * *

Shops and concession stands lined the path, and merchants sold trinkets, souvenirs, and plastic Mary statues.

"Bill, let's get one of those bottles for the holy water."

"You gotta be kidding me, Peggy. You want a plastic Jesus for the dashboard?" He began to sing a song by the Goldcoast Singers from 1962: "I don't care if it rains or freezes, 'long as I got my plastic Jesus riding on the dashboard of my car..."

"Stop! Besides, it's a plastic Mary, and she just might help us through our 'trials and tribulations.'"

"Do what you want. I don't get you Catholics." He kept on humming the song.

"I have one already, so I guess I won't get another." Under my breath I added *jackass*.

But something else caught my eye: a beautiful holy card of Saint Bernadette as a young nun. A relic of brown cloth that had touched her body was attached to the back of the card with a see-through cover that made it look as if Saint Bernadette was wearing the garment. I held the card in one hand, dipped into my purse for a franc, and handed it to the clerk.

"Merci, Madame," the clerk said, carefully wrapping the relic in a piece of newspaper and handing it back to me.

"Merci, Monsieur." I slipped the holy card into my pocket. Bill shook his head in disbelief. I explained, "It's like an insurance policy. You don't know if you'll need it, but it can't hurt to have."

The steep road led to the sanctuary of the grotto; the Basilica of Our Lady of Lourdes adorned the cliff above us like a fortress.

As we approached the outdoor altar, my heart skipped a beat when I saw thousands of people in wheelchairs, on hospital beds, walking with crutches, or on their knees: their families, friends, nurses, nuns, and priests patiently waiting their turn to bring their loved ones to touch or drink the water that trickled out of the ground and pooled in a stone bath. All were expecting a miracle. A enormous statue of Our Lady of Lourdes perched high on a ledge above the grotto, her hands outstretched and a benevolent smile on her face. I felt her presence, a sense of wonder and awe, and reflexively began saying the Hail Mary, tears moistening my face. I turned away from Bill, embarrassed by my sentimentality.

The intonation of the priest saying mass in Latin and the choir's response crackled over the loudspeakers, and incense wafted through the air, mixed with the smoke of the ever-present Gauloise.

"I want to touch the water. Let's get in line."

Bill didn't resist. The misty day and coolness of the grotto gave us a needed respite. I slowly passed under the mossy rocks beneath the statue, knelt down, and dipped my hand in the small trough of water, blessing myself. Bill did the same.

The glacier at Cirque de Gavarnie

Chapter Thirty-Eight

The Hut

Dear Mom,
Just a quick postcard to let you know I'm alive. We'll be hiking
and camping in the Pyrénées for the next few days. We'll be staying
in a hut below the glacier in the Cirque de Gavarnie.

THE SNOW HAD MELTED in the mountains and the rivers
were gushing, clear and beautiful, along the winding road, as
we made our way to the high Pyrenees. In town, we inquired
about hiking and camping and were directed to the ski lifts
used in the summer to take people to the high meadows.

"That beats hiking with our packs." said Bill.

"Let's go," I agreed.

At the top of the slope, we put on our packs and hiked the
narrow trail to the overnight hut, a stone building perched
on a high cliff with a spectacular view of the glacier, Cirque
de Gavarnie. We signed in for the night.

Joining a few men for beers on the deck outside, we
watched the last rays of sun reflect off the snow, a ritual for
climbers and hikers who know their comrades are still out

in the wilderness at the point of darkness. The men passed around a pair of binoculars, pointing to tiny specks on the mountain where the mountaineers were roped together and steadily climbing, hoping to summit by early morning while the temperatures stayed well below freezing.

Climbing glaciers is risky—rocks loosened by the melting snow can fall, and ice bridges can crack and break, sending those who misstep into crevasses and an untimely death. I was astounded by what I thought was an impossible feat and curious as to why people put themselves in such dangerous situations. Thinking about it now, I realize that the mountaineers had more control over their fate than I did at that moment. They knew where they were going and what they were doing. I didn't know where I was going, yet like them, I had no fear.

The hosts set the tables for dinner with tin plates, bowls, and mugs and served a hearty meal of beef and vegetable stew followed by french fries and pounded steaks, a real cowboy dinner at the top of the world. Jugs of red wine lined the middle of the table. The unshaven climbers swigged the wine and wiped their bowls and plates clean with chunks of bread. Bill and I followed suit.

One man stood up and started singing the familiar "Chevalier de la Table Ronde."

"Allons voir," he bellowed, lifting his mug high, and the rest of the group answered, "Oui, oui, oui."

"Allons voir," he shouted louder. Gaining momentum, the fellow hikers sang, "Non, non, non."

"Allons voir si le vin est bon!"

"Let's see if the wine is good," I translated for Bill. We joined in the drinking song, and after each line, regardless if we answered yes or no, we drank, just like the Knights of the Round Table.

It's universal that the big guy in a group will become a target and be picked on in a humorous way, especially if he's an affable American in Europe. So for the next song, the men grabbed Bill, brought him to the front of the room, and taught him all the motions to go with a new song. Of course, he didn't know what the words meant. Two men handed him a mug of beer and showed him the movements. Taking their beers, they touched their beer mugs to their foreheads, nose, mouth, neck, chest and "sex." Bill was a quick study and picked it up right away.

The men sang: "Et porte le au frontibus, au neztibus, au mentonbus, au totonbus, au ventribus, au sexibus, on n'a pas l'plus…"

The group jumped in with the chorus: "Et glou, et glou, et glou, et glou, et glou, et glou…"

All the men chugged their beers in competition to see who could chug the fastest and, in the end, who would stay standing the longest. I'm happy to report that the American frat boy showed well that night, even though he suffered a terrible headache the next day.

By ten o'clock, lights went out and we climbed into the bunks. Two long platforms, one above the other, formed the sleeping area for about thirty people. No privacy. Men, boys, a few women, and some girls all piled into the one room. I curled up in my sleeping bag, happy and tired, but slept fitfully with so many people snoring and farting in such close quarters with the windows shut to keep out the cold night air.

Bill and I left early the next morning and hiked over the ridge to the next valley, descending past lakes the color of emeralds and through forests and beneath trees that lined the rushing river. The outdoors lightened my spirit, and I had a new sense of freedom and adventure. Funny, now that I was away from my French friends, I was less agitated by Bill's behavior and awkwardness. I had gotten such a kick out of watching him sing in French and have a good time with the other hikers. Language didn't pose a problem when drinking and laughing and singing. He was a good sport, and the old guys really liked him—and he'd turned the heads of the few women there. Bill seemed so much more interesting and fun, like he'd been when I first met him. Was it ever Bill who had caused my anxiousness in Bordeaux? Or was it me? I blamed my malaise on Bill. He was just not French enough, but was that his fault?

Bill walked ahead of me on the trail while I was lost in my thoughts, enjoying the beauty and serenity, when suddenly "nature called." I was nowhere near a toilet and the road was wide open, so being discreet was out of the question. I felt panicky. I had no choice but to go out in the open, my upbringing bearing down heavily on me. Certain things were done in private and not talked about in my home. I couldn't yell ahead to Bill, "Hey, wait a minute, I'm taking a shit!" This was totally out of my comfort zone.

* * *

We had only one bathroom for twelve people at home, so one might think that bodily functions would be talked about freely, but that was not the case. First of all, my mother referred to the bathroom as "the blue room," even though it was painted green. It wasn't until I was in my teens that I thought to ask her why she called it the blue room, which my aunts also called their bathrooms.

"My mother thought it was crude to mention the word bathroom in polite company," Mom explained. "So my father suggested that we call it the blue room."

"Was it blue?"

"I don't know. Maybe at one time it was blue, but I remember it being yellow."

Mom never used the correct words for elimination, never mentioning defecation or bowel movement, let alone urination or urine. At my yearly physical before camp, the doctor asked me, if I had regular bowel movements. I looked at Mom and said, "What's that?" I was nine years old.

My mother laughed, leaned over, and whispered, "That's gee-gee."

Our body parts had discreet names too. We referred to our anus, and the surrounding area, as a boofy. Flatulence was politely described as a boofy burp. Admittedly, I passed on this unfortunate behavior to my children, referring to farts as poopy noises.

* * *

I climbed up the side of a hill and hid behind a rock. Having never gone "number two" in the forest, I was a little worried. Squatting on my haunches I looked up at the billowy clouds and laughed aloud at how foolish I must look from above, as if God, Dad, or Shereen could see me. I remembered in psychology class studying about a dream Jung had in which God, in his grandeur sitting on a cloud, defecated on a cathedral. That dream got Jung thinking about God and life, good and evil.

What's wrong with me that I can't talk about taking a dump in the forest, when every human and animal does it? Why am I so uptight?

That day behind the rock I had my own epiphany. I released much more than the rich dinner from the night before. I let go of a pattern of being rigid about my bodily functions and secretions. I pulled up my pants, grabbed my pack, and ran down the trail, passing the day hikers, until I caught up with Bill.

"What were you doing? Taking a shit?" he asked.

"Yep, that's right, I took a shit in the forest."

Crossing the Pyrenees

Chapter Thirty-Nine

Andorra

Hola familia!

Que tal? I've been picking up a few stray Spanish words while in Spain and hope to learn to speak it before Carmen comes next fall. Andorra was amazing, one big shopping country in a valley of the Pyrenees between Spain and France...

I'M NOT A SHOPPER. I wasn't then and I'm not now, so I didn't feel as compelled as Bill to make a beeline to Andorra to find the best deal on cameras. And I had already made my big camera purchase in Spain when I bought my Instamatic Brownie by Kodak. The sting was still there, as I remembered the guys from my program making fun of my cheap American-brand camera while they toted their huge Leica and Canon cameras with changeable lenses and the incomprehensible F-stop.

Bill went into the first camera shop to negotiate a deal. "How much for this one?" He pointed to the Yashica. The store owner gave him a price. Bill scribbled a few numbers on his paper. "How about this one?" and he pointed to the

Pentax on the shelf behind the counter. Again the store owner gave him a price. Bill marked it down on the same paper. This went on for about ten minutes: the shopkeeper taking each camera carefully off the shelf, checking the price tag, and handing it to Bill, who thoroughly inspected it, rotating the black camera body in his hands, looking through the lens, and clicking the shutter.

Laying the last camera down, Bill said, "Too expensive, muy caro." He looked over the array of cameras that now littered the counter and walked out the door with me following him.

"That was kinda rude, don't ya think?'

"Nah, that's what ya gotta do if you want to get the best price. You gotta bargain with these guys."

Bill sauntered into the camera shop next door and began the same ritual, loading himself with ammunition to later go back and bargain with each shopkeeper. I wasn't interested in hanging around until he purchased the perfect camera at the best price, so I told him I'd meet him back at the first shop in an hour.

I walked down the streets, circumventing the displays of local goods, bota bags, and sheepskin rugs, ducking under whole legs of cured ham, and stooping to get by the soccer balls in net bags hanging from the awnings. From time to time, I looked in the windows at the mannequins wearing stylish clothes, thinking, *How impractical.* My mother loved shopping, even though she mostly window-shopped. Funny, the French refer to window-shopping as *lèche-vitrines*, which translates literally as "lick the windows." It was beneath my dignity to lick any windows, and besides I had everything I needed in my backpack.

Tiring of walking on city streets, I sat down in a park and looked up at the mountains. I listened to the birds and watched the kids playing in the fountains while I rearranged my belongings in my pack. I rerolled my cutoff jeans and stuffed them in the bottom, and then I folded my corduroy jacket and pushed it down as far as it would go. The few short-sleeve shirts fit neatly on the sides, filling in the space, and my kelly green blouse went on top so as not to wrinkle it too much. I tucked my underwear and socks in the outside pockets and hung my boots on the straps. Then I took out my book, *A Moveable Feast,* and read a few pages.

It wasn't just that I didn't like to go shopping—I didn't have the money to spend.

∗ ∗ ∗

After Dad died, Mom never did send me my Social Security checks. I didn't like harping about money, but I knew that once I ran out, I would need some cash to buy a flight home. I wrote asking her to put my Social Security check and tax refund in my First Western bank account; I even sent her a blank check in case she needed to use my money to make ends meet. In May I wrote, *Thanks Mom for everything—don't you dare worry about the Social Security $$. I have plenty and don't need the stuff!*

Mom needed the money more than I did, but I never found out what happened to my Social Security money. At the time I thought maybe I hadn't filled out the right paperwork. A few years after returning from Europe, I moved in with a new boyfriend. When her sisters found out, my mother became very upset and called me.

"Peggy Anne, I don't approve. No daughter of mine lives with a man before marriage. You won't get your Social Security check while living in sin." It was only a few hundred dollars, and I hadn't even known she had kept it from me when I was in Europe.

"Mom, I am your daughter, and I am living with my boyfriend. You can keep the check, and I'll do what I want."

Could she have withheld my money because I was traveling with Bill? Perhaps, but it didn't matter. I valued my independence more than money. I remember after freshman year in college, Carmen's parents kicked her out of the house and cut her off financially because she brought a puppy home. She moved in with me in my attic bedroom on Rosemead Boulevard, got a job at Radiance Vitamins, and ate protein pills to survive. Eventually, her parents relented and gave her back her car, paid her college tuition, and sent a hefty living allowance. But she was always sneaking around and in fear that her parents would take away the money.

Not getting money from my parents gave me freedom.

* * *

I looked in my wallet and counted my traveler's checks. I had saved three hundred dollars from my student loans and scholarships, and that money had to last me the next six months. I figured if I spent just a little over one dollar a day, I could stay until Christmas with a little money leftover. I had a plan to outdo Frommer's guidebook, *Europe on Five Dollars a Day,* because that budget accounted for hotels, restaurants, and transportation. Bill and I had agreed to hitchhike, which cost nothing but time. Both of us had sleeping bags so we could sleep on beaches, in parks, or when necessary in campsites, hostels, and cheap hotels. We bought food in markets for picnics, ate from street vendors and in cheap restaurants, and accepted meals when offered.

Our lifestyle wasn't so different from the rest of the youth traveling in the '70s. Flashing the peace sign, "Peace baby!" brought both scowls and smiles as the wave of hippies traveled the world, living off the land and the charity of others.

We couldn't hide being American—Bill at six foot two and me at five foot ten. Our clothes, backpacks, and long hair pegged us as hippies, the spoiled children of conservative America. We bore our nation's culpability of conspicuous consumption and war mongering.

Still, we didn't succumb to the temptation of putting the Union Jack or Canadian maple leaf flag on our packs. Why would we? Most people wanted to emulate us. They wanted to buy our Levi's jeans off our bodies and talk to us about our music, our movies, and our magazines. Some hated us for having more stuff than they did, but they all wanted our affluence and freedom.

In a strange way, I felt superior to the Europeans, even though I barely had two sous to rub together. I had the American dream, the possibility of earning money and a position in society. I didn't have to be born into it.

An hour passed, and I walked back to the camera shop to meet Bill. I caught sight of him coming out of a clothing store. He was wearing a sheared lambskin coat with brown bone buttons and fur around the collar and sleeves. The ochre skin matched the color of his tan. A huge camera hung rakishly across his shoulder, with a few extra lenses dangling from the strap.

"Whoa, cowboy, the only thing missing is the beret." I had to comment on the change from surfer clothes to wearing the local animal.

"Hey, I thought about it—a red or black beret?"

"Don't do it. I was kidding. Nice jacket. Cool camera." Secretly, I was jealous of not being able to buy what I wanted, so I made fun of him, like I didn't need the trappings of material things.

"These sheepskin jackets cost twice as much in the States. I got such a great deal on the camera too! The guy threw in the lens just so I wouldn't walk out of his shop and buy it from the other guy down the street." Bill had spent as much money in Andorra as I had to travel on for the next six months, but I was used to this disparity. My friends had cars at sixteen, lived in fancy homes, and went to private colleges. Dad always said we had more than those rich kids. "You've got each other, and love. You don't need things to make you happy."

La Sagrada de Familia

CHAPTER FORTY

Costa Brava

June 18
Hola familia,
   The drive down the coast is fantastic, but the weather is so
hot, we've been camping on the beaches. The postcard is of Gaudi's
church, Sagrada Familia, a fou (crazy man) built this cathedral
and didn't put on a roof! The architecture in Barcelona is insane.

BILL AND I CHECKED into the youth hostel in Barcelona
and got the lowdown on where to go and what to do. Gaudi's
cathedral, Sagrada Familia, was on top of the list. I was
expecting to see something similar to Chartres or Notre
Dame. The next morning we hopped a city bus, got off at
Avenida Gaudi, and walked across a park of undulating
walls, bright blue-tiled benches with curlicue designs, and
fanciful animal and bug carvings, like a cartoon world on
an acid trip. But when we got to the cathedral, my mouth
fell open. "The cathedral isn't finished!"
   Scaffolding covered a bizarre and unsettling facade.
Light soared through ornate glassless windows, wiggly towers

appeared to melt like candles dripping with wax over time, and convex walls soared above a roofless nave. Catwalks connected the unfinished sections with snails, lizards, and creatures carved into the sand-colored walls, mocking the gargoyles of Notre Dame.

"Maybe we should come back in a hundred years," Bill, the consummate historian, remarked wryly.

The amphibious decorations in the alcoves jarred my sense of the saints' proprietary right, but I found the architecture humorous, striking a chord of disrespect and whimsy.

Suddenly a voice rang out, "Si, mi chiamano Mimi..." We stopped and looked up, our hands shielding the glare of the morning sun. An opera singer, in a full-length black gown, stood on a balcony without guardrails, her head held high, her hands clasped over her heart, and her breasts pushed up in a perfect V. She warbled a long note and disappeared.

"What the fuck was that?"

"Dunno. A lady in black singing?"

Within seconds she reappeared on a veranda and looked down at us, trilling high notes that sent shivers down my spine. No one else was around. Was she performing for us? She again vanished. As we turned a corner, she reemerged on an unfinished facade for her final aria, the radiant blue sky shining through the arches that framed her full-bodied figure and flowing black hair. She took three bows and left.

The workmen hoisted large steel bars up to the men on the scaffolding, as if nothing had happened.

Bill looked at me. "That was totally weird."

"But beautiful," I added, thinking of Dad listening to Pavarotti on the RCA Victrola in the living room. I had thought I hated opera, but this performance changed my mind.

The next day, we headed to the hot and crowded beaches and campsites along the Costa Brava. Big white-bellied Germans lolled in beach chairs around Airstream trailers hitched to the back of Mercedeses. Pasty English families clumped together under big umbrellas, their skin an unnatural lobster red. These vacationers annoyed me by setting their blankets and chairs within inches of us on the beach. We got up to get something to eat. Standing in line at the camp food concession, a hairy man, full of beer, hassled the young ice-cream vendor because he didn't understand German.

"Zwei Eistüten für die Kinder," he yelled, emphasizing the harsh initial sound of each word. His sunburned and salty children cried and pulled at their overwhelmed mother, while the English kids behind us stamped their feet and threw sand in each other's eyes. "You bloody well shut up," cried the mother as the father smacked one.

Bill turned to me. "Hey, let's not stay at the campsite. We can sleep on the beach somewhere farther south."

"I'm all for that." We got our ice cream, threw our packs over our shoulders, and headed back to the main road.

Later that afternoon, a vegetable truck picked us up.

"¿Dónde vas?"

"La playa, por favor."

He left us off north of Valencia on a farm road and pointed to a deserted stretch of beach, warning, "No hay agua, ni comida, ni baños públicos." We smiled and showed him our bag of rice and canteens of water.

After setting up camp on the beach in a secluded cove, Bill started a fire and I cooked the rest of our rice.

"Not much for dinner." Bill was a big boy and needed more, and frankly I wasn't satisfied either.

"Did you notice the fields along the road when we turned off to the beach? Beautiful, tilled rows of vegetables. Hmm," I mused, placing a theatrical finger on my cheek.

Bill laughed. "Really? Well…I don't think anyone's working in the fields now." He stood up, surveying the area. "We could just take a few things…no one would mind."

I hesitated to steal, but I was hungry enough to raid the vegetable patch.

Like naughty children in a fairy tale, we pulled up big bulbs of shallots, shaking off the dirt; popped red, vine-ripened tomatoes in our mouths; and stuffed two oversized zucchini under our shirts. Sneaking back to our camp, we cooked our booty over the campfire, ravenous for fresh vegetables after days of rice and cured meats. An hour later, my stomach cramped and I burped up the shallots. "I don't feel good."

The sun had gone down, leaving a chill in the air. Bill wrapped his arms around me, and in the twilight we watched the campfire flicker out. His body warmth soothed me. For the first time since we left France, we zipped our sleeping bags together and curled up under the stars and waning moon.

The next morning, we awoke to someone in the distance yelling. "¿Qué están haciendo aquí?" A farmer in baggy overalls, his pitchfork raised above his head, came running across the field toward us.

Bill jumped up, pulled on his jeans, and ran across the road toward the farmer. I lay immobilized in the zipped-together sleeping bags, hoping the farmer hadn't seen me. We had trespassed, stolen vegetables, and—the most grievous transgression—were not married and had been caught sleeping together.

In the sixties and seventies, a sexual revolution had exploded at college campuses across the United States, but not in Europe, and definitely not in Spain. An unmarried Spanish woman couldn't be alone with a man. She had to have a chaperone during the courting period.

I lay in my sleeping bag, shamed—"knowing better," as my mother would have said. My head filled with screaming, all the admonitions from my mother, the nuns, the priests, everyone ranting, "Save yourself for marriage. Who wants a used woman? Don't cheapen yourself." I slid deeper into the bag.

I had had plans to be a virgin when I got married, and I held off a lot longer than most of my friends from "doing it," but the social pressure in college overwhelmed me. I knew having sex outside of marriage would bar me from the sacraments of the Church, which barred me from heaven.

* * *

One Saturday afternoon in the spring of my sophomore year, I went to confession, hoping to get a dispensation. Father Tom, a young priest at St. Mark's church in Isla Vista, would surely understand and help me with my sexual quandary.

"Bless me, Father, for I have sinned...well, not yet, but I'm going to Mexico with my boyfriend and his fraternity over Easter break. I think I'm going to sleep with him." I was utterly humiliated voicing such an idea, but I had to try. With my fingers crossed and my eyes closed, I begged God to allow me to have sex just this one time. After all, it was the seventies.

Father Tom placed his hand across his mouth in contemplation. I held my breath. He responded in an unusually low voice for such a young man. "You will be committing a mortal sin if you have sex outside of marriage. I cannot give you permission to do so. Say the rosary and seek Mary's guidance." He slid closed the wooden window.

That was it. There was no wiggle room in my dogmatic faith. I had to make a choice, and I didn't take it lightly. I compromised. I went to Mexico and slept in the same bed as Bill, but I stayed a virgin. As he later said, he "was the only guy that didn't get laid."

Not long afterward, Bill and I ate magic mushrooms on a Saturday and hiked into the hills above Santa Barbara. Climbing to the top of Seven Falls, we slid down mossy rocks and frolicked in the clear pools. Bill spotted a shiny metal piece at the bottom of the river, dove under, and came up with a St. Christopher medal, a surfer saint, with the initials C & M on the back. He handed it to me. "It's for us, Carlos and Margarita." (Those were our Mexican names in Ensenada.) Gently unlatching the chain, he hung the pink and blue St. Christopher around my neck. I wondered if that meant we were going steady. In any event, I took it as a sign from the powers above that we were meant to be together forever.

Lying naked on the rocks, our bodies drying from the chill of the cold mountain spring, I had an "aha" moment while tripping on the frogs "making it" right next to us. One shiny little guy jumped on the back of a sweet spotted frog and moved rhythmically, up and down, up and down. *If they can do it, why can't I?* I thought. I rolled over to Bill and said, "I'm ready," knowing I would marry him.

* * *

I listened to the farmer rant and rave so angrily; I thought he might even hit Bill. Mortified and afraid to show my face, I stayed still and quiet, my head barely peeking out.

I heard Bill speaking Spanish. "Buenas dias, Señor. Mi esposa esta enferma." The farmer stopped yelling.

"Es serioso?" inquired the farmer.

Brilliant! Bill had told the farmer I was his wife, a sick wife. The farmer's voice quieted; he almost sounded sympathetic. He asked Bill how I was feeling. It always amazed me in these Latin countries when the men would raise their voices and fists, as if they were going to beat the living daylight out of someone who crossed them, only to end the argument with arms wrapped around each other's shoulders.

"No esta mejor este mañana." Bill reassured him I was feeling better this morning.

The farmer laughed and pointed to the rows of vegetables, asking Bill if I had eaten too many green vegetables and hopefully not the garlic. Sensing the mood had switched, I hurriedly dressed inside the sleeping bag, got out, and walked over to greet the now jovial man.

"El ajo grande es muy fuerte." He patted his stomach in sympathy for my pain.

"We ate garlic, not shallots! And you wolfed them down," Bill chided. Smiling, the farmer put his arm on Bill's shoulder and insisted on giving us a ride into town.

Rivera is awarded two ears and a tail

CHAPTER FORTY-ONE

The Bullfight

*It's hotter than Hades here. We'll hit Alicante Sunday, then hope-
fully Almeria Wednesday to catch the midnight boat to Morocco. Tell
Nola we saw El Cordobes bullfight, not my cup of tea, but exciting.*

AS WE WALKED DOWN the old streets of Alicante, we noticed a poster in a café window announcing the running of
the bulls each morning during the Fiesta de San Juan and
a bullfight Sunday afternoon.

"Hey, I've always wanted to do that. I'll miss Pamplona,
but hell, I'll run with the bulls here! Then we'll see the
bullfight!"

"It's not exactly what I want to do, but when in Spain...
who are the bullfighters?"

"El Cordobés," Bill said, accentuating the ending, "and
Rivera, a Mexican guy."

"El Cordobés? Wow, he's famous. We should go."

I wasn't a bullfighting aficionado, but my sister Nola
was. She had raved about seeing El Cordobés in Spain in

the sixties, describing bullfighting as an art form, a dance of life and death. Perhaps intellectually that was true, but I hated to see the bull suffer and be killed for entertainment—it was all so barbaric. I couldn't justify the kill, even if the meat did go to feed the poor. Still, I wanted to see the legendary El Cordobés.

As for the running of the bulls, only a fool would do that...and Bill wanted to.

The next day, safely tucked away in a bar window, we watched the *toros* let loose in the street, taking only minutes to run the short course down the cobblestone streets and around the corner to the corral. Bill jumped out of the window and ran amid the crowd of young Spaniards. I was happy he could run with the bulls. It was on his list of things to do. He had sacrificed going to Pamplona in July so I could visit Marie-Paule's sister in Algeria. That's how we traveled.

That afternoon, we queued up outside the arena in the hot sun as people jostled for position in line, shouting the names of the matadors and singing boisterously, raising our expectations of the spectacle. We bought the cheapest tickets, pushed our way through the crowds, and climbed the bleachers, our seats near the top in full sunlight.

Trumpets sounded and the crowd got to their feet, roaring as a bull was led into the ring. Rivera, the young Mexican matador, waited behind a gate as his assistant went into the ring and waved a yellow and magenta cape to aggravate the bull.

With a fanfare, Rivera entered the ring, extending his cape and holding up his killing sword. He dedicated the fight to the crowd. With the skill of a master, he taunted the poor bull, swinging his cape within inches of the bull's horns, dancing a tango of death. He went down on one knee in front of the bull, a death wish. The heated bull snorted and pointed his horns directly at the young matador.

My hands clenched, not knowing if I wanted the bull to gore that awful man or if I feared the animal would kill him. The matador jumped to his feet, the bull charged, and Rivera swiftly leaned to the side, touching the sweaty flank, confusing the bull. The angered animal turned in circles, attempting to gore the young man but only plowing his horns into the dirt. The crowd rose and cheered in unison as the matador continued to bow and kneel before the bull, jumping away in time to avoid a certain death.

"Olé! Olé! Es mejor de El Cordobés!"

With a gallant thrust, Rivera killed the bull instantly. The crowd went wild, throwing flowers meant for El Cordobés. The humble matador circled the ring, accepting the flowers and bowing deeply.

El Presidente, escorted by guards, cut off the bull's two ears and tail and presented them to Rivera, the highest recognition a matador can receive. Rivera went down on one knee, accepting the honor. The crowd rose in a frenzy as he left the ring, a hero.

The next bull stormed the ring to the cries from the crowd, whose desire for blood had heightened. The *pica-dores* assailed the feisty bull with their colorful spears. The trumpets reverberated around the ring, and I was swept up in the moment, applauding for El Cordobés as he entered the ring, magnificently dressed in white brocade with gold thread. He bowed to the judge's box and, in a gallant sweep, took off his black winged hat and dedicated the kill to El Presidente. Applause erupted, and Bill and I cheered as if at a football game.

The bull charged unexpectedly, and El Cordobés re-treated. The crowd booed. He took a few steps back into the ring and lifted his cape. The bull charged again, and El Cordobés turned and ran. The crowd jeered at the cowardly move. A picador came back into the ring to corral the wild beast and speared him with another lance. From a safe distance, El Cordobés attempted to lure the bull to pass under his cape. The bull stood strong. He had won. There was no fight left in El Cordobés, none of the daring maneuvers that had made him famous—just the swish of his cape and the mocking cries of the crowd, which wanted blood.

Defiantly, El Cordobés walked out of the arena. His assistant jumped the gate, ran into the ring, and took the *descabello,* a sword with a short cross piece at the end, and stabbed the bull in the neck, severing the animal's spinal cord and bringing him down. There were no flowers, no ears or tail cut, only the rage of the spectators, a cacophony of hissing, catcalls, and taunts.

Camping on the beach

CHAPTER FORTY-TWO

The Blues

We've seen old fortresses, ruins and palaces. I'm mailing this before we get on the ferry to Morocco. We'll be in Algeria soon, so please write me c/o Marie-Hélène. I gave you the address already.

THE ROAD TO ALMERIA drifted in and out of arid places with high-rise buildings cropping up along the coast and Moorish castles nestled on hilltops. I too weaved in and out of arid places questioning what I was doing traveling so far from home, feeling untethered, having no contact with my friends in France or my family at home—no phone calls, no letters. I fantasized about what they were doing and wondered if anyone thought about me, especially Pierrot. Pining for him made me miserable. I reprimanded myself: *He never loved you,* which made me feel even worse.

I spiraled down, feeling sorry for myself, missing my life in France, and physically aching to return to a past I knew I could not travel back to.

Sitting on the side of the road, I put my head in my hands and slumped over my fringed leather bag. The dull pain in my stomach wasn't hunger, just emptiness. Everyone had deserted me, even my father, but I couldn't go there; it was still too painful, still not real.

Bright heat off the pavement burned my eyes as I looked up and down the asphalt road, waiting for our next ride. Cars sped past us, leaving only the mirage of shiny water.

"Whatcha thinking?" Bill asked innocently.

"Oh, nothing." If he had noticed my mood swings, he didn't know how to handle them. He talked about the mundane: where to eat, where to go, or historical facts. I was afraid we had nothing left in common.

At one point on our trip, I had hoped we could bridge the divide caused by my year away, but I struggled, not knowing if I could love him again. He was a nice guy, a good traveling companion, and we occasionally had sex, but was it love?

Bill never questioned me about what I had done the year we were apart. He never mentioned my blue moods. He accused me of being "on the rag," but that's what guys said when they couldn't handle female emotions. My fits of introspection and withdrawal gave him time to delve into his reading, but it also moved me further from him. I lived two lives that summer, one with him on the road and the other imagining what it would be like to return to France and live my life there with Pierrot. I didn't think about going home to California. I didn't want to face the challenges of making it on my own or the responsibility of helping my family.

At the time, I blamed my bad moods on the food—a little too much grease and a lack of three square meals a day. Maybe my ill feelings came with the lack of sleep, spending nights in fields and on beaches with an occasional night on a boat or in a youth hostel. But mostly, I blamed Bill. I needed someone to talk to, someone who understood and could share my loneliness. I couldn't tell him how much I missed Pierrot.

Swallowing hard, I gave myself a pep talk. *Snap out of it! Make the most of it!* This was my only chance to travel, because when I returned to the states, I would need to support myself, finish school, and get a job. *No one is going to take care of you but yourself.* My dad didn't accept whining, and I didn't either.

Bill sat by my side, relaxed and content to be with me. I looked at him. "What's next?"

"Do you want to see if we can get a ride to Granada to see the Alhambra?" Bill eagerly sought my approval. He had a list of things he wanted to see and places to go, and most of them had to do with wars or mythology. He read aloud from his guidebook, "The fourteenth-century Moorish palace and fortress is a monument to the Muslim reign in the Iberian Peninsula." *He's such a history geek,* I thought.

* * *

We had met my sophomore year in Spanish History class. Tall and tanned, wearing jeans and huarache sandals, Bill walked into Campbell Hall with my best friend, Carmen, and sat between us. Immediately, I was smitten by his Adonis looks. Butterflies swarmed in my stomach when he asked me to study in the library after class. Oblivious to Carmen's feelings, I accepted. Having no interest in studying history, I never missed a class, got a requirement out of the way, and gained a boyfriend I adored.

* * *

Looking into his patient blue eyes, I softened, remembering the day we met. "Sure, let's get off the coast. It's too touristy and slow going."

We got a ride with a young Spaniard heading to the Costa d'Almeria, our destination. He stopped for a coffee while we quickly visited the Alhambra, snapping photos of delicately carved arches that framed the valleys below, of large wooden doors leading to secret gardens with long reflecting pools, and of fountains paved with Moorish tiles.

Early that evening we arrived in Almeria, bought our tickets at the port office, and sat down to wait on the wooden benches with the dark-skinned passengers. Bill opened his book to read, but my eyes skimmed the crowd. The Arab women kept their eyes downcast, their faces covered with headscarves, and, as expected, the men stared unabashedly. I fiddled with our tickets and rummaged through my purse. Nervously, I got up to make sure we had the right ticket, since it was just a blue stub, like the kind you get when you enter a school raffle. The man at the ticket counter told me, "Oui, attendez!" and waved me away.

Crossing at night meant we wouldn't have to pay for a hotel but would sleep on the boat as it lumbered across the strait to Nador, an industrial port close to the border of Algeria known for fishing and, as we soon found out, for smuggling goods from Spain.

As we queued to board the ship, officials pulled people out of line, opening their luggage and bags. Neither Bill nor I had any contraband or dope, but still the guards eyed us suspiciously and checked our packs, questioning if we were selling anything.

Bedraggled from little sleep, we leaned against each other to catch a few winks, nodding off, trying to find a comfortable position on the hard benches inside the smoke-filled cabin and breathing the stale air of sleepers. In a light fog at daybreak, we disembarked along with the other passengers as they dragged their tattered suitcases, some of their belongings wrapped in sheets or carried in baskets balanced on their heads. No vendors lined the streets, like in Tangiers, just fisherman pulling their nets along the shore, making sure not to tangle them before loading them onto dilapidated vessels and heading out to a choppy sea. The shoreline was muddy and marked with discarded buoys, bright blue plastic pieces, and bits of metal siding. A few dead fish and plenty of fish heads and guts rolled up and back with the tide; the stench permeated the early morning air, promising to be unbearable by midday.

We walked into the desolate town and found the youth hostel, where we washed up and got an hour's sleep before being kicked out onto the dusty streets.

"Let's get something to eat."

"Maybe find some coffee too."

It was just after eleven in the morning, and the streets were already hot. We couldn't find the "old town," or any place charming, so we settled for a small restaurant with a few plastic chairs on the sidewalk. The intensity of the heat put both of us in foul moods.

"I sure could use a beer," Bill announced.

"You drink too much beer."

"Hey, it's better than the water."

"You could have a soda.'

"What health benefits do you get from a soda? It's loaded with sugar. At least a beer has hops, vitamins. It's almost a food."

What was I doing with this guy who drank beer in the morning? I didn't want to be with someone with a drinking problem. My mind flashed back to getting ready for high school one morning.

* * *

I had just gotten out of the shower and was putting on my makeup when I heard rustling outside the window. Fearful that someone was peeking in at me, I quickly wrapped a towel around myself and looked outside. My father was rummaging in the ivy under the outside staircase. I watched for a few moments as he found his bottle and took a swig. He wiped his mouth with his bathrobe sleeve and filled his glass of orange juice with the gin. He looked around with a guilty look smeared across his face, making sure no one was watching him, capped the bottle, and hid it back in the corner under the thick ivy. Sickened, I held my stomach and slid onto the bench below the window. Now I had proof my father was an alcoholic. Before, it was only my mother's accusations and fighting, but now I knew my fear was true. I never told my mother about finding Dad's hiding place, and I never confronted my father about the incident. I tried to write him a letter but never sent it. I worried my friends would find out my dad was a drunk, so I kept it secret and let it eat at me.

* * *

Bill's drinking bothered me, but I tried not to harp on him like my mother had done to my father. But that day, on the dusty streets of Morocco, I felt like hitting him and my father who had left me.

Our argument finished with silence. I drank mint tea and he had his beer.

Algerian border

Chapter Forty-Three

Cholera

Hi Mom, If we can get visas at the border we should be in Algeria by the end of the month. Don't forget to write. (Postcard June 21)

ONCE BACK AT THE youth hostel and eager to get out of Morocco, we inquired, "Where do you go for visas?"

The young clerk behind the shoddy desk looked at our map and pointed to a city near the border. "Oujda. A bus leaves in the morning."

After thanking him, we filed down a dirty corridor and up a set of cement stairs that smelled of feces. Passing the lavatories, we read a sign posted on the shower door: L'eau sera désactivé jusqu'à nouvel avis.

"What's that say?" Bill was in a foul mood.

"'The water will be *disactivated* until further notice.' The water's turned off." It didn't feel like a big deal to me. It was a desert after all. Lots of places in Morocco turned the water off during the day while businesses were open.

We went back down to the front desk to ask when the water was going to be turned back on.

"Pas de l'eau." Palms up, the clerk shrugged his shoulders and told us there was no water.

"No water? This is bullshit." Bill heatedly contested the situation.

"Lighten up, Bill, it's not his fault." His anger masked his concern, but I interpreted it as being a poor sport.

The young man aggressively held Bill's stare. Bill turned to me.

"Don't you get it, Peggy? They've been without water for days. They're drinking their own shit. There's a cholera outbreak."

"How do you know?"

"I read about it this morning in the newspaper. You weren't talking to me. I didn't say anything cuz I didn't know how bad it was."

"You're such a worrywart. We'll be fine."

Rumors had started to spread around the hostel that the borders could close any day now until the epidemic was under control. A fellow traveler from Australia described cholera. "It's bloody awful. First your stomach cramps from drinking the contaminated water. Then you get a bad case of the trots, which causes dehydration, so you drink more water, which you shit out again, and then you die. Well, you won't die, but lots of people will."

"How do you know this? Have you had cholera?" I questioned his veracity.

"No, but I've just come from Mali, where it's really bad. My advice is don't drink the water, don't eat prepared foods, and get the hell out of here." He picked up a jar. "Here, have some Vegemite." He put his finger in a brown paste, rubbed a little on a crispy cracker, and handed it to us. We tasted the salty morsel.

"An acquired taste, I'm sure. Thanks," I said. We dug into our packs for our own provisions, and Bill scooped the remaining peanut butter onto a cracker and offered it to him.

Early the next morning, we arrived by bus at the Algerian Consulate to apply for our visas. The line snaked out the door.

I had a pit in my stomach, an urge to eliminate. I turned to Bill and asked, "Do you think I have cholera?" Bill brushed off my question and got in line. *It's all in my head,* I told myself.

A soldier stood at the door, yelling something in Arabic. My palms sweated. People around me shouted in angry voices, raising their arms and waving papers.

"What the hell's going on?" Bill asked.

"I'll go find out. Save our place in line."

I asked a Western-looking French woman at the front of the line what the soldier had said.

"They're closing the border at noon today. Everyone is being checked very closely."

"Why?"

She looked around furtively, and said, "Le choléra, possible un coup."

"You were right, there's a cholera outbreak, and possibly a government overthrow."

Bill immediately wanted to leave. "Let's cross with just our passports."

Our American passports gave us an advantage at border crossings over the poorer countries in Africa, but I still worried about taking the risk of traveling without a visa.

"Let me ask a clerk inside." I wiggled to the front of the line, passed the guard, and squeezed into the small, chaotic room. I walked up to a window and in my most official voice said, "Je suis une Américaine. Je veux voir un representative des Etats-Unis."

Visually intimidated by my moxie, the young clerk nodded and backed into an office. "Oui, Mademoiselle. Un moment."

I signaled to Bill, who stood heads above the crowd, and motioned to him, mouthing *Hurry up!* He pushed his way through the throng.

A *gendarme* came out of the back office. "Passeporte." He put out his gloved hand, took Bill's passport, checked the photo, and stamped it. "How long?"

"A week. We're just passing through," he stammered.

He scribbled his signature and handed it back. "Okay." He looked at me and calmly said, "And yours, Mademoiselle?"

I gave him my passport. Licking his finger, he paged through each leaf: my student visa, last April's border stamps from Spain and Morocco, my photo and US citizenship information. He glanced up.

"Come with me." He took me to a back room.

I turned to Bill and pleaded with my eyes to help me, but he was stopped by a guard and told to wait.

"You have been in Morocco before? No?" A second officer, with more medals on his jacket than the first guy, questioned me from behind an old wooden desk in a sweltering room, an air conditioner humming and sweating in the single window.

I answered, "Yes."

"Why did you come back?"

"I'm traveling with my...umm...my friend." I couldn't lie and call Bill my husband, because my last name was different from his and my passport clearly stated that I wasn't married. I was less confident now. *What if Bill gets to leave and I have to stay?*

"I can't let you cross the border."

"Why?"

"State security." He slapped down my passport. I picked it up and the gendarme showed me the way out.

The French woman's words popped in my head: *Un coup.* There must be another threat on the king's life. Why did I ever come back to Morocco?

I turned back around. "Please, sir, I have to be in Algeria. I have friends waiting," I pleaded. I started to cry. He stopped.

"Show me your friends' address."

I nervously searched through my backpack, praying I had the letter. Next to my traveler's checks I found the letter from Marie-Paule's sister with her address in Algiers.

"You're lucky—you have a place to go." He stamped the Algerian visa in my passport, flaunting his power in front of his inferiors, and handed back my papers.

Regaining my composure, I profusely thanked the officer, telling him he was kind and stroking his ego, not wanting to piss him off. I walked away quickly, keeping a brisk pace, not looking behind me for fear they might change their minds.

Bill caught up. "Whoa, slow down. I almost thought we had another Ensenada situation," he said, referring to spring break when I had almost been thrown in jail.

"Why do I always get caught?" I yelled at him, remembering when the police had hauled me off.

* * *

Last Easter break, I had left Hussong's Cantina with an opened bottle of beer and sauntered down the main street of Ensenada, feeling cocky. "Vive Mexico! Vive!" I called, dizzy with love and freedom. It was my first time in Mexico and my first overnight with Bill.

Wearing a flowered baby-doll dress that showed off my long bare legs, my light brown hair flowing halfway down my back, I was the only girl hanging out with the frat guys. All of us were drinking while their dates shopped.

Bill stopped at a leather goods store and bought a pair of huaraches for himself and a brown leather cowboy hat with a braided band and three fringes hanging down the back for me. Putting it on, I felt like a million bucks...until we turned the corner. Two cops stood there with billy clubs in hand, guns in holsters.

Slyly, the frat guys slipped into a store and came out empty-handed, leaving their beers inside. "Get rid of your beer," one of them whispered.

I immediately dropped my beer in the gutter and kept walking straight to the van and climbed in.

The police followed. "Get out," the younger one said, pointing at me.

Bill stepped in front of him to prevent him from grabbing me, causing the other officer to run over.

"Señor, no hay problema." Bill reached into his wallet and offered him a *morbida,* a twenty-dollar bill, but they ignored him.

"The girl."

In front of everyone, the clean-shaven young policeman pulled me out of the van and questioned me. I lied to cover my ass. "No, I wasn't drinking. No, that's not my bottle."

The *policía* grabbed my arms, one on each side, and took me to the corner market.

"You lied, you littered your bottle, and your boyfriend insulted my integrity. I do not take bribes." The older, heavyset cop recited my offenses while the younger one called the station. "You are going to jail."

I cried and pleaded, telling him I was sorry. "I'll pick up litter in the streets. Please, I'm a teacher at home, please one more chance." All I could think of was the cattle prod they used in Mexican jails on Americans who had been caught with drugs or breaking the law in Mexico. *They'll rape and torture me.*

Bill and his friends followed us to the corner, but the cops turned them away at the market door and threatened to jail them if they tried to intercede on my behalf. I couldn't even talk to Bill. About twenty minutes passed, and the store phone rang. The younger policeman answered it and said something to the other officer.

Perhaps it was my tears or the respect Mexicans have for *la profesora*, or maybe the jails were full...I'll never know, but they let me go with a lesson. "We don't behave so badly in your country, so why do you think you can dishonor us in our country?"

✳ ✳ ✳

Once at a safe distance from the Algerian consulate, Bill hugged me and said, "Good job; you talked your way out of shit again."

Arm in arm, we continued to the limits of town.

On the dusty dirt road, some sweet little children with their father began following us and offered us "petit lait" from their buckets. They laughed as we scrunched our faces at the taste of the sour yogurt liquid from a communal ladle. *Now I remember why I came back to Morocco. I loved the people, their hospitality and the children.*

When we got to the *frontier*, it was closed. Everywhere in Morocco, places shut down in the blistering heat of the day, even the border patrol. We waited under a shady pepper tree outside a large military and police complex, encircled by a high white wall with barbed wire on top. Police cars and limousines entered and exited through a heavily guarded gate, behind which we could see a lush garden.

A young Arab man, around nineteen years old and dressed in Western garb—blue polo shirt and khaki pants—came out of a walk gate and greeted us, asking if he could practice his English. We invited him to sit, answering his schoolboy questions. "Where are you from? How old are you?" The boy was enamored with Bill's size and blond hair and wanted to touch Bill's hairy forearms and measure his size against Bill's standing back to back. Pleased with himself at having made American friends, he invited us to tea. "I live here. My father is the head guard. I will bring you tea." He left.

About fifteen minutes later, he returned through the walk gate holding a tray with a silver pot, three gold-etched glasses, and a bouquet of red, pink, and orange ranunculus. Holding the teapot high above each glass, he ceremoniously poured the mint tea.

"I have a surprise." He glanced around. From inside his pant pocket he pulled out a joint. "C'est le meilleur." He lit a match to the tightly rolled end, drew in a deep breath, and passed the joint to Bill.

"You must be crazy. We're outside police headquarters and you're smoking a joint with the head guard's son?" I hissed, keeping a smile on my face so as not to alarm the young Arab.

"You're so uptight, Peggy; he's taking hits too. He's not going to go rat on me." The young Arab passed the joint to me. I twirled my long braids between my fingers, refusing. Bill toked, holding in the smoke with a goofy grin, and exhaled. "You need this," he said as he passed me the joint.

Against my better judgment, I took a hit, and Bill snapped a photo.

"Why the hell did you take a picture? What if they confiscate your camera? You don't think they wouldn't throw your ass in jail too?"

Angry with myself for taking a hit and fearful of getting caught, I got up to leave. "If we get caught, Bill, it's over!"

I don't know if I meant our relationship would be over or my life would be over if left to rot in a Moroccan jail. Bill chuckled, shook the kid's hand, and left with me.

"Your eyes are bloodshot, and you reek like a stoner. How can we pass the border like this?" I accused him, as if I were innocent.

"Give it a rest, Peggy. No one saw us. And if they ask about my eyes, I'll tell them there's sand in my contacts."

Algerian child on outskirts of town

CHAPTER FORTY-FOUR

As-Salaam 'Alaykum

Salaam ali koum!

We made it to Algeria after a little problem at the border and are heading to see Marie-Paule's sister. Hope there's a letter waiting for me (hint, hint). The coastline around here, which we're exploring, is fantastic. No tourists, beautiful beaches, and one place had a whole Roman town in ruins, situated on a cliff above the sea!

ONCE IN ALGERIA, WE hitched a few slow, long-haul rides through rural areas, dry from the long drought, moving in and out of view of the ocean as it shimmered in the sunlight. With few accommodations for travelers, we camped on desolate beaches, amid Roman ruins, and above the rocky edges of an inland reservoir. Bill was impatient to get to Italy and Greece, and I could understand why. Algeria was a lot different from what I had expected. In my mind, I had envisioned not only a pristine coastline but also an interior of sand dunes amid verdant palms and crystal clear lakes in mountain valleys. But I was wrong. By avoiding tourists, we were also missing the most scenic places.

Hoping to find what I was looking for, I opened the map of Algeria. "There's a lake not far from here. Do you want to camp there?" Bill agreed.

Stopping in a dusty little town near the lake, we marched along an unpaved road strewn with litter and debris, stopped at a market, which was in the front room of someone's home, and bought some provisions for the night. I asked the old man how to get to the lake, and he motioned to a younger boy.

"Mon grand-père ne parle pas français. Follow me."

The barefoot boy, in ragged shorts and a torn shirt, had a grin that reached from ear to ear. Pretty soon, other children followed us up the road, past shanties and onto a mesa. The young boy stopped at the edge of town and pointed in the distance to where we could see rocks piled high, forming what looked to be a dam. Alone we set out across a barren area pockmarked with corrugated sheets of rusted metal, old cushions, and trash clustered in separate piles.

"Must be their dump," Bill surmised. As we got closer, we noticed holes in the ground, large holes covered by burlap or other material.

"Bill, I saw a head pop out of one of those holes." I had the feeling we were being watched.

"I think I saw one too," Bill said quietly.

A beautiful face of a child peeped out of a hole, her big brown eyes gazing at us. She emerged in her tattered dress and put her hand out. My heart broke. This was her home. I fished in my pockets for something to give her and came up with a few coins, not worth even a penny. She grabbed them and retreated into the dark crevice.

As we continued in the sweltering heat, other denizens of the hole-dwelling community peeked out of their hovels, reminding me of gophers with their furtive looks. I tried to smile at them, but they quickly disappeared back into the ground when I made eye contact.

"I can't believe people live like this," I said to Bill as we made our way up the winding road to the reservoir.

"It's sad That's all they have." He paused and said, "Try not to think about it."

At the lake, we set up camp under the lone tree. Bill played around with his camera settings, taking photos of me walking along the edge of the reservoir, silhouetted in the setting sun. The heat was oppressive. I took off my long pants and searched for a place where I could dip in the water to cool down, but the steep sides of the reservoir prevented any contact with the water. By nightfall, we were in our sleeping bags, curled together, feeling fortunate that we weren't living in a hole.

The next day, we left food on the rocks near the sad little town of holes and circumvented the area, averting our eyes so as not to make contact with anyone. I couldn't bear seeing their sorrow.

Later that afternoon, after hours of hitchhiking, we stopped along the coast and climbed down an embankment through some brush and set up camp on a deserted beach where the temperature was bearable and we could dip in the ocean.

Just before sunset, Bill had a campfire going and I was cutting vegetables to put in the boiling water when we heard motorcycles on the road above us.

A few minutes later, two young men about our age emerged from the brush. "As-salaam alaykum!" they called. "We saw the fire. What are you doing here?"

"Uhh, we're camping." Taken aback by the intrusion, Bill puffed up.

"Don't worry, it's good. We'll camp too."

They brought down their saddlebags from their bikes and set up camp next to us, eager to use our campfire.

"You're American?" one of the men asked.

"Yes."

"Ahhh, we love Americans. You have any Marlboros?"

Neither Bill nor I smoked cigarettes, so Bill offered them a beer, which they gladly accepted, along with our meager meal.

We talked into the night, using French and hand signs to communicate, singing Beatles songs and country-and-western tunes. The Arabs recited poetry, using theatrics to express their love—hands over hearts, knees bent, and expressive eyes—as if they were in a silent movie.

They spoke of their dreams, of a future when they would be free like us. "We can't say these things in our country. It's treason. But with you, we are safe."

Unlike American men, they openly flirted with me, even around Bill. The younger one called me *Hamama*, an Arabic endearment, which loosely translates to "my little pigeon." He spoke softly to me in French, so Bill could not understand. "If I could marry you, I will make you my equal. When I drive my motorcycle, you will ride next to me, not like the other Arabs who treat their wives as slaves."

I laughed at his audacity to assume I would be his wife but asked, "Why are the women here treated like property?"

"Hamama, it will take years to change."

I think of him now and wonder if the years have changed him. Does his wife ride next to him in the little sidecar, as he promised me?

Arab men join us at the beach

CHAPTER FORTY-FIVE

Black Panthers

Le 3 juillet
Dear Mom,

   We got to Marie-Paule's sister's place, but she and her husband were in Bordeaux! Bummer, except we stayed with their friends who took us in and fed us. Really great people. They live close to the Black Panthers, so we telephoned them last night to see if we could meet Eldridge Cleaver and his comrades sometime today. I called this morning and couldn't get ahold of any of them so I felt funny just dropping by.

HAVING ONLY THE ADDRESS and no idea where to go, we decided to take a taxi to Cité des Asphodèles Batiment B, Apt. 17, El Biar, a suburb of Algiers. The cab driver couldn't locate the apartment and let us off in a maze of married student housing, rows and rows of apartment buildings. By chance we bumped into building B, climbed the outside staircase leading to the second floor, and found Marie-Hélène's apartment, #17.

A note was tacked to her door: "Peggy, je regrette de ne pas vous voir. Je suis a Bordeaux avec ma famille pour eux montrer le bebe, Maude. Frappez à la porte à gauche. Michel et sa femme, Colette, vous invitent. Des gross bises, Marie-Hélène."

I looked at the note and then looked at Bill, standing at the top of the narrow staircase, loaded down with his backpack, camera, and my bag.

"Soooo? What does it say?" he asked.

"Apparently, Marie-Hélène, you know, Marie-Paule's sister, returned to France with her new baby…" I fiddled with the note, trying to decipher it. The damn French cursive was so hard to read with its curlicues and half-formed letters. "But I think it says to knock on the door to the left and some of her friends, Michel and Colette, will let us stay."

"Knock; I'm tired from carrying all this weight."

The door was only a few feet away, and the walls thin enough that we could hear a party going on inside.

We knocked. The door swung open and a burly, dark-haired man stood there wearing a white chef's apron over his jeans and holding barbecue utensils. "Hey, you must be zee Americans, come in, come in." He put out his free hand to shake. "Michel." We entered.

"Everybodee, zis is…what ees your name?"

"I'm Peggy, this is Bill."

"Oh yes, Piggy and Beel. Enchanté!"

After setting down our backpacks, we joined their small dinner party.

"Do you like bulls' balls?" our host questioned me, holding the knife high as he thinly sliced the meat.

"You mean Rocky Mountain oysters?" Bill was quicker than I was to catch on.

I shuddered, "Ooooh no, I don't eat them," which only made the teasing worse. The French loved to shock Americans with their sophisticated palate. To be a good sport, I tasted one and graciously approved.

Then came the after-dinner requisite political discussion. "You are Marxists, no?"

"No, Communists aren't allowed in our country." Bill naively jumped into the conversation feet first.

"Oh really? I thought you lived in a free country."

The French guests quizzed us on our political stance. Michel pulled in a deep breath on his Gauloise.

"We get to vote," Bill said, but then he started to back-pedal. "Well, we don't agree with everything, like we did protest against the war. Kinda. We got pulled over by the police during the riots." Bill attempted to sound more radical than his ROTC self.

"You know zee Black Panthers? Huey Newton, Eldridge Cleaver?" Michel asked, showing off his knowledge of American radicals.

"Sure, we know them; well, not personally, but we know who they are." I hated to sound so uninformed, so I tried to act cool.

"Well, they're living here in Algiers with two friends, more Black Panthers. Do you want to meet them?"

"Wow, I'd love to meet them." I was quick to answer, and not just to be agreeable. I thought it would be really mind-blowing to meet the leader of the Black Panthers. Bill didn't seem so hot on the idea.

Michel handed me a paper. "Here's zee number."

"Thanks, I'll give them a call tomorrow, you know, just to say hi, from some fellow Americans."

Colette handed me the phone. "Oh no, call them now. You can use our phone." They had called my bluff.

I carefully dialed the number and waited, noting the foreign sound of the ring.

"Allo?" To my surprise, someone answered!

"Hi, this is Peggy O'Toole from Santa Barbara, you know, California, Isla Vista, where we burned the bank." I tried to play the riot card, acted like I was a member of the Students for Democratic Society. "You know, Isla Vista, Angela Davis was just there, people like you." On the other end of the line was only silence, so I continued. "I'm one of you, against the establishment."

"Whatcha want?" The voice was gruff.

"Oh, nothing, I'm in the area and wanted to say hi, maybe stop by?"

"Call back tomorrow. No one's here." The receiver went dead.

I hung up the phone, all smiles.

"Well, what happened?" Bill and the others wanted to know.

"I talked to one of the Black Panthers. Eldridge and Huey aren't in right now, so I'm supposed to call back tomorrow."

"Ahh, too bad" was the communal response from the French.

Bill gave me the evil eye. "You're crazy, Peggy. They're wanted for murder and skipped their trial. I thought the French guy was bullshitting. You really talked to them?"

"Yeah, I'll call back tomorrow," I said defiantly, eager to win the approval of the French while contradicting Bill.

The next morning, I called back and the phone rang and rang without an answer, so we packed up, said good-bye, and headed to the beach.

Algerian baker and family

CHAPTER FORTY-SIX

Letter from Algeria

July 13, 1971
Dear Mom!

It seems like I can't leave Algeria. I've met the most beautiful families and people. They are so friendly! Every time we start to leave a place, someone else invites us to stay.

This nice Arab man invited us to dinner—we ate for hours, couscous, which is a grain steamed with vegetables, meat, hot sauce, and olive oil. (Sorry I can't be too descriptive, it's the second time I've vomited after eating the stuff.) You just can't say no when they offer food. Then they served hot pepper salads, fried fish in tomato sauce, potatoes (I just didn't stop), chicken, lamb... and on top of that the husband is a baker, so we had all kinds of bread. The wife is a wife, a full time job here. This family is a little modernized, but the women still wait until after the men are fed before they eat. The next day we went to his Aunt's house at the beach, again more food, but I refrained from overindulging. The last invitation was for a circumcision celebration, which is a big deal over here. I tried my feet at Arab dancing; it's a belly dance *usually done by the typical 5 feet tall, 180 pound woman—not quite my style, but I tried.*

THE MORNING AFTER ELDRIDGE didn't pick up the phone, Bill and I headed to the beach on the outskirts of Algiers. Walking down a dirt road looking for beach access, past palm trees and crumbling clay walls, we heard a voice. "Allo, friend, would you like to come in for tea?" A man dressed in traditional robes stood under an archway leading to an enclosed community. "Please, I invite you."

Bill hesitated.

I encouraged him. "Let's go."

The Arab smiled and motioned with his hand to follow him. We meandered through a labyrinth of mud brick buildings, ducking under overhead connections of the houses, and climbed down steep stairs into a garden foyer, light sprinkling through overhangs and vines.

"I will tell my wife to prepare the tea." He opened the heavy studded door, slipped out of his babouches, and disappeared.

"Could you find your way out of here, Peggy?" Bill leaned his pack against a mossy wall.

"The Arabs are hospitable, don't worry. This happens all the time." Of course I didn't tell him that sometimes the consequences aren't so good, like the train station incident or the sheik affair.

Within minutes he returned, saying, "Please, please. Come in." He showed us to a room with couches surrounding the perimeter and colorful cushions and pillows for backrests.

Neighbors started to stop by, and our host introduced us as his friends.

"American?" the friends asked.

"Yes, we're from America," Bill happily replied in English.

"Ahh, very good. We love Americans."

From my experience, Moroccans and Algerians treated foreigners as honored guests and seemed genuinely delighted to entertain travelers from as far away as America. Most of these people had never left their birthplace, so it was both a matter of pride—showing off that they had made American friends—and a genuine interest in our culture. I'm not sure if they treated each other with as much kindness. Was it our skin color? Did they look at us as if we walked out of their TV sets, which constantly blared in the background, even in the poorest of areas?

A beautiful young woman entered the room with a large brass tray set with a silver teapot and a half dozen small gold-rimmed glasses. Setting it down, she averted her eyes and slipped back out the door.

"To our American friends," our host said as he lifted the teapot high into the air and let a stream of steaming hot tea pour down into each glass. He handed Bill and me each a glass of hot mint tea while the other men reached for their own.

There was a long silence with smiles and nods.

"C'est très bon. Merci," I said, putting my glass down. Bill took this as a sign that it was time to leave and got up.

"Oh non! Il faut rester pour le couscous." Our host insisted we stay for dinner and poured more tea, this time initiating a conversation with Bill. "You are American? Big one, you're a big American boy. Where from?"

Bill gave him his famous broad smile. "I'm from California."

"Oh, yes, we have family in California. Big families, lots of children. Do you have children?"

This was a tricky question since sex out of wedlock is punishable by death in Algeria, so I answered for Bill: "No, we don't yet, but my mother has ten children."

"Your mother has ten children! I love your mother. Where is your mother?"

"She's in California."

He slapped Bill on the back. "You have a good woman. You can make many babies with her." He translated something into Arabic and the men all laughed heartily, patting Bill on the back.

Feeling uncomfortable with the men joking about making babies, I went into the kitchen. The wife was stirring the couscous while children played on the floor and the other women, presumably relatives, jabbered and peeled vegetables. I stood shyly in the doorway until one of the younger women invited me to join them. She brought me a scarf, which they tied around my head and gave me a little white veil with blue crocheted trim.

"Belly dancing?" She shook her belly, moving her hips sensually around and around.

"Okay," I tentatively agreed as the women pulled me into their circle.

Surrounded by mavens with nimble fingers tapping cymbals to an inner rhythm, the young girl took my hands, shimmying from hip to shoulder, and tried to teach my long, skinny body how to shake rhythmically.

Laughing, the mother pointed to my narrow torso and said, "Mange, mange."

At midday, the gentlemen invited me to eat at their table while the women served us silently and ate the leftovers in the kitchen.

"I can eat with the women," I offered.

"No, you are our guest. You eat with the men. When our women turn fifty, they can eat with us."

"Why fifty?" I was curious what difference that made.

"When a woman turns fifty, she becomes a man. No more babies."

As we left, our host invited us for the next day to his sister's house on the beach. "Tomorrow, we celebrate my nephew's circumcision." He walked us partway back and pointed to her house. "It's the blue house, à demain."

That night, Bill and I slept in our sleeping bags on the beach. In the middle of the night, I dragged myself a few feet away from where we were sleeping and vomited in the cool sand, using the end of my towel to wipe my mouth. Barely back in the bag, I had another emergency and made it to the bush just in time to eliminate what I hoped was the rest of my dinner. I used the other corner of my towel. I returned and crawled in next to Bill and started to cry. I had never been so sick in my life.

"I think I have cholera. I drank the water in Morocco." And to prove the point, I heaved again, only to hear him groan, "That's disgusting."

I took a sip of the boiled water I kept nearby and wrapped myself in my towel, careful not to touch the corners. I sat up alone half the night sniffling and blowing on an unused corner of my towel, making sure I used the correct end for each unfortunate secretion.

Bill woke with the sunrise and took one look at my disheveled hair. "What the hell happened to you?"

"I think I have cholera. I've been up all night vomiting and shitting and blowing my nose. I feel terrible."

He took pity on me and said he was sorry. Then he noticed the towel that I had left to the side of the sleeping bags.

"Don't touch it! I used the corners."

"You used the corners? For everything?"

"Yeah, but a different corner for each thing. I was careful. I've got one corner left and I'm going to wash my face with it."

Bill looked at me incredulously. "What's with using the corners of your towel, Peggy?"

"Don't you use one corner of your towel to dry your bottom half and another to dry off your top? I just needed all four corners last night."

My mother had a system for the twelve people who lived in our house. She had to do the laundry daily, and it saved her a few loads if we remembered to use one edge of the towel for our top and one for our bottom. I tried to explain this to Bill, but unless you come from a large family, it's not easy to understand.

"Just remind me never to touch a corner of your towel," he said humorously. With that, Bill fixed me a cup of coffee and told me to stay in "bed" until I felt better.

Late that afternoon, I awoke to Bill gently poking my sleeping bag with his sandy foot, smiling and red-faced from a day frolicking at the beach and in the surf.

"Hey, do you feel like going to that circumcision party?"

"I've never been to one before, have you?"

"Of course not. No one I know celebrates a guy's dingy getting trimmed."

"Okay, I'll go. It'll be a cultural event."

The party was in full swing when we arrived, people eating and laughing, the stereo blaring Arabic music, children running around with sticks and rocks, and no one minding them.

Our host spotted us and came hurrying over, calling out, "Ahh, my American friends! Welcome, welcome." Everyone greeted us, wanting to shake our hands. The women took me into the kitchen, where once again they tied a scarf around my waist and one for my head. They wore beautiful caftans, headdresses, and silver bangles on their arms.

A girl about my age asked if I went to school and what I was studying. She spoke of her ambitions in science but worried about her future as a female at the university. She asked me to write to her, which I did. Her last letter came in 1972, informing me not to write her anymore, that my letters were being confiscated and communication with the West was forbidden. To this day, I wonder if she finished her degree in chemistry, if she was allowed to work, if she had freedom.

She pointed to my bare arm, took a bracelet off her wrist, and put it on me. "Keep it," she said with a smile.

Bill found me in the kitchen. "Hey, they want to show us the boy."

"What boy?"

"The one who got circumcised."

"He's a boy? Not a baby?"

"I'm not sure, but he's in that room, and everyone keeps going in and out."

I hesitated, watching the people emerging from the room to congratulate the father, grabbing his shoulder and kissing him from side to side.

"Come, come." Our host escorted us with his hand behind our backs into the darkened room.

The poor little boy, who had just turned twelve, was lying in pain on the bed under some light covers. "Look, he's a man now." The father ripped the covers back and proudly showed us his tiny penis, supported by two splints and some white adhesive tape. "He's okay," the father said, rubbing his son's head. "These are Americans," he said in Arabic to his son with such reverence. The little boy smiled weakly, and the father encouraged him to shake Bill's hand and to kiss me.

The culture treated circumcision as a sacrament, a time to rejoice and celebrate, but seeing the little boy's contorted face made me wonder. Was it pain, or was he ashamed to show a woman his penis? I was embarrassed to look at his naked body and projected my feelings onto him. Bill turned away, saying. "It's just too painful to look at."

Arab bargaining with Peggy

CHAPTER FORTY-SEVEN

Selling My Corduroy Jacket in the Kasbah

Dear Mom,
    I sold my corduroy jacket in the Kasbah, the old section of town. It was really funny bargaining with all these Arab men surrounding me. Bill got a picture of me. I got $7 for that old coat, which was just a burden in this hot climate...

I WAS STILL FEELING queasy from my night on the beach, sick as a dog from either the couscous or cholera. The temperature along the coast of North Africa kept increasing. It must have been ninety degrees as we hitchhiked to the edge of town.

"Bill, I can't carry all this crap on my back. It's so hot out." Earlier I'd had chills; now I was sleeveless and sweating.

His clear blue eyes showed concern; he could tell I was still weak from being so sick. "You're not looking so good, Peggy. I'll carry some of your stuff."

I gratefully agreed and let my backpack drop to the ground. He untied my sleeping bag from the top of my pack and handed me my jacket, which had been stuffed under the rope. He retied my bag onto his already overloaded pack.

"Thanks, Bill." I felt good about having him with me on this arduous trip, but it was still difficult for me to tell him so. I wish I had said, "I love you," because at that point in the journey I truly did. But we never talked about feelings. We were always in motion—hiking, sailing, playing volleyball—that's how we communicated, by being active together.

I started to put my burnt sienna corduroy jacket back in my bag when he suggested, "Why don't you just get rid of that old coat?"

I held the coat up, remembering the hours I had spent at the old Singer sewing machine, fitting the pattern onto the material, cutting each piece out, and trying to match the sleeves to the armholes.

"I made this coat, Bill." Sentiment can be a heavy and burdensome thing. I reconsidered. "But I could sell it in the medina."

Having just left Algiers on the road to Tunisia we made a slight detour to the Kasbah in the old fortified city.

Bill and I strolled the aisles of spices, olives, fruits, and vegetables and passed quickly by the butchers with slabs of meat hanging from hooks and live fowl lying on the counter with a rope tied around their legs. We turned down a lane with traditional items: djellabas, scarves, and babouches. Then we curved around to the metalwork, wood carvings, and furniture, and at last found the clothing stalls, filled with used clothes from Western countries and new items packaged in cellophane, and rows of men's dress shoes and ladies' high heels.

I pulled my old corduroy jacket from my backpack and asked a gentleman if he was interested in buying it.

"Voulez-vous achêter mon manteau?" A few other men standing nearby overheard me. Before I knew it, Arab men surrounded me, grabbing for my jacket. I held it high over my head saying, "Attendez! Attendez!" hoping they would wait their turn. "Cinquante dinari, s'il vous plait." I gave a fair price—under ten dollars.

"Fifty dinari!" the first man agreed.

"Fifty-five dinari!" another man offered higher.

A short, well-built man in a blue shirt waved sixty dinari in front of my face, and others began to brandish bills, shouting out their prices.

The heat and crush of the men's bodies and the smell of sweet detergent covering their spicy human odor quickened my decision. I took the money from one of the hands fluttering bills in front of me. The man grabbed the jacket and the swarm of men now surrounded the new owner. Bill laughed and took photos of the melee. I counted my money, sixty dinari (about seven dollars), slipped the bills into my leather purse, slung it across my shoulder, and smiled at Bill with my success.

As we walked away, several vendors followed us. "You sell your blue jeans? I give you a good price." Bill grinned and said no. Another one approached him with money. The merchants persistently tried to buy our clothes. Ragamuffin children chased after us, and the women's smiling eyes peered out behind veils, curious about the procession.

Politely but emphatically, Bill turned around and put his hand up. "Stop. We don't have anything to sell." The men turned away and the children stopped, intimidated by this large, blond man. Then one little boy snuck up behind Bill and petted the blond hair that covered his arm. Surprised, Bill turned. He looked at the mischievous little boy, knelt down in the dirt, and let him and all the children pet his hairy arm. This time it was my turn to take the photo.

Camel driver in Tunis

CHAPTER FORTY-EIGHT

Safe

Mom,

I'm glad I sold my jacket. The pack and sleeping bag that I got before Bill and I started our journey is enough to carry. It's worth it though to be able to camp and not bother too much with hotels. It's safe too cuz I'm with a guy—and don't worry Mom, I'm being a good girl and who cares what the aunts say! Actually every girl should have a protector against these Arabs and Europeans, even though I find them attractive, I'm wary about what they want.

"WHAT WILL I TELL my sisters?" I'd heard this refrain since I was a child and now could only imagine my mother saying it to Nola when she figured out I was sleeping with Bill. I could hear Mom say, as if in the same room, "Where did I go wrong?"

I don't think my mother did go wrong. She instilled morals and guidelines, but I chose only the ones I wanted. As a teenager, I blasted my transistor radio and sang along with Bob Dylan, "The times they are a changin'," and Mom would answer, "Phooey, some things never change," to which I would shoot back, "Mom, you have morals till you change them." Our clashes were few, because more than anything I wanted to please her, to be a "good girl." So I put a spin on my sin. Traveling with a guy was safer in Arab countries, or so I thought.

It was mid-July when we arrived in Tunis, the capital of Tunisia. We had plans to hurry on to Italy by the fifteenth, pick up mail at the American Express office, and have enough time to tour the Mediterranean countries before heading back to France to meet my brother and his wife in late August. We kept moving, meeting people along the way but never staying long enough in one spot to get to know the country and the people. We had no schedule and no reservations, but both Bill and I wanted to cover a lot of territory since we didn't know if the chance would ever come again to see the world.

Our relationship had mellowed into companionship, a comfortable fit of knowing each other's idiosyncrasies and giving in when necessary. I came to the conclusion that I was not in love with Bill nor could I fall in love with him again. Yet I liked him a lot and needed him, and not just for protection. We had fun together, got along most of the time, and agreed on almost everything that had to do with travel. I left sex to chance. If we zipped our sleeping bags together and it felt right, then we had sex.

The first night in Tunis, we met some Tunisian students who invited us to stay with them at their brother's house. Bill and I both agreed that sleeping in a bed would be a decadent pleasure, so we accepted.

After an evening in town, we sauntered back to the brother's house and found three Tunisian men in their twenties sitting around a TV set, watching a black-and-white gangster movie. One of the men got up and showed us to a back room with a single bed. "It's my brother's room. He won't be home tonight."

We got ready for bed and soon fell asleep exhausted from our travels.

Early the next morning, before the call to prayer, I awoke to the light touch of Bill's foot against mine. It was still semidark outside, and the time felt right. I gently nudged back. He began to caress me along my leg, and I slowly gave in to a rhythmic move to entice him to do more. I heard Bill snort, that loud noise that only comes when one is in a deep sleep. I turned toward him as he shifted and curled up next to me, sound asleep. I sat up in bed and screamed! The brother had returned and crawled into his bed and was now lying between my legs.

Startled by my scream, Bill woke up. "What's the matter?" The Arab jumped up and defiantly stood at the foot of the bed.

"Bill, do something! He's been rubbing my leg and I thought it was you."

Bill leaped from the bed half naked and attempted to grab the guy, but he backed away shouting, "C'est mon lit. Elle est une putain, c'est ma putain aussi!"

I grabbed my clothes from off the floor and covered myself. "Bill, get him out of here! He says it's his bed and I'm a whore, so I'm his whore too."

Bill rose up, almost twice the size of the intruder, and pushed him out the door. He lashed back in Arabic, and I'm only glad I couldn't understand what he said.

We dressed in minutes, grabbed our bags, and left the house. Unfortunately, that was our last memory of Tunisia. We caught the ferry to Sicily that day.

Alley near port in Palermo

CHAPTER FORTY-NINE

Mob Killings and Fast Cars

Le 20 juillet
Dear Mom,

Sorry my correspondence has dropped off. Once we left Africa we haven't stopped much, trying to get to Greece. I haven't gotten any of your letters. Write me c/o American Express Athens, Greece. I haven't been writing much, but I think of you all. Tell Terry and Vicki we are still planning on meeting them in Paris late August. Love, Peggy

THE FERRY FROM TUNIS to Palermo took more than twelve hours. We arrived late at night in the Sicilian city and found a cheap hotel in an alleyway near the harbor. The next morning, we awoke to a sunny day in a charming old part of town. We walked down the winding road to an outdoor café overlooking the harbor where we ordered coffee, not mint tea. It was like returning home. Perhaps it was the way the Sicilians dressed or their language that sounded familiar to our ear since it was similar to French and Spanish, or maybe it was the food, which was so recognizable to Americans: pizza and spaghetti. Undeniably, as much as I had loved being in North Africa, I was relieved to be in a world that I understood better.

It was idyllic...until Bill opened the International Tribune and read the headlines: "Leggio flees—accused of the murder of the minister, Antonio Scalione. Mob shooting in Palermo connected to up-coming trial." In small print was a warning to tourists to be aware of violence in Palermo. The latest shooting was a drive-by down some dark alley.

"Bill, that's disturbing. Do you still want to stay here?"

"No, let's get out of the city. I wanted to see the country-side anyhow." He didn't admit to being afraid, but he didn't object to leaving either.

We got our packs from the little hotel, paid our bill, and headed out of town. The first car to pick us up was a maroon race car with decals driven by an Italian race car driver. He had a thin dark face with a prominent nose and slick black hair.

"Ciao, you American? Where you go?"

"We're just heading out of town. Going to a smaller village."

"Ahh, out for a ride?"

"Si."

He told us to get in, revved the engine, and peeled out onto the road, climbing and turning along the beautiful forested coastline with sparkling azure waters below the high cliffs.

"Zees ees a very goot car. Non? I have won many times." He turned to look at Bill and introduced himself. "I am Pietro. I race cars for a living. Do you like to go fast?"

Before we answered his question, he put his foot to the floor. We careened around corners, full throttle on the straightaways. Scrunched in the backseat between our packs, I had nothing to hold on to. Bill sat low in the passenger seat clutching the front, bracing himself.

"Tell him to slow down," I yelled over the noise of the engine.

Bill attempted Spanish to tell him to slow down: "Mas despacio!"

Ignoring our pleas, he kept his eyes connected to the road, his hands glued to the steering wheel, and his foot on the pedal. Surely, I was on the road to my own death.

"Eets okay," he reassured us, clicking the gears increasing the speed. The tires clung to the road as he whipped around a bend, taking a wide berth into the oncoming lane.

Then an unusual thing happened. I gave up trying to control the situation, lapsed into a carefree impulse, and enjoyed the ride. My life was out of my hands. During my whole life I had been keeping things under control, weighing what to say and do. I never trusted other people to take care of things for me; I was always in charge. For a moment, I let go.

Suddenly, Pietro swerved into a gravel parking area in front of a café perched at the top of a hill. Shaken from the ride, I got out of the backseat and crumpled, fearful to continue. A cat has nine lives, and I had already spent several of mine hitchhiking.

Yet Bill was exhilarated. Towering over the young Italian, Bill put out his hand to shake. "Bravo!"

The Italian smiled and offered, "Un espresso?" We accepted. Pietro was small of stature but strode with confidence toward the small, dark bar attached to a lace-curtained restaurant.

"Bill, I don't want to go any farther with Pietro."

"Why not? He's a good driver."

I sipped my coffee and tried to think of a better reason than being scared to death of crashing on some unknown road in Sicily.

"I just don't want to risk it. One time's enough. Don't you want to get to Greece? We can catch a bus to Messina." Again, I took control of the situation.

"Okay. You're right. We're running short on time if we want to see everything before meeting your brother in Paris."

Pietro didn't seem to care when we left the bar. We hopped a local bus to Messina and caught the night ferry. Sicily was a stepping-stone to Italy.

Bill posing as Neptune

CHAPTER FIFTY

Caught in Stone

July 30, 1971
Dear Nola,

We visited the ruins in Pompeii. Do you remember the couple kissing? We didn't see much of Italy, just Amalfi coast, which is beautiful. We went to the island of Capri like you suggested, and had a good time. Leaving soon on the ferry to Greece. Tell Mom I'm fine.

IT WAS THE EGG left on the table, not the contorted or fleeing bodies set in stone, but an egg that was to have been someone's breakfast, that had the greatest effect on me.

Bill and I toured the ruins of Pompeii on a clear summer day when Mt. Vesuvius could be seen in the distance, shrouded by the mist of the heat. We walked the cobblestone paths and peered into the last moments of life, voyeurs of the past.

The frozen family lay curled up in the comfort of their small room, the child in fetal position between his mother and father. *A blessing to die in your sleep,* I thought. *Or was it?*

The table was set, a bowl and that egg…why couldn't I get past the egg? I viewed the horrific plaster casts that caught the child fleeing in terror and the man and woman trapped in an eternal embrace of despair. We passed a pile of human skulls and bones displayed with a scientific explanation of how the ash mummified the remains.

"Did you see that egg back there? It was perfectly preserved."

"Yeah, but what about the dog? It's cool to see a Roman town preserved like this, amazing," Bill said as he stood reading the information in his guidebook.

"They really didn't know what hit them. They had food out for breakfast," I continued.

Why I have such a clear image of the egg is a bit of an enigma. Why not the people? No one was ready for the disaster; no one expected it would happen then. Everyone planned that the next day would be the same as the day before, and so the table was set. I find it sad that the little boy didn't wake up between his parents and run to the table to have his breakfast before going outside to play with his dog and catch the neighbor kissing his girlfriend. His egg was still on the table.

Back on the road, standing on a rocky ledge above the Amalfi Coast, I gazed into the crystal green waters, wishing we had more time to spend in Italy, but Bill was bent on getting to Greece. I looked at him standing on the side of the road, his thumb out, anxious to cover the miles toward Brindisi, where we could make the channel crossing. He looked like he was cut from stone, a Greek god: tall, curly blond hair, strong jawbone, wide shoulders, small waist, and a tight butt.

"Bill, let's just stay one more night. I want to see the Island of Capri."

"That's for tourists."

"Yeah, I know. I remember hearing the song as a kid. It's an island; maybe we can sail over."

* * *

With Bill, I had a strong argument when it came to anything to do with the ocean or boats. When we were in college, Bill had convinced me to buy a sailboat with him, a Lido 14 named *Nifty*, only the N had fallen off so we called it *Iffy*. There is a superstition that it's bad luck to change a boat's name, so we left it as is. We trailered the little fiberglass boat to the harbor and sailed around the other boats, getting our sea legs and checking out the boat's rigging and sails. We deemed it seaworthy. The next day, we planned our excursion out onto the ocean, packed our tuna sandwiches and beer, hooked the boat and trailer to Bill's van, and took off, driving down Hollister Avenue. Jethro Tull was blaring on the radio, and the day was sunny with light winds. Then I noticed another trailered Lido 14 zipping ahead of us on the road, but not attached to a vehicle. My first thought was, *Hey, a boat just like ours!* Iffy continued past us, picking up speed, and Bill let out the proverbial "*Oh shiiiiit!*" as we helplessly watched it cross the divider and ram into the lawn of Raytheon's corporate office.

* * *

Sweat beads formed on Bill's forehead as he stood on the black asphalt, waiting for the ride that would carry us closer to Greece, home of the Olympian gods. "Okay, let's pack it in this morning and go for a swim."

In town there were rows of boats going out to the Island of Capri, so we hopped on the cheapest excursion and headed to the romantic island, jammed like kids on a carnival ride with our packs between our legs.

The ocean spray did its magic, and we were laughing with the other tourists, humming along with the canned song, Frank Sinatra crooning, "Where we met on the Isle of Capri."

Out on the rocky island, we climbed the stairs to the Blue Grotto lookout and continued past the barriers to a secluded beach on the other side. Bill and I jumped off the rocks into the ocean, refreshing our bodies in the cool, deep waters, and dried in the sun. On the way back, I fell asleep on Bill's shoulder, listening to the white noise of slapping waves and Italian conversations.

The next day, we were back on the road to Brindisi, making it to the seaside port in time to catch the night ferry to Greece, home to my big California boyfriend, who identified with all the Greek gods. I loved him.

Greek Orthodox priest

Chapter Fifty-One

Greek Cats

Le 2 âout
Dear Corina,

    How's life at home? Hope vacation time hasn't left you alone to fend for yourself and the little ones. The Greek cats are all right—I know you'd enjoy roughing it here on the rocky islands. Last few days we spent in a small town on a little island. The longhaired, bearded priest let us sleep in the schoolhouse overlooking the ocean. It took an hour to walk down to the shore on these incredibly steep stairs and trails that wound through the village. Met some vacationing Greek families on the beach who invited us to spend a couple of days with them, good food included! At night a fisherman played his accordion from his boat on the water while the Greeks danced on the beach.

    If any of the family wants to write tell them to send cards, letters, money (just kidding) to me c/o Am Express, Istanbul, Turkey. We might be back to Athens to collect mail; none was there when we left on the 26ᵗʰ.

I WROTE A POSTCARD to my cat, Corina. Why not? No one had written me a single letter since I had started my travels with Bill more than two months ago. I missed my family and needed contact with them. I worried I was slipping into another world.

On the ferry from Brindisi to Athens, Gypsy families took over the upper deck—the women dancing, the men singing and playing the mandolin, and the children running wild. The Gypsies were like the Irish in that way: one big family. I wanted to join them but stood by tapping my feet, wishing it were my family traveling the seas.

The boat docked in Athens early the next morning, and a blast of warm air presaged a heat spell. Bill and I could barely endure the high temperature and pollution, so we sought respite in a park, stumbling upon a Bacchanal Festival. Rows of picnic tables were laden with food on red-checkered tablecloths—baklava, moussaka, spanakopita, dolma, and olives. A man in a black beret and striped shirt invited us to join him and his friends to taste their homemade retsina. He handed Bill the first jug to taste. Bill tipped back the clay vessel like a pro, took a swig, and wiped his hand over his mouth, letting out a choking cough. The burly group of men cried out, "It's good, no?" Bill gave a thumbs-up. The next old Greek handed him his brew, and so on, until Bill sat down and passed a jar to me. "Your turn, Peggy. I can't take any more."

I tried a nip and spit it out; it tasted like Pine Sol. "I prefer ouzo," I said. To please me, the man's wife handed me her glass, and the gentleman slowly poured the clear liquid into the bottom. Then he added water to make a cloudy mix of licorice alcohol.

After spending a few hours under the shade of the picnic area, we left—a little tipsy—and climbed the stairs to the Acropolis, high above the overcrowded streets, layered in smog. The juxtaposition of ancient and modern disheartened me; the crowds distracted from the experience. It wasn't until the next day when we drove to Mount Parnassus, home to the gods and the oracle at Delphi, that I discovered the Greece of my childhood dreams.

The fresh mountain air and stillness was a relief from the bustle and heat of the city. Amid the ruins, our guide detailed the history of the oracle, the battles of the Greek gods, and the Peloponnesian Wars. Bill was in his element, but I lost interest and wandered away from the group to sit alone in the amphitheater and ponder the powers of the oracles.

A woman had once told me, "You're like us—you have the powers of a medium," which both intrigued and scared me. My high school friend Carmen and I would call down spirits with the Ouija board until my father caught us in my attic bedroom and declared, "You're selling your soul to the devil. The Ouija board will never work in my house." And it didn't; my father was that powerful. But that didn't stop me from delving into the occult.

Standing on the ancient stones, I opened my arms to the universe and recited a prayer to connect to the other world, to my grandpa, my father, my sister, somebody in my family whom I could reach. Bill found me and snapped a photo. He took the stage, posed as a Greek god, and I photographed him. The mystery vanished.

After leaving the mainland, Bill and I decided to avoid the island of Mykonos, with its nightlife and celebrity viewing. Instead we booked a passage to Melos, a smaller island with no tourists. Disembarking with the villagers carrying their bundles of goods, farming tools, and fishing nets, we walked down the gangplank to questioning looks from the crew.

I too questioned our decision to skip Mykonos as we schlepped our bags up eight hundred meters of steps carved into the side of the hill. Feral cats roamed in the rocks and scurried down alleyways, spreading fish bones in their wake and guardedly eating the heads, scratching at each other, sending low, rumbling feline warnings not to trespass.

The cobblestone streets were lined with whitewashed homes and blue-tiled roofs. A bearded priest saw us wandering and offered us a place to stay in the schoolroom attached to the Orthodox church overlooking the Aegean Sea far below.

While laying out our sleeping bags on the cold, dusty cement floor, I confided in Bill. "I've had some pretty weird dreams."

"You're just tripping on the medication you're taking for your earache," he interrupted. He changed the subject. "Do you want to go to the beach tomorrow?"

In the schoolroom, each empty desk, piled in the corner for summer vacation, had a story of a child, my story. The custodian's closet in the corner held the secret of Carter, the mentally retarded custodian, who invited me to eat with him at lunchtime and then tried to lock me in the dark closet with the mops and buckets. I couldn't tell Sister Stephanie, my seventh grade teacher, because I didn't want to get Carter in trouble. I had been taught to be kind to those less fortunate, and he was less fortunate than me.

I had been having vivid dreams, more like nightmares, in which I was trying to get somewhere and running into dead ends, looking for Dad and Shereen, only to have them disappear. I didn't know if Bill was right. Maybe the hallucinations had been caused by the antibiotics; or the fever I'd had since Morocco; or my active mind, always alert for danger; or my loss of contact with home. At night, as my body fell asleep, I felt my soul creep out like a teenager escaping through the bedroom window for a nocturnal adventure. My mind traveled and twisted the day's events, taking me to the edge of a cliff, looking across the gorge to the ancient town of Constantine, plunging into blue grottos. I looked for Shereen—I knew that if I could get to the other side of the ravine, I would find her.

Something fell. A black feline scurried out the broken window, tipping a chair.

"Bill, can't you imagine the children in their desks?" He ignored me while futzing with his camera. "I think something bad happened here."

"You're making that up, Peggy."

"No, I can feel it."

Even though Bill was at my side every hour of the day and night, he couldn't guide me through my inner journey. My fantasizing, projections, and musings masked my pangs of despair. I was emerging into adulthood without my father, and I feared if I died in a foreign country, no one at home would know until days later. They'd look for me, like they searched for my father.

I closed my eyes and prayed the rosary but was again overtaken by dreams; I visualized myself entering a tunnel, spiraling like a screw, deeper into an unknown world. Lost.

The next morning, we left the schoolhouse to sleep on the beaches with Greek families who had set up camp. I felt better around people, living people, dancing on the shore, eating fresh fish, and drinking the licorice-tasting ouzo from the bottle. It reminded me of family parties where Grandpa played his fiddle while my uncles swung my aunts around and around. My godfather, Uncle Dick, would pick me up off my feet, spinning, spinning, and spinning.

"Grandpa Marren came over on the boat with only his fiddle," Mom would brag, "in hopes of making money to send home to Ireland to his mother and siblings." No one had ever mentioned Grandpa's father. As a young man, Grandpa had played the fiddle at the crossroads in Ireland, where family and friends met to socialize and dance and where the devil passed to snatch the bad children from their mothers. "Stop scaring the children, Dada," Mom would cry from the other room when he told us stories of fairies and witches. I loved Grandpa's world of banshees, leprechauns, and ghosts, the fabric of my childhood.

Bill and I fell asleep under the stars with the ocean lapping gently on the shore, accordion music and whiffs of cigars in the air.

I trusted Mom and my little sisters were feeding Corina and her kittens back home, but I had no real way of knowing. Perhaps my concern wasn't the cat being abandoned but that I was being forgotten.

Dr. Ozal, his wife, his adopted son, his mother and me

Chapter Fifty-Two

Turkey

Le 10 août
Happy Birthday, Mom,

I hear you are getting younger. Hope you get a fat birthday cake and lots of good times. Bill and I are sitting in a little restaurant in Istanbul. It's his mom's birthday too so we both send our best wishes homeward.

Bill and I landed in Turkey August 6 and what a great country—good food, beautiful countryside, and friendly people. The Arabs and the Turks are by far the kindest people I have met. A couple of nights ago we were invited to stay with a Turkish doctor's family. We really enjoyed their company and their neighbors too. The women donned me in Turkish scarves, an ancient apron, and a necklace. They love to give.

I've sent a number of packages home, which haven't been acknowledged. I'm wondering if I goofed up with customs. Let me know, okay?

Tomorrow we strike out for Northern Greece and Yugoslavia. Everything is going fine. Miss you and love you.

Our ship entered the narrow straits of the Sea of Marmara and slowly ferried into Istanbul at sunset. To the west, twinkling lights gave shape to tall buildings, domed churches, and minarets. To the east, across the Bosporus Strait, the large astral face of the moon peeked over the hills. An eerie glow of orange lit the sky as the moon grew and grew like the Christmas tree in *The Nutcracker*, gaining in size and brightness, appearing too close, too large, as it rolled up the hill, smiling.

"Hey, Bill. Is the moon bigger in Asia? It doesn't look real."

Just then, the ascending tide lifted the ferry, knocking it against the dock. The ropes strained and creaked as the deckhands shouted back and forth. My body tensed.

Bill remained calm. "It's a perigee moon, a super moon, closer to the earth so it seems larger. Some say it's a portent of earthquakes, volcanoes, any disaster connected to the moon's gravitational pull." He had a way of speaking as if what he said was the final word, end of conversation.

"And that's supposed to make me feel better? Kinda like 'Bad Moon Rising'?" I felt inferior because I didn't have any scientific information at my fingertips like he did, yet I had an uncanny intuition. Something felt wrong, but I was unable to pinpoint or speak of my malaise.

"Look closely." I turned back to face the lunar orb, seeing the man in the moon, who looked like Jesus. Bill put his arm over my shoulder as if instructing a child. "Astronauts are up there collecting data as we speak."

"Really?" I feigned interest. "Where were you last year when we first landed on the moon?" I asked coyly.

"Huntington Beach with my mom. Where were you?"

"I was in Isla Vista at the Red House," I said, knowing he would be jealous. The Red House was infamous for wild parties, sex, and drugs. "I watched the landing with the sound off on Bemis's big TV, listening to Jimi Hendrix."

"You know Bemis?" I let the question float into the wind, pleased to have riled him.

With the ship securely tied off, we disembarked, struggling with our overstuffed packs, loose items of clothing, and souvenirs trailing off the back. The customs agent searched us, stamped our passports, and told us not to reenter Greece due to the ongoing conflict between the countries.

"We have to cross Greece!"

He ignored my pleas, taking pleasure in his power. "It's not possible. Next." The next passenger in line shoved in front of me.

"Bill, do something. If we can't cross Northern Greece to get back to France we'll have to go through Bulgaria, and that's Communist! Besides it's too far out of the way." I had worried about getting back to Paris in time to meet my brother and his wife with only two weeks left. Besides, I was homesick for the comfort of France.

"We'll worry about it when the time comes." Bill's confidence annoyed me. What did he have to lose? He didn't have family and friends waiting for him.

Sitting on the dock, we organized our stuff that had been rifled through at customs. The moon rose high above our heads, returning to its normal size and creamy blue-white color, more beautiful now that it looked familiar.

We wound around ancient corners of the moonlit streets, stumbling upon the Hagia Sophia, a monolithic Byzantine church with minarets piercing the sky. Stunned by its beauty, we stopped in front of the closed gates. Bill's silhouette was illuminated in the dark, his large pack hanging at his side, his broad shoulders and baggy jeans accentuating his lean lower body. I sighed. I longed to be in love with him, but the spark had once again gone out of our relationship. Now we were just traveling companions, like an old married couple: comfortable, amiable at times and argumentative at other times, but always there for each other.

Why wasn't that enough? At twenty-one, I craved romance, foreign intrigue, and the impossible. *Ahh, Pierrot. Why can't I be with you?*

We found the dreary youth hostel tucked away in an old building near the port. A large red-lettered poster hung behind the desk on a paint-peeled wall: curfew 10 p.m. martial law enforced.

Bill and I were oblivious to the current situation.

Turkey had been under martial law since the previous March after student uprisings and a coup d'état. Little did we know that seven American servicemen had been kidnapped a few months earlier, and Billy Hayes (*Midnight Express*) lay rotting in a Turkish prison off the coast of Istanbul after trying to smuggle hashish out of the country.

Martial law made it sound like we could be gunned down in the street. During the student riots, Bill broke curfew to get me out of Isla Vista when the police pulled us over, threw Bill against the hood, frisked him, searched the van, and threatened to take us both into the station. What could happen here?

"I'm scared, Bill. What if we get stopped or frisked or just hassled? Let's stay in. Anyway, I don't feel good, and my ear aches."

Bill again reassured me, "Stop worrying; it's going to be all right. I'm hungry. Let's go eat."

Leaving our bags in our separate dorm rooms, we took a taxi to the center of town and ate kebabs in a small café outside of the Grand Bazaar bustling with people. But by the time we finished dinner, the streets had emptied, except for soldiers who had taken posts along the rail track, sidewalks, and street crossings.

Bill looked at his watch. "Shit, it's after ten."

We ducked down an alley and found a line of parked taxis, the drivers sitting against a wall on chairs outside of a café, smoking cigarettes, drinking tea, and playing a board game. Interrupting them, we asked to hire a taxi, but none of them would take us back to the hostel. A grizzled man pointed to his watch and shook his head. "No go." We pleaded. Another cabbie wagged his finger.

Bill pulled out a *Playboy* magazine (I don't know why he had it in his daypack) and opened the magazine to the first page of a blond, buxom (what else?) lady in red fishnet stockings holding one hand on her bare breasts and the other pointing to her crotch. The men gathered around him, laughing and jabbing each other.

"What the hell are you doing?" I fumed.

Bill shushed me and continued to show one page at a time making sure that the centerfold remained hidden. My face reddened, angry and embarrassed. Turkish men rarely saw a woman's legs, let alone the bulging breasts and cherry red genitals hid dimly behind a mass of pubic hair.

Bill pulled the magazine away, pretending to put it back in his daypack. The men grabbed at the glossy publication. Judiciously, Bill chose one cabdriver and presented him with the magazine, indicating that he wouldn't get it unless we got a ride.

The cabbie grinned lasciviously, opened the door, and motioned for us to get in. After being assaulted in bed by a Tunisian, I was worried about being groped, possibly raped. The Turk told us to duck down to avoid being seen by the police patrol. I lay in the backseat as he circled through the darkened streets back to the youth hostel. Bill got out first and handed him the magazine. His gold tooth gleamed as he smiled and furtively tucked the magazine under his wooden ball seat covers. "No money, free tonight."

The next morning, people had returned to the streets. They were friendly and helpful, leading us through the maze of shops in the Grand Bazaar, winding up the narrow streets past the artisans pounding out silver plates and past the rows of Turkish delights—rich, gooey pastries filled with almonds and dipped in honey. We stopped at a café and wrote birthday cards to our mothers.

I hadn't seen my mother for a year and had only spoken to her twice on the phone, once at Christmas and again before I left Bordeaux. In my mind, her voice remained unchanged since childhood, the same messages and reprimands, frozen as the good Catholic mother of ten, the addled housewife, forever in her pedal pushers with her hair piled on top of her head with clips and bobby pins. But did I see her as the person she was now, a woman in her early fifties starting a new life without her husband? No, I didn't then. My youngest sister told me later that after Dad died, Mom had gotten a job, learned to drive, made friends, went out dancing, visited her sisters, and left my little sisters and brother to watch the house and our grandma. I knew nothing of this home life. I had already checked out.

After posting the birthday cards, we continued on, walking deeper into the Grand Bazaar to find the leather shops. The stench of rawhides and unfinished leather products permeated the air, but it didn't deter me from buying myself some custom-made pants. Leather was a sign of affluence, a luxury I couldn't afford, but wanted. The owner served us tea and said he would make any pair fit. After tough negotiations and a few measurements, he took the seams in on the chosen cinnabar rawhide pants. I couldn't wear them in the sweltering heat of summer and definitely couldn't roll them up tightly enough to fit into my backpack, so I mailed them home.

* * *

When I returned the following December, I opened the package. The pants reeked of dead animal. I aired them out for two weeks before repacking them to take back to college. That winter, I wore them to outdoor frat parties, hoping no one noticed the foul, lingering odor. But each time I wore those awful leather pants, my skin turned orange, tanned and stained. I eventually threw them away, feeling foolish to have paid twenty-five dollars for those stupid leather pants I had to have, when I had been down to my last one hundred dollars in traveler's checks and some odd coins in other currencies.

* * *

The heat and the smells of the bazaar exacerbated my nausea, which had returned with a vengeance. With every step, my ear throbbed to the point of pain, forcing me to sit on the curb, my head between my legs, spitting up. By the time we returned to the hostel, I was feverish and could barely stand. The concierge gave us the name of a doctor several blocks away. In the oppressive heat, we followed the directions scribbled on the back of a registration form until we reached an old building in a slummy part of town.

"Looks more like an abortion clinic than a doctor's office," I remarked, climbing the stairs to Dr. Sami Ozal's office. Inside, dust balls occupied the corners; straight-backed chairs, chipped and splintered, lined the walls; and there was no receptionist to greet us, only children crying on their mothers' laps. Behind a foggy pane of glass in a door,

I could make out the shape of the doctor leaning over a patient on a table.

"Let's get out of here, Bill. I can't go in there." Even though I had terrible pain, the thought of dirty needles and unwashed linens made me cringe with fear.

"Just ask for painkillers, maybe an antibiotic."

The door opened. The young doctor had a worn look on his face, spectacles on his nose, and a drooping mustache. He called my name. We followed him into a room with a single chair, a table, and cabinets filled with apothecary jars behind grimy glass.

"How can I help you?" he gently asked. He checked my ears, shook his head, and put some drops in each ear canal. Methodically, he filled a syringe. "You have a very bad infection; this is necessary." He gave me a shot in the butt. Next he opened a cupboard, took down a large jar of pills, and shook some into a plastic bottle. "Take two pills a day for ten days, and keep your ears dry. I would like to see you again, maybe tomorrow, but it is Sunday. Can you come by my house to meet my family? I will check to make sure you feel better."

When we arrived the next day, his wife made us tea and gave me an old, but beautiful, handwoven apron. Dr. Ozal checked my ears, and afterward his mother wrapped a scarf around my head and took a strand of beads off her neck and put them on me. They insisted we have a family photo taken together with his adopted son from Germany, an albino boy who wore lederhosen. I started to feel better.

Like a loose electron, I bonded quickly to the nucleus of any family. We left after dinner and planned our departure for early the next day.

1956 Comic, Treasure Chest of Fact and Fun

CHAPTER FIFTY-THREE

Hammer and Sickle

Le 17 août
Dear Mom,

   Traveling in Yugoslavia has been interesting to say the least. The Communist flag is everywhere. We couldn't even go into Albania because it's closed to foreigners. I got my camera and film confiscated for taking a picture of a bridge, oh well, it was just a Brownie and Bill's camera is better.

   Uncle Steve is right; Croatia is the most beautiful place on earth. I'll send him a postcard cuz I know he was born here.

   We're almost back to France. Can't wait, I miss it almost as much as home. Hope to find your letters at the American Express in Paris.

TRAVELING BECAME MORE DIFFICULT as we skirted northern Greece into Yugoslavia, Communist territory.

* * *

   I had a healthy dose of distrust ingrained in me from childhood of the "Commie bastards," as my father had called them. I was taught they were a godless people—tyrants, murderers, and abductors of children in order to brainwash them. Each Friday morning at ten, we practiced "duck and cover" drills at school in case Khrushchev (a bad "Commie bastard" whose name sounded like someone spitting) dropped an atom bomb on us. The alarm would buzz over the loudspeaker, an unrelenting blast of static, *bzzzzip, bzzzip, bzzzip.* We dropped under our desks, arms over our heads. The nun paced up and down, checking that we were tucked under properly. We couldn't make a sound, not even a sniffle, or risk sister's pointer coming down across our ankles.

Friday afternoons after lunch recess, all sweaty and tired, we read from the *Treasure Chest of Fact and Fun,* a Catholic comic book distributed during the Cold War era. One comic strip in the book depicted a family of peasants huddled together and a soldier standing above them, questioning, "Do you believe in God?" In a large bubble the father responded in bold caps, "YES, WE BELIEVE IN GOD!" The next frame showed the family lined up against the wall (which to me resembled the playground handball court). We turned the page to find the firing squad with leveled rifles on their shoulders. "Ready, aim, *fire!*" The last picture showed the bodies of the parents and two children, a boy and a girl, in a pile on top of each other.

Sister Pauline stood in front of the classroom, holding her wooden pointer with a metal hook at the end for pulling down charts, and assured us that the children and parents went straight to heaven, martyrs for their faith. Being the tallest student in class, I sat in the last seat in the last row and could scan the fifty other students in brown uniforms, sitting silently, their hands folded on their desks, backs straight, eyes looking forward. In make-believe anger, our teacher aimed her *weapon,* the pointer, at the smallest child in the first-row front desk and demanded, "Do you believe in God?"

He answered timidly, "Yes, I believe in God."

"Stand next to the blackboard."

Using a husky, soldierlike voice, she walked down the rows, tapping one student at a time. Each child stood up, bravely answered, "Yes, I believe in God," and marched to the front of the classroom to stand against the blackboard, until all fifty of us flanked the wall. Sister Pauline didn't shoot us for real, but she scared the living daylights out of me, and that fear resurrected itself as I crossed into the Communist country.

* * *

As far as I remember, we had no problems getting across the border, but I imagine now that the authorities had bigger fish to fry than two Americans with backpacks. What we didn't know was the discontent brewing in 1971 among the different ethnic groups that had been forcefully united under Tito. Only a few months later, civil unrest broke out in northwest Yugoslavia when intellectuals, students, and nationalists of the Croatian Communist Party demonstrated and fought for greater economic and constitutional autonomy. It was labeled the Croatian Spring.

Without many cars on the road, we hailed down a truck once we had crossed the border into Yugoslavia. We had wanted to travel the coast of Albania, but the country was closed to all foreigners, making it even more enticing. Still, it was cheaper and looked like a shorter route as the crow flies to take the inland route, so we headed into the middle of the country.

The truck lumbered forward and circled onto a new concrete freeway, which seemed odd since there was no development in the area. Perhaps it had been built for tanks. By dark, the driver appeared sleepy and annoyed and was unable to communicate why he pulled off onto a desolate exit. He pantomimed tired and eating, motioned for us to get out, and then drove off, leaving Bill and me at a cloverleaf under the freeway.

"What are we going to do now?"

Visibly worried, Bill's forehead crinkled. "There's not much traffic at this hour. Let's wait until morning."

"We can't just sleep here!"

"Not much choice—I don't see any towns." He took out his map. "Closest city is at least fifteen kilometers. Let's just camp here."

In the shadow of the overpass, we got out our sleeping bags, stowed our packs behind a scraggly bush, and tucked ourselves under the bridge out of sight. I had a fitful night dreaming only to awaken to the nightmare of being exposed, not to the elements, but to the Communists standing over me.

"Up against the wall!" I was frozen with fear and my voice could not form any words; I choked a mumbling, crying sound.

"Peggy, wake up. You're dreaming." Bill was gently pushing my shoulder. "You had a nightmare." He rolled over and put his arm around me, and I quietly told him how scared I was.

"Don't worry; no one's going to come get us." We fell back to sleep, but in the morning my uneasiness returned. At dawn, we got up and gathered our bags to begin another day of hitchhiking.

We emerged from under the bridge, hoping not to be seen by the police after breaking the law by sleeping in a public place. Instinctively, we knew that this was not the place to test the authorities, but it hit us hard when we looked up. In the middle of the weed-infested circle of the freeway entrance stood a tall flagpole bearing the red cloth flag displaying the yellow hammer and sickle flapping gently in the breeze.

After having attended university classes on Karl Marx, demonstrating against capitalism, and extolling the virtues of Communism, my outlook had changed toward the Communists—that is, until I came face-to-face with the regime and witnessed the oppression of the people. As we walked through the towns, there were few children playing outside, not like the playgrounds and streets in other countries. The stores were void of fresh food; only rations of flour and outdated packages lined the shelves. In the south, the sullen people avoided eye contact and conversation, except an old man on a park bench smoking his pipe, unafraid to talk. We sat down and offered him a piece of our stale bread and some cheese. He smiled softly as he broke off a piece.

"Be careful. Do not trust anyone."

But in a naive way, I wanted to trust the soldiers who lined the streets in their green uniforms, the hammer and sickle emblazoned on the sleeves. I wanted them to like me, which was about as smart as trying to befriend a grizzly bear. By being friendly and upbeat, I wanted to demonstrate that not all Americans hated the Communists. In spite of my underlying fear, I considered telling them I was a Trotskyite and had attended Communist meetings in France so they wouldn't hurt me.

Bill took a different approach. 'Just don't say anything, Peggy. Keep to yourself and we'll go about our business. Nothing's going to happen.'

I got up from the bench that faced the small river and walked over to the bridge that led into town. I snapped a few photos. An armed soldier approached me, yelling something in Russian. I looked around to see what was the matter, thinking he couldn't be talking to me. He grabbed the camera out of my hand, ripped it open, and pulled the film out of its spool. All my photos from Greece and Turkey were ruined. By now Bill had jumped to his feet and was at my side.

"No photos." The soldier pointed to the bridge.

Apologizing profusely, I promised, "No more photos," and put my hand out to retrieve my Brownie Instamatic. The soldier shook his head. He noticed Bill's camera and requested he hand it over. Bill hesitated, but he opened the film compartment, handed over his roll of film without relinquishing his expensive Pentax, and walked away.

Yugoslavia may have been the only Communist country to allow tourists, but we never really felt welcome until we arrived in the beautiful Plitvice Lakes National Park in northern Croatia. Walking through pine forests, ducking under falls, and picnicking by a lake under lush trees made us feel more at home than any other place we'd visited. Nature soothed our jangled nerves.

Embankment where Bill and I slept on the Seine

CHAPTER FIFTY-FOUR

Paris Again

August 24, 1971
Dear Mom,

Can't remember when I last wrote but here are the highlights. After island hopping from Greece to Turkey, we returned to Europe by Istanbul, a huge and interesting city but too dirty and having terrible strikes. The Grand Bazaar is an immense building with so many little shops inside where you can bargain with the merchants. I bought leather and gold, the real bargains. Luckily, it was closed on Sunday, or I would have spent all my money. We left Turkey and traveled on to Greece where it was raining. We spent a week in Yugoslavia, saw Croatia and its beautiful mountains, waterfalls, and lakes. We had a horrible time crossing Italy in a day, then stopped in Chamonix to stay with Claire's relatives who were very kind to us.

Bill and I just arrived in Paris yesterday and are waiting in front of the American Express in Paris with two bottles of Bordeaux wine and cheese to welcome Vicki and Terry. Hope the plans to meet work cuz they have to take a ferry from England then rent a car and drive from Calais to Paris. Easier said than done since half of France is closed down for August holidays and no one ever works between noon and four. Consequently, we've planned a long wait—just hope they get here before we pop the corks. I hope there's a letter inside waiting for me!

OUR LAST RIDE HAD let us off on the outskirts of Paris near the Metro Port St. Cloud. The grime of the road stuck to our clothes and faces, making us feel like the vagabonds we were. My appearance hadn't seemed to matter much when we were camping or hitchhiking—the roads were full of kids with backpacks traveling the world—but now that I had entered Paris, I felt as if I were naked walking down the Champs Élysées. Heads turned to stare at us as we clomped down the fashionable street in construction boots, backpacks slung over our shoulders, with sleeping bags, pots, and extra pairs of shoes flopping off the sides. Crossing Place Vendome, we strolled by the Hotel de Crillion and continued along the promenade lined with designer stores: Coco Chanel, Cartier, Hermes, and so many names I didn't recognize.

Catching my reflection in the windows, I saw a poor country girl with braids, wearing the same old green button-down shirt and blue jeans and clunky men's boots. I swore to myself I would come back to Paris as a rich woman and imagined flouncing into the Cartier shop to purchase a diamond necklace. Lifting my head high, I smiled at the smartly dressed ladies going into Angelina's tearoom. They turned away their gazes, not acknowledging me. *I'll be back, dressed to the nines!*

In defiance of their scowls and better-than-thou attitude, I entered one of their holy establishments: Le Ritz.

"Bill, let's check it out." Abruptly turning the corner, we walked up the red-carpeted stairs into the foyer of the elegant hotel. "Act like we belong here and no one will say anything," I coached. But they did say something.

"Madame, do you have a reservation with us?"

"No, we were just looking in case we wanted to stay here in the future." I smirked haughtily, shifted my pack, and walked out the door.

"Well, that was embarrassing. Any other bright ideas?"

"Yeah, let's get tickets for the Comédie Française. It's cheap when you're a student."

We walked a few blocks to the ornate theater, and I purchased two tickets to see Molière's *The School for Wives*. I rubbed the tickets between my fingers, holding them up to show Bill, who was waiting patiently in the shaded plaza in front of the theater.

He smiled his good-humored smile, shaking his head in disbelief. "Now what? We don't even have a place to shower or change."

"Who cares?" My manic excitement continued as I led him into the Metro. "Let's grab some Tunisian burgers and be back by eight!"

Swinging our overladen packs onto our backs, we caught the Metro within minutes and headed for the Latin Quarter. Emerging onto the crowded Boulevard St. Michel, I shouted over the crowd, making sure not to lose Bill. Winding through the cobblestone streets, I found the little Tunisian restaurant where I had eaten with Pierrot last May.

In line behind the Arabs, Beaux-Arts students, and other locals, I looked around as if I might see someone I knew.

"These are the best Tunisian burgers ever," I said, remembering how they had tasted when I was so in love with Pierrot. "You've got to try one. Deux, s'il vous plait." The cook threw the tuna fish and caper combination onto two rolls and handed them through the take-out window.

My first bite didn't taste as good as I had remembered. Feelings get so wrapped up in food. In a flash, I yearned for my old life with my French friends. Resentment welled inside me. *I speak the language, know where to go, and know what to do. I don't need Bill.* Bill didn't let on if he felt my mood go sour. He just ate his tuna burger.

"These are okay, but the ones in Tunisia were better," he said nonchalantly, stuffing another bite of the soft bread into his mouth.

I had forgotten we had eaten Tunisian burgers in Tunis. I hadn't really wanted the burger; I had wanted to relive the night I ran through Paris with Pierrot, before I found out he had a girlfriend waiting for him across town. The hurt resurfaced.

After dinner, the idea of a play didn't sound so enticing, but we went anyway. The theater sparkled and the crowd in the foyer looked like a Renoir painting—women in long black dresses with their hair piled high, men in coat and tie, some with tails. In the lavatory, I changed into my less dirty jeans, covered my stained shirt with my soft lavender poncho, brushed my wavy long hair into a ponytail, and replaced my boots with clogs. The bellman hid our packs behind the fur coats, but we couldn't hide our disheveled looks.

We sat through five acts of the farce, not understanding a word of it. *How pretentious of me to think I could understand Molière in French. I don't even understand him in English.*

We left the theater after eleven with no place to sleep.

"It's not worth spending money on a hotel tonight. Let's just sleep on the Seine." Bill agreed it wasn't worth the money for so little time in a bed, and we had already spent more than we should have on the theater tickets.

We walked along the Seine, descended the stairs to the river's edge, and set our bags down beneath the overhang.

Bill opened his pack and pulled out a bottle of cheap red table wine and a loaf of bread. We sat down on the damp embankment, dangling our feet over the water, and shared our baguette and wine, feeling smug that we were not like the other tourists who floated by on the *Bateaux Mouches,* strands of white lights outlining the boats, the guides speaking harshly over loudspeakers, spotlights shining on the monuments, and little waves slapping up against the embankment.

The wine made everything rosy, so when the *clochards,* Paris's homeless, swaggered down the steps with their cheap liquor and kerosene in bottles wrapped in crushed newspapers, we toasted them with our brown bag of cheap wine. In hindsight, maybe we got too chummy with the denizens of the Seine, but I wanted to be nice to them, to share a song and a few bon vivant words with the leftovers of Paris life.

In the middle of the night, someone snuggled up close to me, making the tiniest squeaking noise, not Bill's resonating snore. I turned over to find a small, dark, middle-aged man curled up next to me, his kinky black hair resting on my clogs, my poncho pulled over his skinny body. I screamed and scared the poor bum out of his wits. He jumped up and backed away, bowing low with his hands in prayer, speaking a rapid, confused Arabic. He turned and ran, leaving his nearly empty bottle next to my poncho.

I stayed awake, thinking about life. Here I was, twenty-one years old, with little money, sleeping next to the homeless in the most beautiful city in the world, and yet I felt blessed. I wasn't condemned or scorned like the men who ate from the garbage cans and ran from the police. I was young, healthy, educated, and an American. I had made the choice to be there. It felt good slumming it, since tomorrow I didn't have to return to the streets to sleep. Something in the human condition says *I'm okay as long as there is someone worse off than me.*

Then another thought crossed my mind. Did this unfortunate man believe that if I had a sleeping bag and a pack full of clothes maybe I should share with him a little warmth? *Whatsoever you do for the least of your brethren, you do for me.* Feeling both sorry for him and guilty for what I had, I admonished myself. *Why didn't I give him my poncho? My father would have.*

At sunrise, the morning bells rang from the towers of Notre Dame. My eyes blinked open to sunlight reflecting on the ancient stones of the old medieval cathedral, slowly changing from gray to purple to a brilliant peach, like in a Monet painting. A dappled path of sunlight crossed the Seine, the garbage trucks rumbled on the street above us, and joggers ran by. Ragged from a disturbed sleep, we rolled up our sleeping bags, not noticing the gendarmes marching down the stairs, rousting the men with their billy clubs. By the time they reached us, we had our packs on our backs. "Il faut partir, tout de suite," the policeman ordered—leave immediately.

By seven o'clock we had shaken off the night in a bistro, sipping café au lait, eating croissants, and cleaning up in the small bathroom at the bottom of the circular staircase.

"We'd better get a place for tonight. I don't think your brother and his new wife are going to want to sleep on the Seine."

"Really?" I said sarcastically. "I know a cheap hotel near the Sorbonne, Hotel Saint Jacques. Five francs with petit dejeuner included." I had stayed there when I traveled with my friends a year earlier. Wistfully, I thought of my first taste of Paris: new friends, the freshness of life beginning.

The plan to meet Terry and his new wife, Vicki, had been set before we left France two months earlier. By noon, we were sitting in front of the closed American Express, unsure if we had any mail inside. We hadn't heard from anyone for two months, but we trusted that Terry and Vicki would show up at Place des Bourges sometime on August 24.

I pondered over the last three months that Bill and I had spent together on the road and knew I could not have done it alone. Along with the weather, my roller-coaster feelings for Bill had started to take a turn for the better. I finished my letter to Mom:

The skies have cleared after a few days of rain and overcast weather—Terry and Vicki will see Paris with sun...At last! They're here! Going to pop the corks in the Tuileries. Will write more later.

Terry and Vicki in front of the Louvre

CHAPTER FIFTY-FIVE

Terry and Vicki

Dear Mom,

We had a great week with Terry and Vicki. We saw so much, Chartres, the Loire Valley, St. Émilion, then Bordeaux.

Terry took us to a three-star restaurant (the best rating in Micheline) in Tours! We ate five courses and drank a different wine with each dish. It must have cost him a fortune. Funny, there was a dog at the table next to us who was served dinner!

I'll check my mail while in Bordeaux—hope UCSB will let me skip fall quarter and still give me my scholarship money for winter quarter.

BILL AND I TRAVELED with the guidebook *Europe on $5 a Day*, and my brother and his wife traveled with the *Michelin Red Guide*, searching out rare properties, chateaux in the Loire Valley, and fine restaurants, while we camped. They invited us to dinner in Tours at La Roche Le Roy, the top culinary restaurant in the region. My dress-up outfit came out of the pack: a short polka-dot dress, lavender poncho, and clogs. Bill had jeans and a Hawaiian shirt, so

443

the concierge loaned him a dinner jacket that was two sizes too small but allowed us to enter the dining room, with tables draped in starched white tablecloths and set with fine china and silverware, the center candelabra casting an intimate light.

"Pegs, what do you recommend we have?" Terry asked as he perused the menu in French. "It's all Greek to me!"

It was my chance to show off. I stumbled along, questioning, "Qu'est-ce que c'est?" and the waiter answered in a simplified French that I could translate.

"The French always start with kir, that's champagne and cassis."

"Do they have escargots? Order that and some frog legs for starters."

"Escargot et les cuisses de grenouilles."

In perfect English, the waiter turned to my brother and said, "I highly recommend that you order the prix fixe meal, which will be five courses and wine pairing." I hated the French one-upmanship but acquiesced to speaking English the rest of the evening.

"That's okay, Pegsy. He speaks lousy English. Your French is much better."

* * *

Terry had always supported me. When my other brothers teased me at home, he made them stop and told me I was the best little sister ever. He paid me to iron his shirts when Mom had made me do it for free. As a teen, when things heated up after Dad started drinking heavily, Terry whisked me away in his car or gave me the keys to his MG to get out of the house. Even though he was only six years older, he was my father figure. Dad confirmed it when he came to

me in a dream. I imagine he sent me the message as he lay
dying, "Terry is your father now."

* * *

A woman who was draped in furs crossed the dining
room, holding a leash with a miniature greyhound prancing
at her side. Her husband followed closely behind. The maître
d' pulled the chair out for the woman, took the leash, and
placed a red cushion down for the dog. Within seconds, the
waiter filled the water glasses and placed a silver water bowl
in front of the dog. When their main course arrived, the
dog ate rare chopped steak. The opulence and waste of the
evening jarred me, thinking of the little Algerian girl who
popped her head out of the hole where she lived to beg for
food and how I had eaten crumbs from the bottom of my
bag to stave off hunger pains.

Terry spent more money on our meal that evening than
I had spent the entire summer traveling. I imagine the cost
of the dog's dinner alone could have fed the clochards who
rummaged through the garbage. The rich food sat heavily
in my stomach and on my mind. I was uncomfortable being
in a place so lavish and unfamiliar to me.

I was happy to see Terry and catch up on family news,
but his visit also revealed how much I had changed. I knew
I didn't want to return to the States.

"Let Mom know I might not come home until Christmas,"
I told my brother as I hugged him good-bye. "I'm going to
find work here, maybe pick grapes."

"Do it while you're young, Peggy. Can't say I blame you."
He regretted not having taken the time to travel as a bum
before marrying and making money. After all the fine hotels
and restaurants, his favorite memory of our trip was the first

445

night in the Hotel Saint Jacques, eating from corner vendors and in local brasseries and pastry shops. Perhaps he would have liked to have slept on the Seine.

Pierrot in Marie-Paule's room

CHAPTER FIFTY-SIX

Le Retour

Le 8 septembre
Dear Mom,
  Guess the kids are back home getting ready for school. I'm in Biarritz with Marie-Paule. It's still hot here and I can't imagine going back to school. Bill is off traveling and I will meet up again with him later to go to Oktoberfest in Germany.
  I hope to get down to Madrid to visit Carmen, but she never gave me her address, and it's over 500 kilometres from Biarritz, so I'm afraid if I make the long journey and don't find her not only I'll be upset but the person I drag along will be furious. Can you call Mrs. Torres and find out her address and send it to me along with some news from home?
  I still don't know if I have to go to school in October. I never got your letter or the package you sent from UCSB.

SUMMER VACATION WAS OVER, and for the first time since I had started school as a child, I wasn't going back to the classroom. The bookends of spring and fall gave way to an eternal summer, something I had thought I wanted. I had no schedule, no one telling me my next step, just an open road. And as exhilarating as that was, it was also terrifying. Bill was my only security, and he had no plans either. But Bill was also a liability, since he didn't fit into my dream. I wanted to be embraced by my friends and live my life again in Bordeaux.

Bill kissed me good-bye at the crossroads of Biarritz and the road to Spain. He looked lonely, standing with his thumb out. Within minutes, a car stopped and whisked him away. A lump developed in my throat. Now I was alone. Hoping to run into Marie-Paule, I slowly walked down the steep stairs that led to Côte de Basque, the beach where I had spent many days in the spring, watching the surf with her, her brothers, Pierrot, and friends.

"Peg-geee! Tu es rentrée!" Marie-Paule recognized my tall slender figure and flowing hair as I walked along the boardwalk. She jumped off the seawall and ran toward me. "Where is Beeg Beel?"

"Salut," I said as we hugged and kissed on each cheek. "He went south looking for surf. He'll be back next week." The truth was, I had asked him to leave.

There was an awkward moment of silence. Marie-Paule realized I didn't have anywhere to go. "Do you need a place to stay? My parents leave tomorrow; you can stay with me in the caravan."

"Sure, I'd love to, thanks." I knew I could always stay with Marie-Paule, but I had hoped to find her with our old group of friends.

I searched for the familiar faces from the foggy day last spring when we had last sat on the crumbling retaining wall, but I only found blond California surfers waiting for the swell to pick up. *How boring.* I had escaped that life and didn't have much interest in any more surfer boys.

"Where's Pierrot and Jacques?"

"They went back to Bordeaux." Marie-Paule made room for me to sit on the wall but didn't introduce me to the famous surfers who came to surf the big waves each fall in Biarritz. That evening, everyone regrouped at the Steak House, buzzing around each other, drinking beers, flirting. One of the waiters, an American, stopped to chitchat.

"Happens every year. Big-name surfers arrive for the contest and the French girls go crazy. The rest of us watch the big events, both day and night."

I knew what he meant. French girls liked to sleep around, especially with Americans, and American boys, well, they liked to sleep with French girls.

For the rest of the week, I stayed with Marie-Paule at the campsite in the caravan and hung out at the beach. When we returned to Bordeaux, I hoped to run into Pierrot. My student visa had expired, so I looked for jobs and talked about getting a place to live, all the time thinking if I found Pierrot, I might be able to stay with him.

One early afternoon, sitting alone in Marie-Paule's studio above her family's garage while she was at the university, I heard a motorcycle pull into the driveway, followed by footsteps on the stairs. The door opened.

"Pierrot!"

"Peg-eee?" He was as surprised to see me as I was to see him. Hadn't Marie-Paule told him I was back? She had been avoiding talking to me about him, but I couldn't figure out why.

Again we held the French embrace longer than usual as our eyes met, so powerful I couldn't imagine him not feeling the same love for me as I had for him. We sat down to catch up on each other's lives, even though neither of us said much. I showed him the lederhosen I had bought in the Alps. Comically, he slipped out of his jeans and tried them on.

"Keep them! I want you to have them."

"Oh no, Peg-eee, they're yours, a good memory."

"I'll get another pair when I go to Oktoberfest." I would have given Pierrot the world, but he always pulled back, leaving me embarrassed by my offer.

Voices below echoed up the staircase. I was sure it was our old group of friends. *The return of good times!* I thought I could recapture the past if we all gathered in Marie-Paule's room tonight, listened to Bob Dylan, and smoked a joint before going to dinner.

"Look who I found!" Marie-Paule burst into the room and greeted Pierrot and me with a bise. Right behind her was Big Bill, dragging his backpack. He had a funny grin on his face, like he was hiding candy.

"Guess who's here?" he teased.

"Umm, Marco? Jacques? A friend of yours?" From the stairwell, I could hear a female voice singing, "Go ask Alice, when she's ten feet tall…" Carmen always sang that song to tease me about my height.

"Carmen!" I ran to the door to find my best friend from first grade through college. She was in her full glory, her long, frizzy hair framing her classic Spanish face, scarves and beads wrapped around her neck, and her matching fringed purse hanging at her side. "How the hell did you get here?"

"Is that the way to greet your best friend? I hitchhiked." She laughed and swiped at my shoulder, grabbing me for a big hug. "Bill and I kept in touch, and he told me he was meeting you here. I've got three weeks before classes start in Madrid."

At first the blend of my two lives appeared seamless, woven together by music, hashish, and friendship. By the end of the evening, we had plans: Bill, Carmen, and I would travel together and pick grapes in one of the many vineyards in the area.

Pierrot slipped out without saying good-bye.

Picking grapes

Chapter Fifty-Seven

Le Vendange

October 5, 1971
Dear Mom,

    I received your letters yesterday and papers informing me that I might get two-thirds of my grant and loan held over for winter and spring quarters. So, I've decided to stay in France to help harvest the grapes to make those great Bordeaux wines. Carmen met Bill and me at Marie-Paule's house and she is also picking grapes. Since I will be earning and not spending money for a couple of weeks that will enable me to travel once again. Bill and I will go to Portugal, a fantastic country according to whoever has gone there.

    I sent most of my clothes home. They'll be at the door one day without me. I miss you and the family but I want to make the most of being here, so I can't promise you I'll be home soon.

BY EARLY OCTOBER, BILL, Carmen, and I had found a small vineyard that took us on as laborers along with a Swedish couple and an Englishman. We bunked together above one of the barns in a comfortable dormitory with plywood dividers demarcating the rooms and simple furnishings for each of us: a bed, a dresser, and a lamp. The open hayloft doors framed rolling hills of vineyards and pastures of grazing cows.

"This place is better than any place we've ever stayed," I said as I happily rolled onto Bill, who was lying on the bed.

"It's so bucolic, and we get paid." He tickled me in the ribs, making me scream.

From the other side of the divider, Carmen yelled, "No hanky-panky you two; these walls are thin."

Bill and I made the bed creak just to tease her.

I was happy to be with my best friend and Bill again, *the happy trio is back,* I wrote Mom, and *I'm not coming home—that is as long as my money holds out.*

We heard the clang of the dinner bell and moseyed on over to the main house across the yard to join the family for dinner in the large farmhouse kitchen. Madame Croizet wore a flowered cotton housedress and a butcher's apron; she was a serious cook. Wearing big black oven mitts, she placed a huge tureen of soup in the center of the table, swearing as the hot liquid splashed. Monsieur Croziet, a round and weathered farmer, bowed his head and said a quick blessing. "Mange."

In abbreviated French and with hand gestures, Madame gave Bill the job of ladling the soup. No one spoke. We didn't have a common language. Monsieur helped himself to the carafe of red wine, filling his glass, then mine, and on down the line, even putting some in the baby's bottle.

"Non, Papa! C'est mauvais pour le bébé!" Bernard, the baby's father, protested.

"Non, c'est bon!" Grandpa yelled.

"Oui, c'est bon pour le bébé!" Grandmother piped in.

The argument continued. The baby started crying, and his mother, a sweet, shy country girl, stood up, grabbed the baby bottle, and poured most of the wine into her glass. She added a good dose of clear water to the bottle, making a pink tincture, and handed it back to the distressed child, who quieted.

* * *

I hated fighting, especially at the table. At home, the ten children lined up along two bars in our kitchen, one bar along the windows for the boys and the other one protruded into the middle of the room for the girls. Mom instructed us not to slurp the soup and to finish all of our vegetables. If we complained we didn't like something, she'd shout back, "If you don't like it, go to another hash house." Her fork came down on the side of a blue plate that was tinged with white chip marks from her banging. Whack, whack, whack! "You better finish your food before Dad gets home or you know what!" Peas got hidden under the curtain and vegetables spit into napkins. If food was wasted, we got the "There are starving children in Armenia" speech, to which, as all children did, we responded, "Then send them the broccoli." But mostly, I sat quietly, hating my brothers for being so bad. Food stuck in my throat. I tensed, not sure when Dad was coming home. When we heard his car on the gravel driveway, someone inevitably sounded the alarm: "Check that the milk bottle caps are on tight!" a clue to the insignificant action that could cause my father to erupt. Larry got the brunt of Dad's anger; maybe it was Larry's swagger or his defiance—he rarely ate everything on his plate—or his sassing back at Mom. Dad got the belt out and after a few heavy swats on his butt, Larry was sent to bed without dessert, once without any dinner at all. Cleaning up after dinner, I scraped Larry's food into the cat bowl, wishing he'd just be good so Mom would stop yelling and Dad wouldn't hit him with the belt.

* * *

As she gathered the empty soup bowls and dropped them in the sink with a clatter, Madame Croizet harrumphed about the baby drinking a little wine. Then she hoisted the large roasting pan from the oven, setting it in front of Monsieur, who deftly cut each chicken into four sections. We passed our plates as he dropped a leg or breast onto each plate while I dished out the potatoes. Madame placed the casserole of *haricots verts*, fresh green beans from the garden, in front of the Swede, who took her turn to serve.

* * *

On Sundays, Dad always barbecued—thick juicy steaks, the best cut from the butcher, or halves of chicken he killed that we plucked earlier in the day. It was always the best meat, perfectly cooked and sizzling hot, piled on our plates with Mom's scalloped cheese potatoes and fresh vegetables, plenty of butter, and homemade apple crisp with ice cream. Grandma came to Sunday dinners, and no one fought in front of her or our other guests. We ate on china plates and used silver utensils. Sunday dinners were special.

* * *

At the end of dinner, following Monsieur's example, we wiped our plates clean with slices of fresh-baked bread, making room for the salad. By now the wine flowed freely from the carafes, even the son's baby was given a little more in his bottle. Madame fussed over the child and rattled off something in French about her lazy son and her no-good husband who drank too much. She looked like a raisin, small and wrinkled with a wiry body that moved quickly and efficiently around the kitchen. Her husband had a rotund belly, short legs, and a demeanor that could change like the weather—one moment he was cheering the group and the next admonishing his wife or pushing his son off the chair, telling him to help his mother. Their son, Bernard, was good-looking and amiable and didn't seem fazed by his parents' behavior. Marion, his dark-haired wife, sweet and demure, tended to the child in the high chair, ignoring the volatile outbursts of her in-laws.

I was uncomfortable witnessing their family fighting, remembering our family dinners and hoping that this meal would turn out to be like our Sunday dinners and no one would get hit. We foreigners sat silently, like an audience watching the life of rural farmers, while I waited for the other shoe to drop.

With great flair, Madame opened the oven with her apron and pulled out a large baking dish of bread pudding with plums and plopped the pan on the table. She flipped over each of our dinner plates and served the piping hot dessert onto the bottom of the dishes, which I saw as a brilliant notion, having been the main dishwasher in my family of twelve.

Everyone pitched in and helped clean up the kitchen. It wasn't like our house where I served and cleaned alongside my mother while the boys and Dad watched TV. The Croizets' lively banter and yelling at each other softened as the family parted, kissing and hugging and cooing at the baby. If harsh words were spoken in my home, they hung around, making life nerve-racking, like tiptoeing around explosive devices. I never quite understood how the French could argue loudly, throw barbs, yell at other drivers, and posture with fisticuffs—and then just as quickly the storm of wrath passed, calm was restored, and they carried on as if nothing had happened. Whereas in my culture, mean words created permanent marks, grudges were held for years, and time had to pass before forgiveness.

Before leaving the kitchen, Monsieur told us to be ready for work at seven the next morning, and Madame added that breakfast was at six.

Up at six and after a hot meal, we joined the local pickers in the fields and worked until six in the evening with a two-hour lunch, similar to dinners. When in the fields, we called for the panier, either Big Bill or Heavy Harold, the Englishman, both of whom had the height and strength to carry the large basket across their shoulders. Bending over branches, hunched next to each other, Carmen and I chatted, caught up on the gossip in California, and complained that hard labor wasn't for us.

Two weeks later, we toasted the end of our vendange. Down in his wine cave, Monsieur Croizet handed each of us a bottle of wine from the year of our birth and some advice. "If a good wine in your cave does not taste as good as it did the year before, invite your friends over to finish off the rest."

My last days in France

CHAPTER FIFTY-EIGHT

The Last Letter Home

November 22, 1971
Dear Mom,

I just finished washing all my dirty clothes from our last journey south to Madrid to visit Carmen after the vendange, then up through Portugal and along the northern coast of Spain, a remarkably green and beautiful place, so different from the arid plains around Madrid. Near Santiago de Compostela, the great pilgrimage cathedral dating back to the Middle Ages, we cruised the main bar district with all the local Spaniards. They got this great custom of eating little hors d'oeuvres and shellfish with a nickel glass of good wine! That's at eight in the evening and they don't eat dinner till ten. Crazy hours!

Nov. 28—Sorry I never mailed my last letter (enclosed) but I've been stalling to find out when I can get home. Bill was drafted, so we'll be heading home soon, but I don't have any money.

I need to get to London, where I can find a cheap flight on Freddie Laker. Can you sign my scholarship check (go ahead and forge my name) and send me an international money order? I'll be in Paris at Nicole Cardinaud's home—you have the address.

It was late November. Bill went to see the big surf in Biarritz, and I stayed in Bordeaux to say my good-byes. I walked through the Jardin Publique, past empty park benches, barren trees, and dismantled flower beds, knowing I had to go home. I no longer had a reason to stay. Marie-Paule had made plans to live with her sister in Algeria. Marco, now stationed in Paris, never came home on the weekends. Jacques had disappeared from the scene; it was rumored he flipped out. Pierrot had quit school and moved in with his girlfriend, Sian.

I revisited my old haunts. At the corner café on Place Gambetta, the waiter, in his crisp white apron, set two tables on the sidewalk, one on each side of the door, and then tucked the wire-backed chairs against the windows facing the park. I went inside and ordered a bowl of French onion soup to warm up.

My student visa had expired three months earlier, and my recent application for a work visa had been denied. I didn't have enough money for a plane ticket home or enough cash to live in France without a job.

Bad news came in a bundle. Last week, in front of the American Express, Bill had opened a letter from the Selective Service. His face dropped. "I'm drafted." He gave me a big bear hug.

I sank into his full body, buried myself in his sheepskin coat, and wept. After all the shit I had given him, I felt horrible that I might lose him. I didn't want him to leave for good, and no way did I want him to go to war.

"Why can't you be a conscientious objector? Just ignore that letter." I hadn't expected to be so sad and angry.

"I don't have a choice; my student deferment lapsed last year. I'm lucky it took them this long to find me."

Lucky? I was pissed off our government could snatch a brother, a friend, a son, and place him in a jungle to kill or be killed. How was that lucky?

"I can't believe you'd follow what they say just because you got a letter."

"Peggy, it's an induction letter. I'd go to jail if I didn't show up."

"If you go to Canada, you'd be alive, not in jail."

This conversation had played out so many times with my brothers and friends over the past five years. Young men had enlisted and died, like my brother's friend Vince, a Green Beret. Boys went to Vietnam and returned home, only to put a bullet in their head, like Michael, my cousin. Some got "lucky" and served in Germany, like my brother Ted; and some dropped acid and freaked out, never to recover, like my friends Brian and Larry; and others served and carried the nightmare for a lifetime.

The waiter brought my soupe de l'oignon. It was too hot to eat. I dipped my spoon beneath the crusty bread covered in gooey cheese and savored the smell of sweet onions soaked in the rich, salty, brown broth.

I'll miss France. My sadness came from an unrecognizable depth and lodged in my throat. I needed closure to my frayed final days in Bordeaux, a salve for my disappointments and dashed hopes. The entire time I had traveled with Bill through North Africa, Eurasia, the Macedonian Peninsula, and Europe, I had held onto the dream of making France my home, rekindling friendships, and having Pierrot fall in love with me. The thought of never seeing my friends again was unbearable.

It had been a stroke of luck in the first place to get to Europe. I would never again have the finances, the time, or the opportunity to live in a foreign country. That just didn't happen in my family. My year abroad was an anomaly.

I stirred my soup, mixing the broth and croutons, sipping the nectar. I fantasized about what would happen if Bill left and I stayed. Would I have a chance with Pierrot?

I loved Pierrot, but that was stupid. We had never had a physical relationship, but I sensed he loved me. He always did something to encourage and sustain my love for him. Back and forth, I relived all the sweet things he had said to me, his lingering looks, his embraces, and all the good times we had spent together. Had I misread him?

My logical mind twisted back to Bill, a good guy who'd stuck by me as we traveled and fought for six months. I was so comfortable with him. He understood me even when I exasperated him with my ambivalence, my moods, and my downright meanness, like when I told him I didn't want him around. But did I love him? I no longer idolized him, but I would be lonely without him. He was so loyal. I wrote him a short poem in memory of our time together:

> *A fire, a feeling, a memory not so far*
> *Of silent beaches echoing a guitar*
> *Old wooden boats*
> *And sheepskin coat*
> *Cuddled between soft down*
> *The warmth came with you being around*

I didn't want to sit alone in the café any longer.

The soup had cooled down. I ate my fill and wiped the bottom with the soft interior of a baguette. I got the waiter's attention and asked for the check: "L'addition, s'il vous plait."

As I waited, I teared up, thinking of saying good-bye to Marie-Paule. I couldn't say good-bye forever. Smiling to myself, I replayed our first conversation on the stairwell in the Bordeaux library:

"*Why do you look so sad, California?*"

"*I have a term paper due, and I don't read or write in French.*"

"*Don't worry; everything will be okay. Do you want a ciggie?*"

"*Sure.*"

I wished I had a cigarette now.

I had never seen the mummies of St. Michel, so I spent the afternoon as a tourist in Bordeaux before my dinner engagement with Pierrot and his new girlfriend. I walked down the gray streets to the cathedral, went inside the cavernous vault, lit a candle for my father and sister, paid two francs, and descended the stairs to the crypt.

It was already dark outside when I emerged from the creepy exhibition of exhumed bodies. I arrived at the soot-smudged building that housed apartments above a closed bakery across from the quay; the merchant ships had docked and the prostitutes lingered in the shadows. I pulled my jacket tight and wrapped my scarf around my neck against the cold November air, heavy with dampness. As uncomfortable as it would be meeting his girlfriend, I had to see Pierrot before I left.

Searching the residence list, I found his name: *Gulundo, Pierre, fifth floor.* I pushed the brass button, still questioning if I should have come. Lights were on in the top apartment, and I could see shadows on the wall. I rang the doorbell again, this time harder and longer, until the buzzer sounded and the door clicked. Pressing my weight against the heavy cast-iron door, I turned the handle and entered the nearly black interior. Once inside, my hands groped for the illuminated light switch on the wall. Dim lights flickered on, and I saw an endless staircase circling upward, jutting off to small landings on each floor. Voices echoed down the shaft from above me, and then I heard footsteps growing louder. I began climbing the stairs and came face-to-face with Pierrot on the second landing.

"Salut, Peggy." He kissed me lightly on both cheeks.

"Salut, Pierrot; comment ça va?" Flustered, I sounded stilted and formal. It had only been a few months since I had seen him, but a lifetime had passed during those months.

Standing in front of him on the landing, I wanted to ask, *Why didn't you tell me you were in a serious relationship?* How foolish of me to have hoped to return to those days with Pierrot on the beach, running down sand dunes, high on life and drugs, picnicking in the fields, and talking of revolution.

Sian, a tall, gorgeous woman in a housewife apron, stood at the top of the staircase and greeted me at the door of their tiny, unheated quarters. Stepping inside, I saw a tablecloth on the floor in the main room, with pillows at each place setting. Pierrot offered me an aperitif while Sian busied herself in the kitchen. A baby's gentle whimpering leaked from under a closed door down the hall. Sian came out of the tiny kitchenette with a plate of halved avocados filled with shrimp dressed in Dijon mayonnaise. I sat down on the floor, keeping my coat on.

She set the platter in the middle of the tablecloth and brightly said, "Pierrot said you were from California. I thought you would like avocados." She spoke in a brogue, a light, lilting accent I didn't recognize.

"Of course; I haven't had one in over a year."

How could they afford avocados? Neither of them had a job. She watched me as I took my first bite. The avocado had not ripened and tasted bitter, but I thanked her for such a wonderful surprise.

Sian was Welsh. We chatted in English about how difficult it was to find work as a foreigner in France. I commiserated, since I too had been looking for a job. Matter-of-factly, she told me Pierrot had dropped out of kinesiology school to earn some money by making leather sandals to help pay their rent.

"We're so happy living simply," she assured me.

I didn't believe her. No one could live so poorly with the responsibility of a child and still be happy. I would be worried sick and definitely would not waste my money on avocados.

"We're getting married; then I can work in France." It suddenly dawned on me—she had exactly what I wanted: to live in France, get a job, and marry Pierrot.

"Congratulations." I looked at Pierrot, who was following the conversation but didn't speak enough English to contribute. He gave me an enigmatic smile and said he would go check on the baby.

"Can I see the baby?" I wasn't sure whose baby it was.

He nodded, and I followed him down the hall while Sian cleared the tablecloth for the next course.

We could hear the water running in the kitchen and the oven door squeak open. Stopping in the hallway, he held me the way I had always wanted him to hold me. I pulled back. "Is that your baby?"

"No." He spoke softly, sweeping my long hair away from my face. "The baby is Sian's. I'm not married, Peggy." He kissed me. "Tu me manques." In broken English, he promised we'd always be more than friends that we had a spiritual connection, which confused me even more than his embrace.

Was he playing with my head, or had he really missed me? Had I blown my chance when I left last summer? Was I more than a friend? For a moment I thought I was in a movie, and Omar Sharif was about to swoop me into his arms and carry me down the fire escape to a life of bliss. Or was it always an act?

He took a pair of sandals off the shelf in the hall where he kept his leather-making goods. "C'est pour toi." He handed me the sandals, but I could see the size was wrong. Patiently, he brought out his leather workbag and took out a sheet of blank paper and a thick pencil. In the hallway, he outlined my foot. "I'll make them tonight and bring them to you at Marie-Paule's tomorrow." He never showed up the next day, but three years later we met again by chance on the beach in Biarritz, and he had saved my sandals.

Tiptoeing into their bedroom, we walked over to a makeshift crib in the corner. Under the glow of a small lamp, a dark-haired child lay sleeping with his thumb in his mouth, curled in a ball against the cold draft from the leaky windows.

"What's his name?"

"Kepa." In Basque that meant Pierre, but I didn't question him again about who the father was.

"I don't have a present for him, but can I leave him my jacket?" I took off my coat and laid it over the baby as Sian walked into the room. "He's beautiful," I told her, holding back my tears.

She held onto Pierrot and then leaned over and pulled the coat around the baby's ears. "Thank you, Peggy, but you will be cold."

"No, I'll be okay. I'm going home."

Epilogue

After leaving Bordeaux on a clear December morning, I stayed for a week with the Cardinauds in their country home outside of Paris while waiting for my money order. With nothing to do during the day but wait, I had time to miss my friends and to fear going home, not knowing what to expect after being gone so long. Bill had flown back to California ahead of me to report for duty. After saying good-bye, I lost contact with him. How could that be after traveling together for six months? He went back to his life as I returned to mine. I didn't even know if he served in the army or where he went. Neither of us kept in touch, and neither of us looked back.

The money arrived, and I booked a ticket on the train and ferry to London. England was the first English-speaking country I had been to in more than a year and a half. I couldn't understand the telephone operator when I called to get my passport and visa in good order before buying an airline ticket.

"Pardon, I don't understand you."

The woman on the other end of the line repeated herself, in a language not clear to me, so I tried French.

"Je ne comprends pas."

She again repeated herself, this time louder and with an annoyed twist in her voice.

"What language are you speaking?" I yelled, not comprehending what she was saying to me.

"I am speaking the King's English," she curtly replied, enunciating each syllable.

I got a cheap flight on Freddie Laker. As if sealed in a time capsule, I flew all night and arrived in LAX on December 18, after being gone sixteen months. My sister Nola picked me up and brought me to her house in Playa del Rey, from where I had left so long ago. My goddaughter Marren, no longer a baby, and I walked to the duck pond to feed the ducks. That next day, Nola drove me to Temple City High School for the CIF championship game to watch my baby brother, Dennis, bring his football team to victory. Larry and his new girlfriend Joanne sat in the bleachers next to Mom and said hello between the cheering. Larry teased me about my clothes and boots. Mom scooted over to make room and told me she had made lasagna for dinner. My little sisters, now fourteen and seventeen years old, hung out with their friends. It was an all-American scene: cheerleaders, football, Coke, and hotdogs.

I was welcomed back warmly, but no one kissed me on both cheeks or hugged me.

The gap between my family and me felt greater than when I was alone in Europe. What mattered to me didn't seem to interest them, and vice versa. They were wrapped up in their own world, a world that was now foreign to me.

Back home on Rosemead Boulevard, I found the boxes of clothes and presents I had sent on ahead. The Camembert cheese and can of foie gras were unopened in the back of the refrigerator. At Christmas, I uncorked my bottle of wine that Monsieur Croizet had given me, a sweet dessert wine from 1950. Terry and Vicki appreciated that. Mom got her Santon dolls and loved them. Eventually, I returned to the fold of my family—teasing and joking, holding back my feelings. I let Marie-Paule, Pierrot, and the Delannes fade, distancing myself from the pain of being torn away.

I returned to Isla Vista for the winter semester of my senior year. The youth seemed placated now that the Vietnam War was coming to an end and the troops were coming home. The hippies and radicals had morphed into the beautiful people, shallow and self-absorbed...so bourgeois. My point of view on society, politics, and other cultures had radically changed; I got my job at Devereux back, and a fellow teacher at the school labeled me a Communist. The media rankled me. The news reports seemed so myopic—they seemed only to view events from the Western perspective. People drove bigger cars, lived in bigger houses, and stored milk and eggs in refrigerators instead of on windowsills. Everything came in packages, and the trash piled up outside our doors and along our freeways. To make life in the States more bearable, I didn't talk about politics or how things were done in Europe. Instead, I moved into a mental space, a selective amnesia, telling myself that Europe was another place and another time. My year abroad became more and more dreamlike, and I questioned what really happened.

I didn't fit into my own culture, and yet I had never fully adapted to the French culture. Caught in between and lost, it was easier and less combative to stash my memories into a fold in my brain, visualizing two giant waves of gray matter rising up on either side of my year abroad and enveloping it deep into the crevice so that it vanished like the valleys between the swells of the ocean.

AFTERWORD

Forty years later...

IN MY MEMOIR, SECTIONS of my letters have been copied
from the actual aérogrammes and postcards my mother saved
in her burgundy satchel. The letter I wrote to my father was
never sent nor saved, but its content is etched in my memory. I
did receive letters when abroad, but I didn't keep them. Mom
wrote to me, but she really never sent a single long letter. I
could depend on her to send all of my official papers and
money orders, and she was kind enough to send my boots,
clothes, and a fruitcake at Christmas. Thanks, Mom. Vicki
sent a long Christmas letter with photos and chocolate chip
cookies Carmen wrote letters about Bill and how he missed
me. She sent photos of Isla Vista beach on a windswept day,
making me cry. Bill, well—I only remember asking Mom if
she had heard from him, but I'm sure I received a few letters.

My mother died at eighty-seven years old, rich in life
with her children and twenty-four grandchildren and five
great-grandchildren. Mom always counted her blessings in
the number of children. In spite of her losses and hardships,
she managed to remain positive until the end of her life.
To quote her on her deathbed, "I never cried in my wine."

Marsha *La Blonde*, my roommate, returned from France to care for her mother, who died of cancer in 1973. We are sister-friends (she married my sister's brother-in-law) and have stood by each other through deaths, births, marriages, divorces, and partnerships.

Claire, my high school friend, returned to France as the international consultant for Apple, a new company then, and lived in Paris for more than forty years. In honor of our time together, she quotes from *Casablanca*: "We'll always have Paris." Our friendship continues and we meet yearly with Carmen, my oldest and dearest friend, at the beach house.

Marie-Paule and I have remained close. She calls me her American sister; our children are like cousins.

Last year, I returned to Bordeaux with Marie-Paule to revisit our old haunts. She photographed me on my doorstep on L'Abbé de L'Épée, and I wondered who lived there now.

I knocked. A few minutes passed, and a woman in her fifties opened the door. I explained that I had lived there forty-some years ago. She stood blocking the doorway, but I was able to peek around her and noted the same black-and-white checkered floor and chandelier in the foyer. "I normally don't answer the door when I'm working. I'd love to ask you in, but I can't right now."

Disappointed, I replied, "I understand." As an afterthought, I added, "Are you a writer?"

"Yes, a novelist, and I have a deadline to meet."

Next, we met up with Pierrot and Jacques. Our ages and bodies had changed, but we were who we were. The four of us laughed about the Moroccan party, the trips to Biarritz, and our other adventures. Pierrot showed me photos of his grandchild. He and Sian were divorced years earlier. The four of us strolled through the old *quartiers*, now gentrified. Unfortunately, Le New York Bar had undergone a makeover and was now all chrome with no game room—unrecognizable to me.

There is one discrepancy in my memory: whose baby was in the apartment on the last night at dinner with Sian and Pierrot? I had left my coat for a baby that night, but Pierrot told me that Kepa had not yet been born. The last chapter is how I remember the night.

I didn't see Bill until ten years after we had traveled together. I found out he never went into active service. It was an awkward meeting; I had just had my first child and didn't have time to visit. We didn't speak again until a few months ago when I called him to check some facts. Similarly, we had both taught school, had been married the same number of years, and have children the same age. He sent me the photos in this book.

Our memories synced.

Acknowledgments

EVERY WEEK I ESCAPE to Maureen's home in the hills behind Santa Barbara for writing class. I thank Maureen Murdock, an internationally acclaimed memoirist and my teacher, for sharing her years of knowledge as a writer and holding me to a high standard. I thank the women in my class who share their stories in the specialized art form of memoir in a safe haven. Their gentle, and not so gentle, criticism made me look deep into myself and kept me honest over the past seven years while writing my memoir, *Then I Won't Seem So Far Away*. I salute our core writing group: Carolyn Butcher, Wendy Lukomski, Hilary Klein, Olivia Harris, Deborah Gunther, Peggy Garrity, Eugenia Hoyne, Vicki Riskin, Hilary Kreiger, and Mary Anne Contreras, and extend my deepest gratitude.

A breakthrough in my writing came after a workshop with Tom Jenks. Thanks, Tom, for your wisdom and the opportunity to read for *Narrative Magazine*.

And to you, Dorothy Allison, I could never be as brave as you are in your writing, but I'm braver because of you.

And my thanks goes to my family, both living and dead, grateful for the love we all feel for each other. Thanks, Mom, for holding us together during the tough times (and I appreciate that you saved my letters). And Dad, your voice is forever with me. "May peace and happiness reign in our household."

My three daughters, Marie Claire, Erin, and Annick, have been my inspiration and muses as I tell my story of when I was their age. When they were young, around ten years old, they found my diary from when I was sixteen, which I said they couldn't read until they were sixteen. I told them, during the seven years of writing my memoir, that they couldn't read my book until they passed the age I was writing about. They all have now surpassed me in so many more ways than age.

And to Richard, my husband, who read and reread my chapters and book, careful not to change anything except the grammar, both French and English, I thank him for his patience, love, and understanding.

* * *

In remembrance of my French *maman,* Madame Françoise Delanne, "Fafache," who passed away today, November 7, 2014.

On the doorstep of 77 Rue de l'Abbé de l'Épée, 2013

About the Author

AUTHOR PEGGY O'TOOLE IS a teacher who received her masters of arts degree and teaching credentials from the University Of California, Santa Barbara. She remains active in the community as a member of the Dean's Council, and supports student teachers. She spends much of her time traveling extensively and writing memoires that she shares at local readings. Married with three grown daughters, she lives in Santa Barbara with her husband Richard.

APPENDIX

Timeline: Era of Counterculture from Sixties to Early Seventies

1950-1991 **The Cold War** between USSR communist states and Western capitalist states. The Soviet Union (USSR) and the United States increased espionage.

1968 **The Vietnam War** becomes the longest war in American history: December 22, 1961, marked by the first death of an American serviceman, to March 29, 1973.

1954-1968 **African-American Civil Rights Movement** marked by non-violent protests and civil disobedience (bus boycotts, sit-ins, Freedom Rides, marches) and emerged into violence in inner-city riots: Watts Riots, Los Angeles (1965)

Assassinations in USA:

November 22, 1963 **President Kennedy** is assassinated.

February 21, 1965, **Malcolm X,** a civil rights leader, is assassinated Black uprising spreads across America.

April 4, 1968 **Martin Luther King, Jr.** is assassinated.

June 6, 1968 **Bobby Kennedy** is assassinated.

October 1966 **The Black Panthers Party** started by Bobby Seale and Huey P. Newton, influenced by Malcolm X teachings,

October 1968 **The Black Student Union** (BSU) took over North Hall computer center at University of California, Santa Barbara and renamed it "Malcolm X Hall."

1960-1969 **Students for a Democratic Society (SDS),** a student activist movement, joined forces on campuses across the United States to oppose the Vietnam War and racial discrimination, and to promote women's liberation.

1964-1970 **Free Speech Movement** takes root on Berkeley campus and spreads throughout the University of California campuses and across America.

1967 **Hippie Movement**: Love-ins; Rock Festivals; drug culture and use of LSD; communes.

1967 **Psychedelic Movement**: Timothy Leary, "Turn on, tune in, drop out." Drugs: LSD, peyote, psilocybin mushrooms, marijuana, mescaline influence the counterculture philosophy, literature, art, music, and styles of dress.

1969 **Rock Festivals**: Woodstock Festival (New York) 1969 and Altamont Free Concert (California) 1969.

1968 **Women's Liberation Movement** first nation-wide conference

1969-1974 **Gay Liberation Movement** urges transsexuals, lesbians, drag queens, and gay males to "come-out." (LGBT Rights movement continues 1972-present.)

1968 **Democratic National Convention** in Chicago is site of demonstrations and police brutality.

September 24: **The Chicago Seven** trial commences. Abbie Hoffman, Jerry Rubin, Tom Hayden, Bobby Seale, et al., are charged charged with conspiracy, inciting to riot, and other charges related to countercultural protests. Bobby Seale is released due to lack of evidence.

September 1968 **FBI Chief J. Edgar Hoover** publicly termed the Black Panthers "the greatest threat to the internal security of the country."

1965-1970 Cesar Chavez, **Latino American civil rights** activist, succeeds by instigating boycott on grapes, marching, and strikes to organize unions (United Farm Workers) in support of farm workers and Hispanics.

November 20, 1969: **Native American** protestors occupation of Alcatraz until June 11, 1971.

1969-1970 **Angela Davis**, a Black professor at UCLA, is fired and imprisoned for her communist political beliefs and inflammatory speeches.

February 25, 1970 **William Kunstler**, a defense attorney who represented Chicago Seven, spoke at the UCSB stadium on campus and afterwards the students took to the streets where the police brutally beat a student inciting the **Isla Vista riots** and the burning down the Bank of America building. Police curfews were enforced periodically and intermittent rioting, protests and demonstrations continued until the university shut down classes early in June.

April 22,1970 **First Earth Day**, to mark the massive 1969 oil spill in Santa Barbara, California.

1970 **Religious Movement**: Hippy ethos rejected of mainstream religion for occult, spiritualism, Buddhism, Hinduism, Transcendental Meditation, and new Jesus Movement

Events in Western Europe and abroad:

May 1968: **Protests and Demonstrations**: Centered in Paris, French students and workers united in the "Grand Strike," and nearly toppled the government.

The counterculture movement took hold in Western Europe, with London, Amsterdam, Paris, Rome and West Berlin rivaling San Francisco and New York as counterculture centers.

1968 **ETA,** an armed Basque nationalist separatist organization, waged guerilla warfare against **Generalissimo Franco,** the fascist ruler of Spain.

In 1968 in Carrara, Italy, the **International Anarchist Federation** was founded. 1969 The Piazza Fontana bombing was attributed to the anarchists.

26 April 1971, the Italian-French-Iberian far-left terrorist organization made its last officially recorded bomb attack in Italy.

12 March 1971, **Turkish coup d'état**, carried out by military, universities closed, Martial Law invoked.

1971 **Attempted coup of Hassan II**, dictator and King of Morocco.

In 1971, Soviet Union leadership under **Breshnev** applied pressure on **Tito**, the dictator of Yugoslavia, to assert control of the Communist party.

1971 **Croatian Spring** revolutionaries prepare to break from Yugoslavia.